CONNECTED HISTORY

Connected History

Essays and Arguments

Sanjay Subrahmanyam

VERSO

London • New York

This expanded edition published by Verso 2022
First published in India as Is 'Indian Civilization'
a Myth? by Permanent Black 2013
© Sanjay Subrahmanyam 2013, 2022
Chapter 21 © Sanjay Subrahmanyam 2012, 2022

1 3 5 7 9 10 8 6 4 2

Verso
UK: 6 Meard Street, London W1F 0EG
US: 20 Jay Street, Suite 1010, Brooklyn, NY 11201
versobooks.com

Verso is the imprint of New Left Books

ISBN-13: 978-1-83976-238-3
ISBN-13: 978-1-83976-240-6 (US EBK)
ISBN-13: 978-1-83976-239-0 (UK EBK)

British Library Cataloguing in Publication Data
A catalogue record for this book is available from the British Library

Library of Congress Control Number:
2021947277

Printed and bound by CPI Group (UK) Ltd, Croydon, CR0 4YY

For

ANMOLE

*Many wars are fought
across the mediocre
foxholes of the head*

Contents

Preface

Though my first professional publication as a historian—on the fascinating subject of trade in the Kanara port of Basrur in the seventeenth century—dates to the end of 1984, I had already begun publishing journalistic pieces as an idle undergraduate in the late 1970s. A fair number of these were written for Trevor Drieberg, a genial Sri Lankan burgher and Marxist who lived in Nizamuddin West, which in those days was mostly a scattering of bungalows and old houses not far from the Jamuna's west bank in New Delhi. Drieberg ran an information service called 'India Backgrounder' and took what I delivered; other pieces were written for some of the less respectable Delhi magazines of the time (such as *Probe India*) which permitted freelancers; and I also wrote music reviews, of both rock and jazz, for the ephemeral midday newspapers of the time. Occasionally, I showed good sense in taking the precaution of using a pseudonym. Even if these pieces paid at most a few hundred rupees—sometimes as little as fifty—it seemed a sizeable amount of money for that phase of my life, and allowed me to indulge in my favourite pastime of purchasing second-hand books and vinyl records, and even paid for some train journeys to visit friends in places like distant Kalimpong.

As I became serious about research, I abandoned other forms of writing through most of the 1980s. In the early 1990s, I again had the opportunity to publish in some of the Delhi newspapers, first the *Economic Times* and then the *Times of India*. This was largely because some of my former students from the Delhi

School of Economics joined the editorial staff of those papers and kindly asked me to write for them. I am unable to trace most of those articles, which may be just as well, though I am secretly pleased to occasionally see one of them in particular, on the idea of the 'middle class' in India, turn up even in scholarly citations. I continued to publish in the newspapers, as well as magazines such as *India Today* and *Outlook* (often book reviews) through the later 1990s and early 2000s, by which time I had moved from Delhi to Paris. Sometimes, I was even published on the same day and in the same paper as my father, K. Subrahmanyam, whose journalistic production, though on the very different subject of security and international relations, was rather prodigious compared to mine.

I would probably never have done anything with these lighter pieces had it not been for two facts. First, a couple of years after joining UCLA in 2004, I was approached by the *London Review of Books* to write for them and began to do so on rather diverse subjects once or twice a year. These were unusual pieces for me, long reflective essays around the books under review, frequently over 3000 words. After a few years, as often seems to happen with the *LRB*, my dealings with them ceased. However, as these pieces accumulated they came to the notice of Rukun Advani, who had been publishing my scholarly work since 1990 (when, as an editor in Oxford University Press, he accepted one of my early books, *Improvising Empire*). Rukun was astonished to find not only that I could write on topics that were not arcane and lost in the depths of time, but that, unlike some of the 'heavyweight' scholarship which he claimed was his antidote to insomnia, he could read what I wrote without falling directly into the arms of Morpheus. He has been the principal motor behind putting together this collection and must therefore share at least some of the blame.

Unlike a large number of my contemporaries in Delhi University, I have never been tempted to write a novel or even publish a short story. Still, I do love literature, but am certain that—as in the best Hindi films, like *Muqaddar ka Sikandar*—this is unrequited love. It has been my privilege over the years, however, to have known some great writers and translators and to work with them. Amongst them I would number A.K. Ramanujan (whom I knew all too briefly, alas), but above all Velcheru Narayana Rao and David Shulman. They have always set an unfailing standard of taste and translation for me. I hope someday also to turn like them to the work of translation. (A historian, when he does his work, is anyway something of a translator.) For the moment, though, I hope the unfootnoted ideas and critiques here will meet some of their expectations.

My thanks to the many friends and colleagues who have commented on and criticized these *pièces d'occasion*. They are more than I can count. But thanks above all to Caroline Ford, who has always encouraged me by word and deed over the past decade in these offbeat pursuits.

The book is dedicated to an old friend, who in the late 1970s and early 1980s taught me more about literature, music, and aesthetics than either of us would care to remember.

Los Angeles
October 2012

Acknowledgements

The translation of the poem by Unamuno is new (not earlier published). Thanks to Anthony Pagden for help in its revision.

The chapters that comprise this book have all been revised for publication, the revision in some cases being heavy and yielding a substantially enlarged version of the one first published. The sources of first publication are listed below.

Chapter 1 appeared in *Outlook*, 20 August 2001.

Chapter 2 appeared in the *Times Literary Supplement* (London), 24 December 2010.

Chapter 3 includes materials from an article in *Outlook*, 5 July 2004, and another article in the *Telegraph* (Kolkata), 8 August 2004.

Chapter 4 appeared first in the *London Review of Books* (*LRB*), vol. 29, no. 18, 20 September 2007, pp. 26–30.

Chapter 5 appeared in the *LRB*, vol. 29, no. 21, 1 November 2007, pp. 7–9.

Chapter 6 appeared in the *LRB*, vol. 30, no. 21, 6 November 2008, pp. 42–3.

Chapter 7 appeared in the *LRB*, vol. 31, no. 23, 3 December 2009, pp. 27–30.

Chapter 8 appeared in the *LRB*, vol. 31, no. 3, 12 February 2009, pp. 28–9.

Chapter 9 appeared in the *LRB*, vol. 31, no. 16, 27 August 2009, pp. 19–21.

Chapter 10 appeared in the *LRB*, vol. 32, no. 23, 2 December 2010, pp. 25–6.

Chapter 11 was commissioned by the *LRB* in 2011, went as far as the proof stage, but then never appeared.

Chapter 12 appeared in *The Guardian* (London), Saturday Review, 14 February 2009.

Chapter 13 appeared in *L'Homme*, nos. 187–8, 2008, pp. 93–104.

Chapter 14 appeared (in French) in *L'Histoire*, no. 355, July–August 2010, pp. 70–6.

Chapter 15 appeared in *India Today*, 6 October 2008.

Chapter 16 appeared in the *Economic Times* (New Delhi), 11 September 2011.

Chapter 17 appeared in a very different version in Dharma Kumar and Dilip Mookherjee, eds, *D. School: Reflections on the Delhi School of Economics* (Delhi: Oxford University Press, 1995), pp. 254–61.

Chapters 18 and 19 have not been published earlier.

Chapter 20 appeared (in Portuguese) in *Cultura: Revista de História e Teoria de Ideias* (Lisbon), vol. 24, 2007, pp. 253–68.

Chapter 21 appeared in *Books & Ideas* (Paris), 27 January 2012.

To Die Dreaming

MIGUEL DE UNAMUNO (1864–1936)

'In fact, he said to himself, it seems that my destiny is
to die dreaming.'
—Stendhal, *The Red and the Black*

To die dreaming, indeed, but if one dreams
of dying, Death is but dream; a window
into the void; not to dream a Nirvana;
so that Eternity at last masters Time.
To live today under the sign
of a yesterday that unravels on the morrow;
to live chained to revulsion,
is that really living? And what do we learn from that?
To dream of dying, is that not to kill the dream?
And to live the dream, is that not to kill one's life?
Why insist on it so much then?
Why learn something you will only forget,
while deciphering that unforgiving frown—
that abandoned heaven—of the Eternal Master ?

(translation from the Spanish
by Sanjay Subrahmanyam)

1

Is 'Indian Civilization' a Myth?

Two radically different conceptions of India have informed discussions amongst both academics and normal human beings in the past few decades, and it is the tension between these two conceptions that I wish to treat here. On the one hand, we have the view that 'India' as we know it was invented in the not-too-distant past, probably by the British, or perhaps by Indians and Britons acting together in the period of colonial rule. This is what we may call the constructivist approach, one that from its academic origins has percolated to other parts of elite Indian society which have, willy-nilly, absorbed the best and the worst of postmodernist gobbledygook by now. There is of course some truth to the notion that the idea of India altered significantly in the nineteenth and twentieth centuries, but one may legitimately doubt whether the whole thing was made up in recent times as a sheer act of will.

The second view, which is radically opposed to the first, and which today finds more extensive political expression than academic support, is the idea that some very stable and autarchic notion of India has been around for a very long time, indeed from the time when a classical Indian civilization put down its roots in the Indo-Gangetic plain. This is a view that sees Indian society in terms of three (or two-and-a-half) phases: a formative one, ending at the close of the first millennium of the Christian era; a second phase of confusion and decline that is roughly coterminous with Islamic rule; and then a third—which may yet be incomplete—of resurgence and a return to the roots. We can all identify the crudest versions of the last in the writings of the ideologues of the RSS or their Neanderthal counterparts elsewhere, including rabble-rousing European journalists in India, but the problem is that this view is far more widely shared than one often suspects.

Some thoughts on 'India' as a term may be useful to set the stage. The word itself derives, most of us know, from the medieval Arabic term 'Hind', which is itself a deformation of the far older and far more limited 'Sind'. When one reads the Arabophone encyclopaedists and geographers writing in medieval times, it soon becomes clear though that they are quite ambiguous as to the limits of 'al-Hind'. Of the core areas there is little doubt: everyone includes the Indo-Gangetic plain from the Punjab to Bengal. But the status of the peninsula is already less clear, and we know that, as late as the fifteenth and sixteenth centuries, 'Hind' and 'Hindustan' sometimes did not include the Deccan and areas south of it. If this minimal view exists, there were also other writers who thought in medieval times that Indonesia, Thailand, Cambodia, and (in a few odd cases) even Yemen belonged to Hind. All in all, we have three major geographical categories that stand out in these materials: Hind, Sin (or China), and 'Ajam (the Persian-speaking area). The problem was that the borders of the three were not unambiguous.

What of people in the Indian subcontinent? Did they have some definite notions of the limits of their identity? Once again, matters are far from clear. One measure could be the limits of the spread of Sanskrit or of Brahmanic culture, but both of these take us far into Central Asia on the one hand, and South East Asia on the other. Nor do the epics, and the limits of their spread, prove particularly helpful. It is true that the partisans of a theory of 'Greater India' wished in the 1930s and 1940s to make grandiose claims on this basis for the extended limits of Indian sovereignty, but such claims could be equally made then by India's neighbours using very similar sorts of evidence. It may nevertheless be useful to reflect a little bit on the 'Greater India' thesis, and its corollary, namely the idea of the 'Indianization' of cultures elsewhere. At the heart of the matter is the notion that at some distant point in the past, say about AD 500, the concept of 'Indian civilization' had already been perfected. Everything of any importance was in place: social structure, philosophy, the major literary works. Then, we can imagine the process of 'Indianization' as the transportation of these elements to distant lands such as Cambodia or Champa, to be transplanted in more or less fertile soil.

But little in the history of South East Asia actually provides much comfort to this view. At the same time, we must ask ourselves whether it is really convincing to think of an Indian 'civilization' that had been perfected as long ago as the Gupta dynasty. Many writers in the twentieth century have held to this view. These include some of the best-known Western Orientalists, such as A.L. Basham and Madeleine Biardeau. But the protagonists of this position also include writers from V.S. Naipaul to Jawaharlal Nehru, whose *Discovery of India* is quite remarkable from this point of view.

The central idea here is of India-as-civilization, and it very soon becomes the same as a notion of closed India. Indian civilization is portrayed as self-sufficient and homeostatic, and it can only export culture but never really be influenced by the outside save in a negative sense. Somewhat paradoxically, in view of his later reputation as an apostle of secularism, Nehru seems by and large to have accepted a very negative view of Islam. This is why he portrays the situation in India after AD 1200 in negative terms, as the decline and atrophy of an already perfect civilization. Writing more recently, Naipaul draws upon similar images, adding to it a dash of the 'clash of civilizations' thesis:

the faultline between Islam and Hinduism (which can be read as 'Indian civilization') passes for him through the heart of the subcontinent.

One of the examples that Naipaul chooses to illustrate his sad tale of medieval decline is the fate of the imperial state of Vijayanagara in the Deccan, portrayed by him as one of the last bastions of Hindu civilization that held out against the Muslim invader. Now, most historians of Vijayanagara today would see matters rather differently. They would point to the dependence of Vijayanagara on Muslim military specialists and horse-traders, Portuguese firearms, and an imperial ideology that was based not on ancient precepts but newly-formulated sectarian ideas from the fourteenth and fifteenth centuries. In terms of court ritual, fiscal structure, and imperial style, Vijayanagara shares far more with the Bahmani sultanate and its successors at Bijapur and Golkonda than with the Pallavas and Cholas. Politically, the rulers of Vijayanagara were as often allied to these sultanates as opposed to them, while amongst their major rivals and enemies were the Gajapati rulers of Orissa. In order to understand this, however, we need to see India not as a civilization but as a crossroads, as a space open to external influences rather than a simple exporter of culture to its neighbours.

Where did this misunderstanding arise, and since when has Vijayanagara been seen as a Hindu kingdom struggling against Muslim enemies? One part of the answer lies with the Portuguese in the sixteenth century. Looking for help against the Muslim rulers of peninsular India, they thought the 'Gentile' kings of Vijayanagara were their natural friends. By the middle years of the sixteenth century they had partially given up this illusion, but some parts of it persisted into the views of later writers, including those from Holland and France. It may be useful at this point to insist on one particular fact. It is clear that most of these writers were not liars or prevaricators; they did not simply make up things about India. What they did, however, was read Indian society selectively and produce an image of it that, while often based on true elements, was also one in which these elements had been shorn of their real context.

Still, several centuries after the arrival of Vasco da Gama on Indian shores, there was no single dominant idea of India in writings by Westerners: several contradictory views existed, depending on whether one wrote from Madurai or Agra, whether one was Protestant or Catholic, whether one knew Persian or Sanskrit, and so on. However, by the late-eighteenth and early-nineteenth centuries, a new homogeneity can be found in views of what India was. This picture, produced by Western Orientalists and their Indian assistants, tended to focus on Sanskrit as the true source of Indian culture (demoting Persian in the process), and there was also a search for an Indian Golden Age. Minority voices contested this view, but they were few and far between. Indian popular culture was also largely set aside in favour of an obsession with high culture.

It is remarkable that both Indian reformers and neo-traditionalists of the nineteenth century bought into this view, and a strange complicity came to exist between these two apparently opposed strands. The epoch from the twelfth to the eighteenth centuries was portrayed in dark hues, and if some felt Westernization was the antidote to the malady, others proposed a return to the 'real' roots of Indian civilization. But what was this pristine culture to which a return was proposed? In the case of South India, many 'purists' found such immaculate culture in Carnatic music played on the violin (actually an eighteenth-century import from Europe), or dances performed to the texts of the great sixteenth-century poet and composer Kshetrayya that also came precisely from this 'dark' period! In North India, ultra-purists insisted that Dhrupad should be favoured over Khayal, and invented a bogus Vedic genealogy for the former, forgetting that it was heavily influenced by Mughal court culture. As for devotional religion, such as we know it today in India, most of it is the product of the period from the fourteenth century onwards, whether in Maharashtra, Punjab, or Bengal.

This takes me to an observation of the poet and literary critic Velcheru Narayana Rao, who has often argued that all we have real access to in our past is that part which goes back five or six centuries. Beyond that, we have intellectual constructions and wishful thinking, but little that exists in our everyday life which connects us instinctively to things so distant from us in time. So, ancient India is not a reality for us in the same way as medieval India, and it can never achieve the same status. Further, this intermediate past is one which we can only think through in terms of the idea of a crossroads, where not only did regions and regional cultures influence one another, but things came and went from far more distant lands, whether Europe, Central Asia, Iran, and the Ottoman empire, or South East Asia and East Africa. It will do us no good to pretend that these processes of exchange were not linked to violence. Empires were built and cities sacked; religious sites were desecrated and political opponents massacred. This was the way it was in our part of the world, just as it was in medieval Iran, the Germany of the Thirty Years War, and the empire of the Incas. This is the only past we have, and we had best make as good a job as we can of it.

Take the example of the Indian connection to Africa—this is one that has been really neglected. On the one hand it is linked to the Indian Ocean slave trade, since Africans were brought as slaves to serve in the states of medieval India; on the other it is linked to the complex history of western Indian merchant communities who profited from Africa and the African trade. The point to be made is that it will simply not do to always portray Indians and Indian society as victims of the greed and depredations of others while conveniently whitewashing those parts of our own past that do not suit us today. In similar vein, the relations between Indian traders and moneylenders and peasants in Central Asia were often exploitative, a fact that partly explains the resentment against Indian traders in the early years of the twentieth century.

Some of my Indian intellectual friends believe it is their task to use history in order to demonstrate the illegitimacy of Indian nationalism. This is not my view, nor do I believe that historians are really up to this task. The point I wish to make instead is that we have by now come to terms in surprising measure with a truly traumatic period in our not-too-distant past, namely that of about two centuries of British colonial rule. No one really questions the existence of key institutions that the British left behind in India; there is no current proposal to dismantle the railway network or blow up the city of Kolkata simply because they were created under colonial rule. The same holds for the status of the English language, which has if anything grown stronger in India in the last three decades. It would be truly bizarre if the price to be paid for this acceptance of the legacy of colonial rule were to be the transfer of nationalist resentment onto an earlier period in order to cast the blame for everything that is wrong with Indian society today on medieval invaders from Central and West Asia. True, all nationalisms seem to need negative stereotypes in order to shore up their self-images. But a national culture that does not have the confidence to declare that, like all other national cultures, it too is a hybrid, a crossroads, a mixture of elements derived from chance encounters and unforeseen consequences, can only take the path to xenophobia and cultural paranoia. A last modest suggestion: if cultural cleansing is to start in India, we might begin by returning the khaki shorts of the RSS to their place of origin.

Some afterthoughts may not be out of place here on these questions. On 1 June 2004, the Royal Geographical Society in London held a debate whose motion was 'The British Empire was a Force for Good'. The motion was supported, amongst others, by the historian Niall Ferguson, the recent one-man industry justifying empire, both British and American. In extremis, he made use of a shallow but ingenious counterfactual argument: If Indian soldiers had not fought in the Second World War, he argued, Hitler would not have been defeated. These soldiers were recruited by the British empire, therefore the empire was a force for the good. QED! The motion was passed by a popular vote of the audience.

Such an argument has a familiar ring to it. It could be used, for example, to defend Stalin and the gulag. Without them, surely Hitler would not have been defeated either. We can thus easily see where such opportunistic arguments take us. Reading through the public debate in India after Prime Minister Manmohan Singh's remarks to the convocation of my former university, Oxford, puts me in mind of some of these exercises. As I see it, Singh was careful to not simply praise the British empire; he first criticized it, on the basis of some rather bogus statistics produced by Angus Maddison on the change in India's share in world GDP, allegedly 22.6 per cent in 1700 compared to 3.8 per cent in 1952. No one knows what India's GDP was in 1700. But let us admit a part of the premise and say that India's share did fall over these years. Three questions then arise. First, was this fall the result of British rule? Second, in the absence of British rule, what was the most plausible alternative? Third, is this the most useful way of looking at the effects of British rule in India, and of British imperialism more generally?

Singh also implied that while the economic consequences of British rule were negative, the global effects on liberal institutions and political culture were really quite positive. These consequences cannot be measured in numbers (though the issue is worth thinking about), nor were they planned or intended as positive by the British, which is unfortunately implied in Singh's remarks. Despite periodically using the rhetoric of paternalism, it is clear that British colonial policies were not primarily designed to promote economic growth in India. The British often and insistently said this themselves. Growth between 1800 and 1950 was thus slow and fitful, and many other parts of the world (including Japan's colonies in Taiwan and Korea) clearly did better than India.

It may be argued very plausibly that some institutions that came under British rule, such as the railways, would have come even without such rule. After all, many modern institutions fell into place in Iran, nineteenth-century Latin America, China, Japan, and parts of South East Asia (e.g. Thailand) that were not colonized. Why is it a plausible assumption then that Britons, whose primary allegiance was to Britain, would have done better for India than Indians? Would any historian of Britain be willing to accept, say, that Britain would have performed better economically if only it had been ruled over by Indians? So, much depends too on the answer to the second question: If not Britain, then what? Here, each writer will have his own alternative scenario. Had the French under Bussy conquered peninsular India, would French colonial rule have produced a better outcome? Perhaps French revolutionary republicanism would have worked marvels on India. I have my doubts, but we cannot simply measure this by looking at France's performance in Algeria. Would India not have fragmented into many small states in the absence of British rule? I have my doubts about that too, since I believe that the Mughal empire left a powerful cultural and institutional legacy of cohesion, which we tend to neglect today because of Hindu right-wing rhetoric.

But the most important question is the third. The British empire was a complex and multifaceted motor. Two aspects of it are worth keeping in mind. First, the British practised selective forms of acculturation, which were less brutal than those of the Spaniards in America but also less nuanced than those of the Ottomans. Unlike the Spaniards, British attempts at conversion to Christianity remained muted for the most part, but in this they were not that much more tolerant than the Ottomans. Again, linguistically, the Ottomans encouraged far greater diversity than either the Spaniards or the British, and the interplay of Persian, Arabic, and Ottoman Turkish led to a great literary and cultural efflorescence. However, acculturation is always a many-sided process. It was not just a question of what the British brought to the table, but the cultural resources that other parties disposed of. In the settler colonies, where indigenous populations over time came to have a highly reduced role, metropolitan culture could impose itself with far greater ease and in the face of far more limited opposition than in South Asia or East Africa. Even the contrast between New Zealand and Australia, with the latter possessing a far less resilient indigenous demography and culture than the former, is instructive in this respect. This is why the British empire produced such different outcomes in different parts of the world, and even within South Asia itself. It is also why nostalgia about British rule is not equally shared. Second, despite Ferguson's arguments, most historians of even Britain today would admit that 'modernity' was not something that the British produced domestically and then exported. Britain and British society were also deeply affected by the empire. Therefore, we cannot see what happened in colonial India simply as a transfer or a gift—not even a poisoned gift. By once more making the colonial encounter in India a meeting between rigid, timeless, Indian society and its frozen values, and egalitarian and fair-minded Britons, we are caricaturing India. We are also caricaturing Britain. There is comfort in this, but only for those comforted by clichés.

2

Back to the Future
Why the West Rules the World*

For some years now, we have frequently been told in universities that the historical profession is in a crisis and that no one wants to read history any more. At the same time, despite what is sometimes claimed, especially by over-enthusiastic publicists and their academic accomplices, there is currently no shortage in the market of large books of general or popular history making ambitious claims to attract the attention of distracted potential readers. The evidence can be found in any bookstore (if one still exists in your city). If bookstores such as Borders and Barnes & Noble often carry a section amusingly entitled 'oversized anthropology' (apparently referring to large-format works), there could easily be another called 'overweight history' for books that weigh in at between 600 and 1200 pages. The greater part of such books are produced by trade publishers, or are otherwise 'crossover' books from university presses trying to edge into the trade market. In the past two decades this proliferation of doorstops has been accompanied by ever more stringent restrictions on academic history books, especially by first authors, which are often expected to be under 300 (or even

---

*On Ian Morris, *Why the West Rules—for Now: The Patterns of History and What they Reveal about the Future* (London: Profile Books, 2010).

250) pages and heavily subsidized in one fashion or the other. Even so, they usually cannot be found in Borders or Barnes & Noble. This growing polarization of the market—short books in ever-shrinking printruns and enormous volumes aiming at massive sales—has struck many of us by now, especially when one is approached, at least three or four times a year nowadays, by agents or trade publishers asking that one abandon one's usual modest monographic mode to write the next mammoth blockbuster. Like the population at large, history books too now seem to lurch between the obese and the anorexic.

Why the West Rules—for Now is clearly not a part of the second category. Its author Ian Morris is a prolific, distinguished, British-educated historian of the classical period in Europe who teaches at the prestigious Stanford University after having taught in Chicago. According to his Stanford biography page he has written some fourteen books, mostly on ancient history and archaeology, including some quite wide-ranging ones such as *The Greeks* and *The Dynamics of Ancient Empires*. He is also a field archaeologist who has directed digs in Italy and Greece, and participated in others elsewhere. Though presumably trained initially in the humanities, Morris, like many who navigate between history and archaeology these days, is far more open to the hard sciences and their techniques than the run-of-the-mill historian, and he is particularly attracted to quantification. He is also drawn to both physical geography and sociology as disciplines, and further seems to draw much inspiration from economics. All this means that one sees clearly from the outset that he is distinctly more inclined to methodological positivism than the greater part of the historical profession today. Yet it is precisely by seizing on positivism that he hopes to appeal to a larger public, even arguing—right from the subtitle of his book—that history is some sort of predictive science that reveals clear patterns and trends about the future.

The questions that Morris ostensibly sets himself are, first, why 'the West' dominates the world at the current time, and, second, how long this domination can be expected to last. These are questions which, as he himself notes, have a history of their own. When initially posed, say, in the sixteenth century by Iberian historians of the 'discoveries' (both in America and Asia), they asked how long Europe would dominate the 'four quarters of the world', restricting their use of Europe furthermore to its western part. When presented in the eighteenth and nineteenth centuries again, the question once more focused very largely on Europe. It was only in the twentieth century that this category, 'the West', seems to have come to the fore, mainly as a way of uniting Western Europe and the United States in a single history. Oswald Spengler's *Der Untergang des Abendlandes* (1918–22) was obviously a central text in speaking of the West as a historical object, albeit in decline. The Chicago historian William McNeill's massive *The Rise of the West: A History of the Human Community* (1963), interestingly absent from Morris's large bibliography, was the key work which enshrined this question (why did the West dominate over the Rest) as the central one around which history curricula came to be taught in many places in the world. Now, 'the West' here was a curious and treacherous term. Anti-Islamic, and also anti-Catholic in the inclinations of many of its users, it excluded Central and South America more often than not. It included the territory of the United States, but only from rather late in the eighteenth century, or even later. (US history is, incidentally, still not taught in many Western Civilization courses.) It excluded large parts of Eastern and Central Europe. Greece played an essential role in its origin story but dropped off the map by the medieval period, and even more so when it fell under Ottoman rule. 'The West' therefore was not so much a place as an idea, an ideology even. It was like the proverbial knife where the blade was replaced a few times, and the handle a few times, but it was somehow still the same knife. Of course, this had its advantages. In this form the West came to be stripped of any racialist connotations—of a sort that the idea of 'European civilization' certainly had had in the late nineteenth century.

The continuing centrality of the 'Rise of the West' issue is demonstrated by the immense academic popularity of a work that is somewhat unexpectedly at the polemical heart of Morris's own book, namely Kenneth Pomeranz's *The Great Divergence* (2000). A specialist of Qing China, Pomeranz argued that, at least in economic terms, it was difficult to argue for a divergence in living and other standards between China and Europe until late in the eighteenth century. He further suggested that both China and Europe were large and diverse and that comparisons between the two should be focused, more narrowly than had been the case hitherto, on concrete and comparable regions in well-demarcated periods. Nevertheless, he did not see the 'divergence' as deep in either its causes or consequences, but rather as a relatively short-term phenomenon with causes that came largely out of political economy rather than culture. Pomeranz was concerned not with the 'West' but with Western Europe, and even that region he defined rather precisely. His explanations were largely short-term and conjunctural (rather than structural) in nature, as opposed for example to older works by authors like Mark Elvin in his *The Pattern of the Chinese Past* (1973). They were also limited in their extent and ambitions, at least initially. To be sure, not all economic historians agree with Pomeranz's use of evidence, but there has been a real and fruitful debate around the work because the sorts of measures that he employed were not merely accessible and comprehensible, but already in quite general use.

In contrast, Morris wishes in this work to argue for the significance of a long-term perspective on how 'West' and 'East' might have diverged, indeed one that might go back even 20,000 years (if not to the ape-men 1.6 million years ago). He assures us from the outset that he is interested in the hard facts of geography and not in mushy cultural definitions. Therefore, he wishes to treat West and East as 'geographical labels, not value judgments'. Unafraid of essentialism, he argues that the best way to deal with the matter is to take the Eurasian landmass and, looking at its 'westernmost' and 'easternmost' portions, treat them as 'the West' and 'the East'. This occurs early in the book, and I must confess that I found this a rather logically muddled and unpromising beginning. We all know that West and East are directions, and hence relative. As we also know, America lies to the east of China. Why should these directions then be deployed to develop fixed and hardened categories of place? Furthermore, what about other directions such as Northwest and Southeast? Finally, why must we never be allowed to go beyond the number 'two' for our categories? Naturally, if we admit that the world has historically been made up of many (and shifting) spatial categories, and is not really amenable to treatment using binaries, the fundamental premises of this book begin to appear rather quaint.

As one goes through the remaining twelve chapters of it, however, the significance of these initial choices becomes clear. Morris knows a great deal about European history in the classical period, and is also comfortable both with archaeological literature on earlier epochs and writings on later medieval and modern Western Europe (especially modern England, from which he draws for a disproportionately large number of anecdotes and vignettes). He is, incidentally, never shy of wandering away from the 'westernmost' end of his landmass in search of scarce data. As a foil to this 'western' material he has decided to choose one other place, and for this he has, for whatever reason, gone to China (though one gathers he does not read either Chinese or Japanese). In effect, therefore, the book is organized for the most part as a set of enduring contrasts between Europe (especially—but not always—Western Europe) and China. The rest of the world, at best, makes mere cameo appearances. West Asia occasionally appears, in relation for example to the beginnings of Islam. South Asia is almost entirely absent in any substantive way, being saved for some quite casual mentions; in fact, by one of Morris's own ever-changing definitions, it even seems to fall into the 'West' rather than the 'East'. Africa disappears largely after prehistory. This is historical cherry-picking, to say the least. One naturally understands that to take South Asian or African history seriously would mean not merely an effort of erudition, but also an attack on the unremittingly binary mentality that characterizes the whole work. But since when have historians been afraid of complexity?

The heart of the exercise for Morris is the construction of something he terms the 'index of social development', with social development being defined as 'societies' abilities to get things done'. He believes that such a quantitative index should and can be constructed over the very long term, and that this will enable the historian to determine the periods when the 'West' has dominated the 'East', and vice versa. Such an index ought, in his view, to be composed of four elements: he terms these energy capture, organization, war-making, and information technology. Now each of these elements, if taken seriously, is in fact incredibly complex in itself. Yet Morris believes that each can be quantified within a small margin of error, and then combined by some process of weighting to produce a single grand index number. Readers who have the patience can go first to the appendix of the book, and then to the author's website to see how this is done. Morris then argues that only two significant possible objections can be raised to his index: by those who believe that such comparisons are 'dehumanizing'; or by those who believe that he has made narrow definitional or empirical errors. The former set of critics, he believes, will have 'to find another way to explain why the West rules or to show why we should not be asking that question at all', while the latter will be 'forced to come up with better indices of their own'.

For my part, I believe that this hubristic exercise is fraught with insurmountable problems from start to finish. Morris's ideas of 'West' and 'East' are more or less meaningless. The elements he chooses to quantify are highly debatable. Even the elements he chooses are for the most part not really quantifiable save in a grossly arbitrary manner. It is, further, entirely arbitrary to weight them and arrive at a single index number. The whole exercise appears, frankly, to be a form of mumbo-jumbo or naïve pseudo-science wherein the apparent accuracy of the numbers reflects no more than the qualitative instincts and prejudices of the author. If one asks fifteen historians who believe that the 'West' and the 'East' exist and have existed in a meaningful way for thousands of years to draw such graphs, you will probably get as many answers as historians. If this is meant to be the public face of history today, it is a singularly odd one.

Yet it is this index which apparently shows us 'the shape of the history that has to be explained', and which drives the structure of the book as a whole. There is plenty of erudition on display here, but it has the general effect of throwing handfuls of confetti in the air to distract one from the relentless march of the parade. That parade is essentially a rather dull affair, in which West and East each have had their moments of domination. Apparently, the East's turn will come again in some years, later in the twenty-first century or perhaps early in the twenty-second. Yet, we are told by the author, by the time this happens West and East may no longer exist separately in any meaningful way. Is there not a rather odd contradiction between this conclusion and the premise of the whole exercise? And what are we to make of the closing (and quite messianic) claim that 'only historians can explain the differences that divide humanity and how we can prevent them from destroying us'?

Morris is not afraid of a whole series of issues that most historians have a difficulty with. I have already pointed to his blithe indifference to essentialism. A series of scattered and quite bizarre counterfactual (or 'what-if') vignettes, written using a bag of clichés of the 'it was a dark and stormy night' variety, enough to make Snoopy wince, also make it clear that he has no problems whatsoever with anachronism. But there is also the absolute devotion to teleology, which ensures that all his graphs are in general unidirectional. In one of the apparently playful moments in the work, Morris cites the 1985 film *Back to the Future* in which a white American teenager time-travels thirty years to 1955. Here he begins to play Chuck Berry's songs to the astonished audience at his prom. They are at first appreciative, but then quite disgusted when he begins to use Eddie Van Halen's tapping and other techniques. There is a lesson here concerning teleology, one which Morris (himself a former heavy-metal guitarist) might want to reflect on.

There is no denying the wide reading and extensive erudition that Ian Morris has mobilized to write this book. I could find few obvious errors of fact and citation in the areas I was most familiar with. In regard to China, he has consulted extensively with historians of the area to familiarize himself with the relevant secondary literature. These are thus not the problems with the book. The problems in it lie elsewhere, and, keeping binaries at bay, are three in number. The first is the mistaken view that history is a predictive science. This is in fact belied by the muddled conclusion, where the author—faced with his own incapacity to make clear, concrete, and falsifiable predictions—muddies the waters endlessly and then falls back on messianic statements such as 'the next forty years will be the most important in history'. The second problem lies in his embrace of an indefensible quantitative methodology. It is really no good saying that if you don't believe my estimate of how many angels can dance on the head of a pin, you had better provide better estimates of your own. Finally, the unremittingly Bertie Woosterish tone in which the book is written, apart from being silly, suggests the author does not overly trust the intelligence of his readers. Perhaps on account of too much undergraduate teaching, Morris has fallen into using a style that is a parody of itself. The book is peppered with ghastly sophomoric jokes that set one's teeth on edge. Perhaps the medium is the message. Perhaps this is really a joke played on us by an erudite and accomplished scholar who has decided to metamorphose for a while into a synthesis of Nostradamus and Aunt Dahlia.

3

Secularism and the Happy Indian Village

In July 2004 the editorial staff of the Indian newsmagazine *Outlook*, in which I had occasionally written prior to that date, invited me to respond to an essay by Ashis Nandy they had recently published, which was in turn a response to an earlier essay in their pages by the journalist Kuldip Nayar. I did not suspect their motives, which I later learnt were somewhat less than innocent. Though I was no great admirer of Nayar or his work, Nandy's piece somewhat annoyed me, not only on account of its tone and content but because it was the repetition of a worn formula that he had by then deployed numerous times. I knew Nandy personally, although not very well, and had had some social dealings with him, especially in the late 1980s and early 1990s when I was a young scholar who had freshly finished his doctoral degree. On the other hand, Nandy by the late 1980s was already very well known both in India and the West as the author of a number of arresting and provocative works. Our first dealings were during the time of the anti-Mandal agitation in Delhi, and I recall that on this matter we had largely tended to agree. Later, in the course of the 1990s, our relations grew somewhat estranged, especially as a result of a conference in New Delhi in 1998 on the consequences and meanings of Vasco da Gama's 1498 voyage, where we clashed publicly. Earlier, I had usually dealt with him in private surroundings, or at best with a few friends like D.R. Nagaraj who did not treat him with any great reverence. Now, I came in particular to dislike his habit of surrounding himself in public with acolytes who would not allow one to question him or debate with him even when he made the most outrageous and factually inaccurate statements—which he frequently did, simply as a matter of provocation. At any rate, this may help to contextualize my brief comment on him in *Outlook* entitled 'Our Only Colonial Thinker', reproduced below.*

The essay by Ashis Nandy, 'A Billion Gandhis' (*Outlook*, 21 June 2004), demonstrates once more that this celebrated Indian psychologist and maverick thinker is exactly as dazzlingly clever as he is tiresomely repetitive and profoundly ill-informed. And he is as innocent of the facts about India and her past as he is of Europe and hers. Armed with this blissful innocence, he can then brilliantly develop paradox after paradox. That none of his facts has any basis in reality has rarely fazed him. So let us begin with his view of the history of concepts. Nandy claims that 'the concept of secularism emerged in a Europe torn by inter-religious strife, warfare and pogroms'. When and where did this happen? In the France of Charles IX and Henri IV? During the Thirty Years War? Can he give us some specific periods and societies? No. Because Nandy's Europe does not exist except in his own imagination. It is a non-place that only exists to be an 'anti-India' and he believes he can attribute anything he wants to it just because it tickles his fancy.

In point of fact, the term 'secularism' has very little purchase in most European or indeed other Western societies as a part

---

*With minor syntactical tweaks but no substantial change.

of normal political vocabulary. Even today, no one in the political sphere talks much about 'secularism' in the United Kingdom, Germany, Italy, France, Spain, and Portugal, or in the United States, Argentina, and Brazil. Neither Tony Blair nor Mrs Thatcher has ever used the word in a speech that I can remember. The only Europeans who use some sort of term like it are the French, with their idea of *laïcité*. But the French did not mean this term to be one that mediated between religious groups. Rather, it had to do with separating the state from one particular religion, Catholicism, in the French Revolution and its aftermath, leading up to the well-known Separation Act of 1905.

This is not quite the same thing as 'secularism'. Europeans do talk of 'secularization', but this simply means the turning away from religion, the fact that churches are less and less attended, and so on. The idea of 'secularism' propagated in nineteenth-century Britain by George Holyoake and then Charles Bradlaugh (who founded the National Secular Society in 1866) was for the most part linked to promoting rationalism in education rather than education through religious schools.

It is therefore a profound error to assume that 'secularism' is a common word in political use in the West that has simply been transferred to India as an 'imported idea'. In reality, the term has a political weight in India that it has never had in the West, and it has acquired a deep meaning and significance in India that many Europeans simply don't understand. Thus, 'secularism' has become almost as Indian a word as 'preponed' or 'denting' (removing a dent in a car).

This said, Nandy deserves applause for suggesting that one should look to traditions and political concepts that have long existed in India for notions of tolerance. But one equally wishes he practised what he preached. What is Nandy's own record on this matter over the years? He has never deigned to study Indian history. He has no idea what took place or what people thought

or wrote in India before colonial rule. When pressed, he refers
to the *Ramayana* and the *Mahabharata* as if this were the sum
total of India's past. His own knowledge of colonial history is
essentially limited to the British, and to Bengali authors under
colonial rule. What sort of intellectual resources are these, if not
those of 'the dominant, colonial culture of India's knowledge
industry'? Not only has Nandy never read a single work from
the fifteenth or sixteenth century, he does not even read those
who write about these texts. Truly, to be a 'great thinker' one
must first be a great innocent, one who can blithely claim—as
Nandy does—that India never had historians before colonial
rule. Apparently Abu'l Fazl came from Mars.

Nandy appears at his worst when he wishes pompously to
hand out lessons. He wants others to learn from 'the concept of
convivencia' that apparently existed in medieval Islamic Spain.
Did anybody in Islamic Spain ever use this 'concept'? So far
as I know—unlike him I have studied the history of Spain for
that period—no one did. This idea was imposed on the Spain
of that time by romantic modern historians, and it is no more
indigenous to it than 'secularism' is to Mughal India. And the
idea that Spain in this epoch was 'the only truly plural polity
Europe has produced in the last one thousand years' is simply
another example of what passes for scholarship in some circles.
It is just another case of the Golden Age syndrome.

So perhaps Nandy should begin by reflecting on the rather
widespread forms of 'obscene arrogance' and not hand out
lessons before doing his homework. If he does so, I am sure he
will find plenty of examples of tolerance not just in the villages
that his rather tired populist rhetoric wants to hold up as an
example, but in other parts of Indian society in both the past
and present. But it may involve harder work than producing the
cotton candy that passes for cleverness in 'indigenist' circles.

And it may also involve the sad admission that given his
romantic adulation of India's Hindu past, his desire to preserve

indigenous 'purity', his mythification of an ahistorical Europe, and his links to the lachrymose tradition of the romantic underside of the so-called Bengal Renaissance, Nandy is today—now that Nirad Chaudhuri has passed on—our only true colonial thinker. He may be a colonial romantic, but that does not make him any less colonial in his mentality.

Within days of the publication of this provocative—though brief—essay, an avalanche of responses appeared, some in the weblog of *Outlook* itself (which was not controlled, let alone censored, by a webmaster), but also in the form of a vast number of emails, often extremely violent and abusive, directly sent to my electronic mail address in Oxford. A substantial number came from the United States, Canada, and Europe, but since much that happens on the internet is done under the cover of anonymity, it was often impossible to verify the real locations (let alone the names and identities) of the protagonists. The editorial staff of *Outlook* obviously were delighted by the controversy and helped stoke it, not only by choosing provocative titles for the letters but also, in one case, mischievously altering the content of a letter so as to render it more aggressive. I eventually responded in the form of a letter that the magazine deigned to publish, which ran as follows:

> Attacks on 'secularism' as an ideology in India have, in the past 15–20 years, come from two quarters. One's the predictable, Hindu majoritarian view that claims that Hindus (especially high-caste ones) have been discriminated against in the name of secularism. Such people, who include the usual roster of shrill, strident, self-pitying Non-Resident Knicker-Dharis (NRKDs)—many of whose letters one finds in response to the recent articles on 'secularism' in *Outlook*—are really beneath contempt, hardly worth arguing with. Let's leave them to their Modi-worship and pogrom fantasies.

The second attack, with which my essay was concerned, is largely from 'indigenist' authors who claim that secularism was inauthentic, un-Indian, a slavish imitation of a model that came from elsewhere. I argued that the Indian idea of secularism does not come from elsewhere. For where could that 'elsewhere' be? The model does not fit the UK, or most of the rest of Europe. The US, to my mind, is hardly a secular polity, and no one dares affirm 'secularism' as a value there amongst the major political figures. Samuel Huntington has recently laid bare the conservative (and widely shared) understanding of what America stands for: it is Protestant, English-speaking, intolerant of difference. No wonder the NRKDs can find no place for their political programme there, and so must try and spread it in India. The French Republican ideal of *laïcité* is an aggressive homogenizing model, which has little to do with 'secularism' as understood in India. Secularism as discussed and understood in India is in large measure not an imitation, but *sui generis*. It may not be an old word in India, but it has something profound to do with an older set of practices and even institutions. This secularism is not the same as some wishy-washy idea of 'tolerance'. No one ever will claim to be intolerant. No doubt even Mr Modi and Mr Togadia will claim to be tolerant. The NRKDs probably believe they are tolerant too. My concern is that the authors of the second type of critique of secularism, whatever their initial motivations, have become increasingly complicit with those who hold the first view. None of this means one has to defend the Congress and its record on secularism, which is pretty abysmal. This is a red herring, and should be treated as such. The real question today is hence whether writers like Ashis Nandy—whose work I have followed with close attention for over 20 years—can be happy that their primary constituency is to be found among aggressive, upper-caste Hindu majoritarian critics of 'secularism'. Is Modistan really what the indigenists are looking for?

I do not wish to imply that all the responses, whether in the blogosphere or in print, were unreasonable, let alone abusive. But relatively few of them had taken the real content of what was being said into account. 'Knicker-Dhari' was, incidentally, a phrase that I did not invent, it was used by many New Delhi bureaucrats of the time who were tired of the BJP. At any rate, assumptions were made that I was a mere apologist for the Mughals, a spokesman for the Congress Party, a card-carrying Marxist, and the like. Even as intelligent an essayist as Amit Chaudhuri fell into this trap and wrote an extended comment on the matter a few weeks later in the pages of the *Telegraph* from Kolkata. He portrayed Nandy as a lonely intellectual David fighting an establishment Goliath, of which I was the designated representative. This was so sufficiently far from the truth that I once again responded, with some irritation. This piece, entitled 'A Guru and His Followers', published in early August 2004, appears below.

I was initially interested to read Amit Chaudhuri's extended two-part essay in *The Telegraph* (25 July and 1 August 2004), 'Distant Thunder' and 'A Climate of Opinion'. But my interest soon turned to disquiet, for I found that his essay was simply another one in a series he has written expressing his own admiration for Ashis Nandy's work while simultaneously misrepresenting the position of Nandy's rather diverse critics (see his 'On the Nature of the Indian Gothic', *The Hindu*, 6 April 2003). I am hence constrained to reply, albeit somewhat more briefly, than Chaudhuri.

Many of Chaudhuri's basic assumptions are largely unfounded. Let us begin at the beginning. It is quite untrue that public airings of intellectual differences are rare in India. One has only to read the *Economic and Political Weekly* to know this is incorrect. These debates and disagreements are not simply about territorial identities, but very substantive affairs, say between Ramachandra Guha and Peter D'Souza, or Partha Chatterjee and Ranajit Guha. I am unclear where Chaudhuri derives his information for such *ex cathedra* pronouncements from, or whether he has in fact looked into this matter carefully.

This initial misconception then leads to a series of others. It is equally incorrect to pose Nandy as a Lone Ranger, a marginal crusader against an undifferentiated establishment of 'liberal intellectuals' composed of Romila Thapar and Sanjay Subrahmanyam, both industriously engaged in writing official 'secular' textbooks to brainwash the masses. To begin with, anyone who has followed the field would know that my own relations with official historians and the history establishment of the Indian Council of Historical Research—from Irfan Habib to Ravinder Kumar—have been anything but consensual. I have never written a textbook, and have no intention of doing so. But I have taught in universities, which I suppose will be regarded as a sin by some.

Nandy chose not to take up a teaching position himself, when he could easily have had one in the University of Delhi. This is because it was possible for him to have a very comfortable career as a full-time researcher in an institution that was quite well funded by mainstream agencies both in India and abroad (from the Indian Council for Social Science Research to the Ford and Rockefeller Foundations). It is a conceit to believe that this bestselling author of the Oxford University Press and Princeton University Press, whose books are used in cultural studies and postcolonial studies courses in many parts of the world, is simply a marginal figure, a minority voice, an eccentric. He is in fact a kind of guru, and even the get-up of his books—where he is prominently featured on the front cover (rather like the J. Krishnamurti Readers)—testifies to this.

So what are the constituencies of this guru? Clearly, Nandy has several. His anti-science, anti-modernity, and anti-technology writings appeal to a part of the Indian middle class which revels in its guilt, and so flocks to buy his books. His clever essays on cricket, Satyajit Ray, Kipling, or Tagore, strike a chord with the Amit Chaudhuris of the world, or a certain brand of Subaltern Studies and postcolonial studies thinker. But there is a third category of writings, for which Nandy has found a constituency in the extreme right wing of Hindu nationalists, because of his position on sati, or secularism; I also recall a rather frightening occasion at the SOAS in London, where he rose to make an impassioned defence of the RSS as true freedom fighters against the Emergency. Whether this is his intention I do not know, but he has certainly not disavowed this constituency. I do not have to caricature him in this matter, since the fact is that Nandy is very good at caricaturing himself, especially when he appears in public arm in arm with the likes of Claude Alvares. The deluge of hate mail (and believe me, there was a lot of it, often unprintable) that poured in when my critique of his position was published in *Outlook* essentially came from this lot, often resident in the United States and Canada, but also to be found in Bangalore, Calcutta, and Mumbai.

So who does not find Ashis Nandy today 'significant, provocative and necessary'? The dying breed of orthodox Marxists do not, since he never fails to attack them for being complicit in Stalinist massacres and the like. Neither do most Dalit intellectuals, who find his defence of an imaginary, bucolic, rural India—a place free of violence and with everyone living together in peace—not just false but repellent and deeply patronizing (and, as Chaudhuri would put it, 'discriminatory, exclusivist, and unegalitarian'). And, I have to say, most sensible historians who have read his bizarre essay ('History's Forgotten Doubles'), which Chaudhuri too has read but passes over in silence, on how history must be gotten rid of and myth revived, can only wish that Nandy had fewer followers than he does. This has nothing to do with membership of Chaudhuri's completely invented bogeyman group, 'a new "secular" ruling class, [that] began to form, after the death of Indira Gandhi, around Rajiv Gandhi, in Delhi.' This claim is not simply irresponsible and utterly bogus, but pernicious and deeply offensive, if Chaudhuri means to say I belong to such a group. I cannot have much respect for an author whose stock-in-trade consists of such low canards.

So, to my last point, namely what this in fact has to do with the heritage of the Bengal Renaissance. Far from being 'utterly heterogeneous', it is clear what this movement did epitomize. It meant accepting the premise that a 're-naissance' was needed in India, after some form of Dark Ages. It meant rejecting the pre-colonial centuries and harking back to a classical Golden Age, whose contours were conveniently provided by Orientalists. This is what I mean when I see Nandy as a colonial thinker, namely his utter subservience to Orientalist clichés regarding India's past. In this Nandy is like Ranajit Guha or Dipesh Chakrabarty, other thinkers whom Amit Chaudhuri much admires. Their position may be ostensibly anti-colonial, but in fact—no matter what their internal divisions—they are all prisoners of the very same heritage as the Chaudhuris, both Nirad and Amit, as well as of the Greater India theorists of the inter-war period. Amit Chaudhuri's own essay drips with cultural cringe, with his gratuitous references to Eliot, Blake, Lawrence, Auden, and Whitehead, who are obviously the defining points of his universe. Ranajit Guha makes similar gratuitous use of the *Mahabharata*. But the point of departure is the same.

Is there a way out of this bind? There is, if one looks to other writers, such as Gautam Bhadra, or Partha Chatterjee (at least in his critique of Ranajit Guha). But to take this another way, one must have read more of, say, Alaol, Daulat Qazi, and Bharatchandra, and less of Bankim and Tagore. That may yet be a distant dream.

Indefatigable polemicist that he is, Amit Chaudhuri was not about to let me have the last word and responded again at great length, pointing out how much better his command of Bengali was than mine (a matter I was not about to dispute), and attempting to score as many trivial debating points as he could. In the process, he unfortunately failed to address the two central points in my short polemical essay: his quite mistaken and rather insulting characterization of my political position as deriving from a 'secularist' grouping around Rajiv Gandhi (which was no doubt the result of his lack of knowledge about the academic politics of Delhi); and his curious portrayal of Nandy—an enormously influential and powerful intellectual with a very extensive (but also rather erratic) following both in India and the West—as a pathetic underdog. There, we might say, the matter rested, with the exception of a few further minor sallies from Nandy's disciples, sometimes in the form of craven reviews by them of his most recent books, which they made occasions for attacking his critics.

I have had occasion to think the matter over in the intervening years, especially after discussing it with serious interlocutors in less heated circumstances than those of 2004. Was I wrong to write these short essays? I would still wish to defend my case up to a point. No doubt it was quite foolhardy to launch an attack on 'the heritage of the Bengal Renaissance' in the leading English-language newspaper of Kolkata; I was likely to have few sympathizers in that city in regard to that position. I was thus tactically wrong to write the second essay, and also to widen its scope to attack (as one blogger bluntly put it), 'well, half the world'. But polemics sometimes have their own inexorable logic. Nevertheless, I continue to hold to the view that while Nandy, like any intellectual, may not be responsible for the more extreme views of his followers, he also has a particular proclivity towards rhetorical excess and deliberate and irresponsible provocation. An inspection of his works from about 1980 to the present day shows a progressive simplification of his positions, a widening of claims, and a corresponding ratcheting up of the tone.

And so finally to the question of *convivencia*, secularism, and tolerance as alternative terms. Anyone who uses the first of these terms is obliged to return to its inventor, the twentieth-century

Spanish historian and ideologue Américo Castro, and also to his critics. The usage, as is by now well known, is part of a modern myth of a Golden Age of Spain before the expulsion of the Jews and Moriscos, which can hardly be reconciled with the fact that the several centuries before 1500 were occupied by constant wars in Iberia, as well as the broad and unkind trend called the *reconquista*. Most of the states that were in this competition had a dominant religious group, and then also more or less tolerated minorities in a subordinated role. This, to my mind, can hardly be the model for any future state in the space of India, unless it is a model of a dominant Hindutva with its 'tolerated' minorities. This brings us in turn to the question of 'tolerance', a concept of so sufficient a vagueness that it can have no consequential institutional let alone legal meaning. One community can exercise enormous power over another and yet claim to 'tolerate' it. These usages remain, in my view, red herrings. This is not to say that there should be no debate on secularism in South Asia; on the contrary. But it cannot be meaningfully framed either in terms of these false alternatives, or indeed in terms of the equally false opposition between desirable purely homegrown conceptual products and undesirable imports.

4

Indian Political History and Ramachandra Guha*

I t may seem a little perverse to begin this essay on India by invoking a most influential historian of France who died in May 2007, Eugen Weber. A colleague of mine and a formidable presence at my university UCLA, Weber (b. 1925) was as prolific as he was eclectic, an Anglophile with an ironic—even acerbic—humour, who famously wrote a book in 1976 on how France became a proper nation by transforming 'peasants into Frenchmen'. But the Weber I knew, and exchanged banter with on some occasions in the last years of his life, also had an Indian past of which he felt periodically obliged to speak, although he spoke to me of it with discomfort (and not only from embarrassment because he initially mistook me for a Sikh). For Weber, though born in Bucharest, migrated to England to study in Windermere, served in the Second World War as captain (and possibly as chaplain) in the King's Own Scottish Borderers, and in the course of this service spent the mid-1940s in India, as well as stints in Belgium and Germany. Eventually demobilized in

*On *India after Gandhi: The History of the World's Largest Democracy* by Ramachandra Guha (London: Macmillan, 2007), xxvi, 900pp., and *The Clash Within: Democracy, Religious Violence, and India's Future* by Martha C. Nussbaum (Cambridge, Mass., and London: The Belknap Press of Harvard University Press, 2007), xviii + 403pp.

1947, he went to Cambridge, and the rest (once he gave up his initial idea of pursuing a career in law) is history, mostly French history. However, Weber did continue until the end of his life to harbour a certain affection for India, and visited it on more than one occasion in later years, besides keeping up a marked taste for spicy curries. It was an affection that was tempered though by chilling memories of the religious violence that he had witnessed at very close quarters in India in 1946–7, as part of the birth-pangs of the modern Indian nation, which he never forgot; hence his discomfort.

Weber is best known for his account of how the modern French nation was built in the course of the late-nineteenth and early-twentieth centuries. It is an account involving roads and railways, schoolrooms and stern *instituteurs*, and of the production of homogeneous 'Frenchness' (as both reality and myth) from the diverse *terroirs* that still existed in 1870. It is either a version of modernization theory, as some of its critics have claimed, or a rather sly account of the modernizing pretensions and projects of the Parisian elite, or even both of the above—as Weber himself sometimes gave out. Devoid of pretentious jargon, or any explicit nod in the direction of the social sciences, the work has been a sort of model, whether implicit or explicit, of how to write modern national histories ever since its publication thirty years ago. One may even be tempted to see its distant shadow cast on Benedict Anderson's account of how print capitalism helped create the 'imagined communities' that are today's nation-states.

No such master-account as that of Weber has existed so far for the modern Indian nation-state, partly because historians of the subcontinent have usually shied away from reaching beyond 1947, leaving that task to political scientists, sociologists, and omniscient travellers. The curious practices of Indian archives and their keepers have not helped either, as documents are declassified and allowed into the public domain on a very erratic basis. When my wife, herself a historian of modern France (and a critical admirer of Eugen Weber's work) asked me some years ago to recommend an accessible work on the history of modern India, I was left nonplussed. The market was hardly saturated. Sumit Sarkar's sweeping but dense account in *Modern India* did not extend beyond 1947; the collective volume entitled *India after Independence* by Bipan Chandra, Aditya Mukherjee, and Mridula Mukherjee was really a stodgy, snore-inducing piece of nationalist-Marxist writing from the rank and file of plodders at New Delhi's Jawaharlal Nehru University. Though an admirer of some of his novels, I really could not subject her to a diet of Sir V.S. Naipaul's bile-infused travelogues such as *An Area of Darkness*, and his later incarnation as an apologist for right-wing Hindu nationalism in *India: A Million Mutinies Now* had little to recommend it either. Eventually, I settled for Sunil Khilnani's *The Idea of India*, an urbane, readable, and somewhat personal account by a historically-minded political scientist who, coincidentally, had initially worked on France and published a first book entitled *Arguing Revolution: The Intellectual Left in Postwar France*. Khilnani's work on India is not to everyone's taste, but it has some virtues, including its mellifluous style and its assumption of very little prior knowledge regarding that part of the world. It also has one rather notorious vice, namely its author's weakness for the personality and ideas of independent India's first prime minister, Jawaharlal Nehru (1889–1964), whose biography he has been writing now for some years.

It could only be a matter of time before this wide historiographical breach was filled. The task that Ramachandra Guha sets himself in his massive account on 'India after Gandhi' is not quite one of telling of the Indian *fin des terroirs* (the first French title of the translated *Peasants into Frenchmen*). But it is still the story of the building of a rather improbable nation-state from a fragmented political landscape, and as such it is primarily a political narrative. Eugen Weber does not appear in it, and even Max Weber, who wrote extensively on India, has no more than a cameo role. But like Eugen Weber's work, it is primarily a narrative account, expertly and fluently written, and has apparently found its way to the top of the non-fiction bestseller list in India (a list that is itself, paradoxically, a form of fiction since no one really knows how much of what is sold). It is also a work that shies away from jargon or from any overly explicit use of the social sciences and their apparatus.

While this may have been easily explained in Eugen Weber's case, since he was a humanist with no training in the social sciences, it is perhaps more surprising in that of Guha, who actually has had a rather unorthodox career. Initially trained as an economist, he then moved into historical sociology (tempered with anthropology), to produce a first book-length work on the history of an environmental movement in the Himalayas. Over the past two decades, he has continued off and on to work on the environment, in the form of general histories, comparative reflections, and tracts with a more contemporary flavour. A second interest of his has been the history of anthropology, largely through his engagement with the life of the missionary-turned-anthropologist Verrier Elwin, on whom he has written a successful book. A third aspect of Guha's work is the history of sport in colonial and post-colonial India, and above all cricket, on which he also writes in a more popular vein. Guha has also, since the early 1990s, refused a stable position in the academy and makes a living from writing and lectures, including two regular columns in the Indian newspapers *The Telegraph* and *The Hindu*. He is probably the best-known public historian in India today, and the one whose books and essay collections—rather than those of Partha Chatterjee and Romila Thapar—the visitor is most likely to find in a middle-class drawing room. Ironically, if he has a rival in the public domain, it is not an Indian, but the Delhi-based Scotsman William Dalrymple, with whom he does not quite see eye to eye for complicated reasons having to do with their relative positions on British imperialism and Indian nationalism.

The reader of his weighty book will come quickly to the conclusion that Guha is indeed an Indian nationalist, albeit a moderate and self-critical one. He is also a self-defined 'liberal', a word that actually has no real resonance in the world of Indian politics today, but which is meant to suggest a distance both from Marxist historiography and that of the right-wing Hindu nationalists who have a firm hold on power in New Delhi. It is from these standpoints that he sets out to produce an account of India since 1947, focusing on why India has remained a democracy against the odds, while using the 'techniques of the narrative historian' rather than of the social scientist. The emplotment (or *mise-en-intrigue*, as Paul Ricoeur might have it) is straightforward enough: there are forces that divide India, and others that serve to keep it together. Amongst the first set of forces, there are four in particular, all large and impersonal: caste, language, religion, and class, which operate at times singly and at times together. As for the latter forces, which are still unexpectedly winning the game, they are less evident. In closing his prologue entitled 'Unnatural Nation', Guha assures us that 'they have included individuals as well as institutions'. But how much of each, one is entitled to ask, and in what combinations?

Guha himself seems in no doubt about this. His tale is told in five somewhat unequal sections. The first, 'Picking up the Pieces', takes up the immediate aftermath of Partition and Independence, beginning with the assassination of Gandhi in January 1948, and sets the stage for what follows in some 120 dense pages; the second, somewhat longer, section is tellingly entitled 'Nehru's India', and carries the story to about 1957 when it seemed that Nehru's plans for a modern, industrialized, secular India could really be implemented; the third part, 'Shaking the Centre' then chronicles the declining years of Nehru, including the disastrous war in 1962 with China; the fourth part, 'The Rise of Populism' carries us through the complex cycle of the rise to power, temporary eclipse, second rise, and ultimate murders of Nehru's only child, Indira Gandhi, and then her own older son Rajiv; while the fifth and final section, where the author in his own words 'moves from "history" to what might instead be called "historically informed journalism"' takes us from the late 1980s to the present. The balance is clear enough though: the Nehru years are at the heart of the book, and manifestly also closest to the author's own heart.

The good philosopher-king, succeeded by the scheming, corrupt, and spoilt princess-in-waiting, and then by the well-intentioned but weak, pouting, and feckless little prince. Now this looks rather like the dynastic history that early modern historians like myself used to practice (Nehru as Charles V, Mrs Gandhi as Philip II, Rajiv as Philip III, and so on), but is that really Guha's fault? The raw materials of modern high politics in India are, after all, largely dynastic, as indeed they are to some extent in Pakistan and Bangladesh. But there are also choices that Guha makes which further this tendency. The most important of these is his decision to 'humanize' his history by consistently highlighting the place and role of individuals, of whom Nehru and Indira Gandhi appear most prominently. This is not to say that there are not a good number of Rosencrantzes and Guildensterns around; in fact, the book abounds in deft portrayals of all kinds of leaders, from communists such as Namboodiripad in Kerala, to separatists in the north-east and Kashmir. There is even the Polonius-like Iyengar Brahmin from Tamilnadu, C. Rajagopalachari, wagging his finger and advising all and sundry to neither a borrower nor a lender be. This is a good strategy when one is writing popular history, because individuals and their biographies are indeed the regular stuff of such history. But for all his deftness with portraits small and large, one is actually relieved when Guha the social scientist periodically re-emerges to tell us of the planning process and its pitfalls, or the still-abiding problems of poverty and caste in a 'globalized' India, or even when he evokes Durkheim to discuss the issue of recent farmers' suicides in rural India.

There is no doubt that this is a dazzling book in many ways. Its prose is always attractive, and it is a real page-turner with a sureness to its essentially chronological organization. The different regions of India get a fair and balanced treatment, not always the case in such histories. Besides memoirs, monographs, and essays, as well as contemporary newspapers, Guha has also plunged into certain important archival collections, such as the papers of Indira Gandhi's right-hand man of the early 1970s, P.N. Haksar. But it is not a book that will satisfy all discerning readers, particularly those inclined to a more inclusive social history, who will hence find the biographically-oriented political narrative a little overwhelming. Others may carp at the small place given to culture, or even to sport—one of Guha's own preferred domains of interest. But the problem does remain of how one organizes a narrative history in the absence of a powerful central thesis such as that proposed and defended by Eugen Weber, and which, as we know, had its own insistent critics as well. Individuals and their actions, in Weber's view—for all that he was a humanist— eventually fade into relative insignificance, save as voices that are used to articulate one or the other position. There are no real heroes or villains in his conception of the making of modern France, which is a far more diffuse affair than the individual projects of Napoleon III or Georges-Eugène Haussmann.

What could such a central thesis *à la* Weber have been, had Guha chosen hypothetically to pursue such a line? We should note at the outset that this would not really have required Guha to deal with matters he has left aside (for his book is indeed astonishingly comprehensive in the way it deals with a variety of themes), but rather to reorganize the materials to highlight a particular thrust or set of thrusts. The first possibility would have been to focus centrally on social mobility and its limits in India over the past sixty years. This would have meant dealing jointly with two of the issues that Guha indeed sees as central challenges to Indian democracy: namely, caste and class. Moreover, he is well aware of the potential fecundity of this particular line of enquiry and writes that 'as a laboratory of social conflict the India of the twentieth century is—for the historian—at least as interesting as the Europe of the nineteenth', adding that 'in India the scope for contention has been even greater [than in Europe], given the diversity of competing groups across religion, caste, class and language.' From such a focus, the real question to be answered would be how India, despite the fact that it has effectively provided so little opportunity for economic and social mobility over the past sixty years, has nevertheless been the site of such limited social violence (seen in comparative terms). I stress that this is not to understate the actual violence that takes place in both towns and the countryside, both the assertive, bloody aspects and the quiet violence of everyday oppression. But it is all the same remarkable how different this still is from the situation in Latin America or much of Africa. The violence of a city such as Mumbai (formerly Bombay), much dramatized in recent years by writers such as Suketu Mehta in his *Maximum City*, does not really compare with São Paulo, Mexico City, or Lagos.

The answer sketched out by some would stress the complementary relationship between the political system and the social and economic processes mentioned above. To writers such as the prolific Paris-based political scientist Christophe Jaffrelot (and he is only one amongst many to make the point), the political system in India effectively diverts energies that might have exploded violently in other societies. In his work entitled *India's Silent Revolution: The Rise of the Lower Castes in North India* (2003), Jaffrelot plots the rise to political office of a large number of lower-caste men and even some women. A

particularly dramatic instance of this was that of the so-called
'bandit queen', Phoolan Devi (1963–2001), who belonged to
the *mallah* caste of boatmen in the northern Indian state of Uttar
Pradesh. After serving out eleven years in prison for her activities
as a bandit, she was actually elected to the Indian Parliament in
1996 on behalf of the Samajwadi Party, but was eventually shot
by assailants outside her home in New Delhi. Revenge was given
as the apparent motive behind her killers' actions, and most of
them belonged to far higher castes than her. But alongside this
rather lurid story one can also plot the entrepreneurial use of the
political system by those who could certainly never have been
recruited into the Indian Administrative Service, and even less
the Bank of America. The pool of industrial entrepreneurs in
India still remains depressingly limited to a small group of castes
(with relatively few exceptions), but politics has opened up in a
way that it has not in neighbouring Pakistan or Bangladesh.

In other words, the Indian world is in concrete terms not
much like that of Eugen Weber's France, where a relatively
limited and coherent elite set out to 'modernize' the rest of the
nation in both discursive and institutional terms. Rather, it is
the political elite itself that has been transformed from the time
of Nehru to the present day, in ways that are of course deeply
disturbing to upper-caste voices and points of view. To be sure,
this has also gone hand in hand with what has been termed the
'criminalization of politics', with large numbers of legislators
in India today being either convicted felons or facing criminal
charges of one sort or the other, rather than being lawyers like
Gandhi or Patel. However, this cannot be separated from the
larger problem of how the limits placed upon mobility by class
and caste jointly have been addressed in a democratic political
framework. This is a theme that has long been dear to the heart
of one of Guha's mentors, the liberal sociologist André Béteille,
and has now been addressed by political theorists farther on
the left such as Partha Chatterjee, who have posited a lasting

distinction between the tea-and-biscuits politeness of 'civil society' and the rough-and-tumble of 'political society'. Whether or not one wishes to accept such a potentially rigid distinction, it could certainly provide the guiding theme for a discussion of the past sixty years.

An alternative strong hypothesis might have focused on the issue of regions in India, and various centrifugal and centripetal forces that inhere in a space that still remains more populated and, in some ways, more complex than the European Union. Guha again does invest a good deal here and there in discussing the problem, but largely in relation to two sets of issues: first, where region is read through the prism of language and linguistic divisions; and second, in relation to the northern and north-eastern border states which have posed a long-term challenge to Indian political unity. However, we are now aware that sixty years of independence have, if anything, sharpened regional disparities in India, not so much in cultural terms (where some homogenization can be discerned) but in regard to the basic human indicators, including demographic ones. It is thus possible to draw a diagonal line sloping from right to left across the centre of India (a sort of 'St Malo-Geneva line' in reverse), and discern sharp differences above and below the line in terms of rates of population growth, infant mortality, the economic status of women, and the sex ratio. This can be posed as a more complex problem still, once one factors in the role of a limited number of mega-cities as growth poles, where peasants are allegedly being transformed into programmers. In this context, Guha cites Amartya Sen as worrying that 'one half of India will come to look and live like California, the other half like sub-Saharan Africa'. But as significant as this mere fact, which may also characterize growth in the age of globalization in China, is that such economic and social differences could well manifest themselves regionally (and here, once again, the regional comparisons with China are relevant). In other words, even as a number of the older cultural conflicts based on considerations such as language, as well as 'ethnicity' (in particular, the celebrated and somewhat bogus divide between Aryans and Dravidians) have been resolved, other longer-term regional differences have persisted, and even become aggravated, with every prospect of further aggravation as both politics, and political economy, become more rather than less decentralized. Guha, no doubt anxious not to turn his narrative into another boring tract in the social sciences, hints at some of these issues, but eventually sets them aside for his preferred method of exposition based on vignettes. In this process, he gains a large audience, but misses the opportunity—if that is the right word—of a real argument with others in the field.

The problem of emplotment finds a quite different solution in Martha Craven Nussbaum's book, which is less than half the size of Guha's doorstop of a tome. Nussbaum is a celebrated philosopher and a classicist who, from an initial training in Hellenistic philosophy and the interpretation of Aristotle, has begun in recent years to write far more widely on issues of development, feminism, and public affairs. Her interest in India stems from personal dealings over two decades with a number of prominent Indians (especially the family of Kshiti Mohan Sen and Amartya Sen); in her preface, she compares this to her conversion from an 'elite WASP heritage' to Judaism and 'the cause of the underdog in my own country', and adds that she is equally 'sure that my passion for India (and particularly for Bengali culture) reflects a similar enthusiasm for the colonial underdog.' Nussbaum apparently celebrates the Indian Independence Day on 15 August 'enthusiastically' in Chicago, while even Indian ambassadors abroad have been known simply to go through the motions on the occasion. This is a rather more curious form of (vicarious) Indian nationalism, arguably, than that of Ramachandra Guha, who still lives in Bangalore.

Nussbaum's book deals with religious violence in India, and

more particularly with Hindu majoritarian violence organized around groups often called by their three-letter acronyms such as the RSS, VHP, BJP, and so on. If the work can be identified by genre, it is primarily a sort of travelogue, reviving the narrative form of philosopher-as-traveller most famously associated with the French doctor (and disciple of Gassendi) François Bernier, in seventeenth-century Mughal India. Martha Nussbaum is manifestly a liberal, but apparently in the American sense of a left-leaning Democrat. Her heart is certainly in the right place, and her intention is to be Socratic, open, and engaging while dealing with her Indian interlocutors, who include a number of rather unpleasant defenders of mass violence (and perhaps even some perpetrators thereof).

Given the fact that Nussbaum's book is (by her own claim) intended 'for an American and European audience' with a view to act amongst other things as 'a loudspeaker' for views already expressed in India by other, presumably less famous, scholars, I suppose I am not its ideal reader. If this book does indeed raise awareness in the West of the acuteness of certain forms of politico-religious tension in India and the role played by a number of clearly identifiable groups in organizing and justifying mass violence, that alone would be laudable. But if it is intended as a work of genuine and deep scholarship on India, questions can and should be raised. A work like this can easily cause embarrassment amongst those devoted to the same political causes as Nussbaum, and judging by responses on internet websites may already have done so. It will be easy enough for those who wish to mock this book and its political message to point to its errors of historical fact, its eccentric views regarding Indian scripts and the difference between Hindi and Urdu, and debatable points of view on a variety of other questions on which Nussbaum is simply paraphrasing, or repeating, what she has been told, without being able to apply any of her own considerable critical faculties to the questions at hand.

Perhaps with a view to getting around this recurrent problem, or perhaps simply by way of adherence to a generic convention, Nussbaum resorts in a good part of the book to first-person narratives of her own personal experiences, including interviews with a number of the dramatis personae. But the philosopher-as-traveller (however omniscient in tone) still finds it hard to pull off a Naipaul or a Christopher Kremmer. These interviews are rather stylized and follow quite predictable plots. A physical description of the interviewee is usually presented: Arun Shourie has 'a long straight mustache, restless burning eyes, a bald head fringed with thick gray hair'; Romila Thapar has 'a stately bearing, a deep, mellifluous voice, and elite, British-accented English', and so on. Where Nussbaum is sympathetic to their views, they are presented with a minimum of fuss; where she is not, they are often presented rather condescendingly, as psychologically inadequate or disturbed persons, as much to be pitied as they are to be censured; only occasionally does she find someone really beyond the pale. There is also a periodic (perhaps involuntary) genuflection to reflexive anthropology, such as when we find Nussbaum on a January morning in Delhi 'wrapping my shawl vainly around my cotton *salwaar kameez*', since she cannot persuade her taxi driver to drive with his windows closed (normally a simple task for non-philosopher travellers). I must confess that the significance of her apparel on the occasion still escapes me.

At the end of these interviews, interspersed as they are with reflections on Gandhi and Tagore (who Nussbaum greatly admires), and Nehru (for whom her admiration is more mitigated) one is really left no wiser than by reading the Indian newspapers on an intermittent basis. This is a classic case of preaching to the converted, and not a single person who does not share Nussbaum's views at the beginning is likely to change their mind by the end. One even feels the philosopher's talents, passions, and splendid analytical skills have been wasted sadly in this exercise. The constant references to Tagore, and his relevance to India today, are particularly ironic since even the Bengali *bhadralok* bourgeoisie have now shown signs of moving beyond his Deist vision, and somewhat monotonous and romantic message. Yet Nussbaum continues to insist that 'India needs Tagore today even more than it needs Nehru and Gandhi', as if these were the only three significant thinkers or points of view available in modern India. One can only see the traces here of her excessive dependence on expatriate Bengali informants, suggesting that Chicago today is no more than an intellectual suburb of Kolkata.

Yet, the publication of Nussbaum's book by a major university press in the US, and the reviews of it that have appeared in many non-academic magazines and journals (including *The Economist*) might suggest that even the bad times are good. Interest in the Indian subcontinent is clearly at a high in the Atlantic world today, after years when Japan, Korea, and China were at the centre of attention where Asia was concerned. The price to be paid for popularity is, at least in some measure, the resort to one or the other form of expository simplification, more or less justifiable. Unlike the past, the trade press is an option that is open now to most of us who work on India, and not just to novelists and travellers alone. Mother India can come out of the closet at last. More will be heard.

5

V.S. Naipaul's Pride and Prejudices*

I n a wonderful short story called 'Haha Huhu', written
in Telugu in the early 1930s, Vishvanatha Satyanarayana
(1893–1976) describes an accidental traveller to England: a
gandharva, a flying half-man half-horse from classical India,
who loses his wings and crash-lands in Trafalgar Square. His
encounter with English society as he lies captive in his cage
and waits for his wings to grow back becomes the occasion
for Satyanarayana to comment wryly on many things: among
them cultural difference, the nature of scientific progress, and
the resources that Indian culture may still possess even though
under colonial rule. It is not a romantic text, nor is it a militant
call for the revival of old Hindu values. But Satyanarayana,
who had a distinctly modern literary sensibility while being
wholly immersed in the long literary tradition of Telugu and
Sanskrit, is not much read today outside Andhra Pradesh. His
gandharva ends the story by soaring off into the sky, destination
unknown, calling out to his perplexed English captors that he'd
never seen a 'more childish race'. It's a subtle piece of work, but
Satyanarayana's version of the encounter between the West and
the non-West has nearly been lost to us.

*On *A Writer's People: Ways of Looking and Feeling* by V.S. Naipaul
(London: Picador, 2007), 193pp.

The fame that eluded Satyanarayana has been granted of late to other authors from India and of Indian origin, mostly writing in English. In their forefront is the author of this collection of opinion pieces and reminiscences. A quarter of the way into it, V.S. Naipaul offers the reader an insight into his thinking:

> I had criticised others from my background for their lack of curiosity. I meant curiosity in cultural matters; but the people I criticised would have had their own view of the relative importance of things and they would have been astonished by my lack of political curiosity. As soon as I begin to examine the matter I see that this ignorance of mine (there is no other word for it), this limited view, was an aspect of our history and culture. Historically, the peasantry of the Gangetic plain were a powerless people. We were ruled by tyrants, often far off, who came and went and whose names we very often didn't know. It didn't make sense in that setting to take an interest in public affairs, if such a thing could be said to exist.

Naipaul is here using history to explain the difference between his own sensibility in the mid-1950s and a half-century later. In his youth, Naipaul recounts, he believed that 'things ran their course; elections took place, and the United States and Great Britain continued much as they had done'. This otherwise incomprehensible indifference to current events is seen by him in 2007 as possessing one major virtue: 'When I began to travel I saw places fresh.' But has he seen 'places fresh', as he claims? Or is he no more than a prisoner of his history and heritage? It is a question worth asking.

Many people have strong opinions about this Trinidadian expatriate, including the reviewers and interviewers he regularly deals with. The dividing line is essentially political, a fact that might be disquieting for a creative writer. In this respect Naipaul is more like Solzhenitsyn than, say, Joyce, whose appeal can transcend (or confound) traditional political divides. In the case of Naipaul, those on the left, especially defenders of the 'Third World' and its hopes, from Edward Said to Michael Gilsenan to C.L.R. James (who had decidedly mixed sentiments), more or less uniformly find him and his attitudes troubling and sometimes bigoted. He is portrayed as a self-hater and Uncle Tom, a product of the sorts of complex that Frantz Fanon diagnosed. On the other side are the conservative writers—those who might see Ayaan Hirsi Ali as a major intellectual figure—who celebrate Naipaul as an original voice, a writer who provides a searing, politically incorrect indictment of all that is wrong in the modern world: Islam in its various manifestations, the grotesque dictatorships of Africa, the squalor and self-inflicted misery of much of the Third World, the failure everywhere of projects of *métissage* between the West and non-West. A few fence-sitters meanwhile play down the significance of his non-fiction and praise his fiction, his pared-down style and capacity to write precise, economical, somewhat repetitive English. Naipaul is a prototype that has now been cloned many times over in the Indian subcontinent: the fiction writer who is also a travel writer with pretensions to omniscience. One can see why Pankaj Mishra may read and review Naipaul with an Oedipal frisson. *Vatermord* or ancestor worship? It can be a hard choice.

The five essays in this volume mostly revisit earlier moments in Naipaul's work. The first essay refers back to the Caribbean of Naipaul's childhood in the late 1940s and is largely concerned to deflate the reputation of the poet Derek Walcott through a clever exercise in condescension and faint praise. Walcott and Naipaul, both Nobel Prize winners, have long been rivals, in both a literary and a political sense, and the bitterness remains. Walcott has referred to Naipaul as 'V.S. Nightfall', while Walcott for Naipaul is a 'mulatto, of old mixed race', who has chosen to 'put himself on the black side'. His poetry is seen as deliberately giving matters 'a racial twist'; it would seem that his talent quickly ran out and that he had to be 'rescued by the American universities'. The black or 'Negro' culture of the Caribbean is one for which Naipaul has no sympathy; he tells us, for example, without citing a source for the incident (he does not seem to have been present), that 'in 1945, when newsreels of concentration-camp sufferers were shown in Port of Spain cinemas, black people in the cheaper seats laughed and shouted.' Why? Was it schadenfreude because they were black and poor? A case of Louis Farrakhan *avant la lettre*? A simple lack of empathy with their fellow man? No answer or analysis is provided. We are meant to conclude that even the English, whatever their colonial past in the Caribbean and India, would not have been so cruel.

The second essay, 'An English Way of Looking', moves on logically and chronologically to the moment when Naipaul began his writing career in England after getting a degree from Oxford (where he had been sent on a scholarship from Trinidad in 1950). In 1957 Naipaul was befriended by Anthony Powell, who helped set his literary career on a firm footing. After Powell's death in 2000 at the age of 94, Naipaul was asked by the editor of an unnamed literary weekly to write about him. Naipaul notes that in spite of their long friendship he was not acquainted with most of Powell's work, and adds, characteristically: 'It may be that the friendship lasted all this time because I had not examined his work.' When he began to read Powell, he 'was appalled . . . There was no narrative skill, perhaps even no thought for narrative.' The indictment, presented as an exercise in fairness, precision, and truth-telling, continues page after page. There is again a hint of condescension—it turns out that Powell's book reviews were at least better than his fiction—and at the end of the chapter a rather deft trick. He attacks—on moral grounds—those who attacked Powell in the past, thus deflecting attention from his own moral position. One of these unnamed critics, who, Naipaul says, called Powell 'the apotheosis of mediocrity', is accused of being a 'false friend', full of 'rage or jealousy'. Philip Larkin's unkind remarks about Powell are summarized and termed 'the most awful abuse'. Auberon Waugh's review of one of Powell's collections of essays is called typically 'cruel'. These, then, are all apparently the acts of Powell's 'enemies'. Of what motivates his own cold and sneering regard, Naipaul does not tell us.

I myself have no great enthusiasm for Powell's fiction, though it is really rather too harsh to call him a mediocre writer: some people whose views in these matters I respect, such as Perry Anderson, even consider him the greatest English-language historical novelist of the twentieth century. It is the lack of self-awareness in Naipaul that is troubling. How is his attack so different from that of others? Naipaul's subtitle is 'Ways of Looking and Feeling': are lucidity and self-awareness not a part of 'looking' and 'feeling'? These questions are not answered in the third essay, entitled 'Looking and Not Seeing: The Indian Way'. This is a long chapter, clearly meant as the heart of the book. It sets out a thesis of sorts, even if one risks mortifying Naipaul with the accusation that he has composed something as contemptibly academic as a thesis. The chief problem with Powell, the chapter seems to suggest, was that he wrote about a society 'at once diminished and over-written-about', and he could not rise above it. There is only one kind of narrative fiction that Naipaul understands to be properly modern: a sort of late Victorian, realist, slightly constipated fiction with a thoroughly old-fashioned narrative, an economical use of words, plenty of natural description (countryside, gardens, townscapes), and so on. The nonsense of post-Joyce, post-Svevo, post-Musil narrative, the 'literature of exhaustion' once celebrated by John Barth, can and should be flushed down the 'latrine' (one of Naipaul's favourite words). Naipaul then sets his ideal against his imagined enemy: what he terms 'the self-serving "writing schools" of the United States and England'. He attempts to parody the writing-school technique in one of the least humorous passages in this rather solemn book:

> You begin (at the risk of using too many words, like Hemingway) with language of extreme simplicity (like Hemingway), enough to draw attention to your style. From time to time, to remind people, you can do a very simple, verbose paragraph. In between you can relax. When the going gets rough, when difficult or subtle things have to be

handled, the clichés will come tumbling out anyway; the inadequate language will betray itself; but not many will notice after your very simple beginning and your later simple paragraphs. Don't forget the flashback; and, to give density to a banal narrative, the flashback within the flashback. Remember the golden rule of writing-school narrative: a paragraph of description, followed by two or three lines of dialogue. This is thought to make for realism, though the dialogue can't always be spoken. Chinese and Indian and African experience sifted down into this writing-school mill comes out looking and feeling American and modern.

The problem is that all this—save the 'American'—looks and sounds more like Naipaul himself than, say, Arundhati Roy or Vikram Seth. Do the Indian Naxalites in Naipaul's novels not sound as though they have been ground and thoroughly sifted through his own authorial mill? Is this not more lack of self-awareness?

It would appear that for Naipaul there is only one way to be modern, and that is to be Western. All other societies have failed in this respect—the Enlightenment is not mentioned but it lurks offstage—and therefore can only look; they cannot see. Further, as we must recognize through the case of Powell, being Western is necessary but not sufficient. And for people from non-Western societies, the task is far more difficult. Naipaul devotes a good twenty-five pages of his third chapter to the only real exercise in empathy and affection in the book (aside from the passages mentioning his own father), and these pages are to do with Gandhi. He sees Gandhi as a sort of village idiot and incompetent in the first years of his life in Gujarat: coming to England to study law saved him and gave him a critical perspective on India, which he then sharpened in South Africa. Expatriation was the key to seeing. Naipaul admires Gandhi because he imagines him as a version of Naipaul: a man from a traditional, non-Western society who escaped that society and its blinkers to produce a critique of it (and a political movement to implement that critique). By these means he learned to see. Like Naipaul, he rose above the prison of his origins to imagine an India that was hygienic, cleansed, and reformed.

To make this point more dramatic, Naipaul summons up a contrasting figure: a man who left India and yet saw nothing. This is in order once more to support his thesis: leaving India (or Trinidad) is necessary but not sufficient. This other man is to Gandhi, in short, what Derek Walcott is to V.S. Naipaul. The man Naipaul chooses is Munshi Rahman Khan (1874–1972), a Muslim Pathan from northern India who emigrated to the Dutch colony of Suriname at the end of the nineteenth century and wrote a multi-volume autobiographical work called *Jivan Prakash* (loosely: The Light of Life). It has never been published in its entirety, and it appears to be in a mix of various dialects of western Hindi, such as Bundeli and Awadhi. What seems to be a radically abridged Dutch translation has recently been translated into English, and it is only to this last version that Naipaul has access; it is as if a reader in Gorakhpur were reading Naipaul in Maithili after the text had passed through a Japanese translation. Naipaul seems confident nonetheless of the soundness of the conclusions that can be drawn from this double-distilled translation, even on matters of style, while scholars such as Mohan Gautam at Leiden University continue to pore over Rahman Khan's complex manuscript.

Naipaul is deeply disappointed, but also manifestly satisfied, by the poverty of this autobiographical narrative. He finds Rahman Khan to be a narrow-minded, semi-literate character incapable of producing a real modern narrative. 'He has no feeling for the physical world about him', Naipaul complains. When Rahman Khan is moved as a potential indentured labourer from one depot to another in northern India, 'he gives no description of these depots'. The problem is that Naipaul has little purchase on Rahman Khan's world, which he simply assumes was very similar to that from which he believes his own grandparents came, in the northern Indian state of Uttar Pradesh (earlier the United Provinces). This is the world that he evokes in the passage about the 'peasantry of the Gangetic plain', 'a powerless people . . . ruled by tyrants, often far off, who came and went and whose names we very often didn't know.' These distant tyrants might be British, but I suspect that they are really meant to evoke Muslim sultans. The use of 'we' is also disingenuous, as if intended to suggest that Naipaul has some sort of unmediated access to the world of the Gangetic plain when, in fact, his knowledge of even standard Hindi is rudimentary. Nor need we credit the clichéd vision of an apathetic peasantry, indifferent to the march of history, that he describes.

Rahman Khan was the author of two brief but well-regarded collections of poems, *Doha Sikshavali* (A Didactic Collection of Couplets, 1953) and *Jñan Prakash* (The Light of Knowledge, 1954), and was a respected figure in Hindi-speaking literary circles in Suriname. He began writing *Jivan Prakash* in his late sixties, and it seems that a political agenda lay behind it. He saw himself as an apostle of Hindu–Muslim unity, and buttressed his claims through his knowledge of the Tulsidas *Ramayana*, a sixteenth-century retelling of the Sanskrit epic that was very popular in the Caribbean. Rahman Khan presented himself explicitly as an exegete of this text, and even wrote verse in its broad style. One of these poems runs:

Two groups came from India,
They were called Hindu and Musalman,
Both of them were full of affection,
Like two brothers born of the same mother.

This was wishful thinking and hardly the entire tale of Hindu–Muslim relations in the Caribbean. But the point remains that Rahman Khan was deeply immersed in regional Hindi culture, and this included the so-called Hindu epics, many of which are regularly acted and recited even today by Muslim performers in popular theatre such as the annual Ramlila. This is not Naipaul's view, however. Rahman, he tells us, may have participated in 'a composite Hindu–Muslim culture of the region' (the Gangetic plain), but we can be certain that 'this composite culture has now vanished'. Even more extraordinary is his claim that 'Rahman, remarkably for a Muslim, knew Hindi very well'. As Naipaul sees it, Muslims must speak something called Urdu; Hindi is for the Hindus. Which makes Rahman Khan incomprehensible for him rather than a fairly common, if unusually articulate, type.

It is clear, then, that the deeper world of Rahman Khan, born in the Hamirpur district of western Uttar Pradesh, is not as familiar or accessible to Naipaul as he would have us believe. He repeatedly suggests that Rahman's whole account is nothing more than a 'brightly coloured, *Arabian Nights* world', full of holy men, magic potions, and gilded kingdoms. It is certainly not realistic, and does not meet the imagined standard that Naipaul has in mind. But historians and observers of Indian society have never taken the view that Gandhi's autobiography was the measure of all first-person writings. This is why others will make more of Rahman Khan's writings than Naipaul can, since they will want to read them for what they are rather than what they are not.

The fourth essay, 'Disparate Ways', takes us on a detour before returning once again in the concluding pages to India and Indians. At first sight, it seems out of place. An initial, fairly tedious, section is devoted to a bald contrast between Flaubert's deft narrative technique in *Madame Bovary* (this for Naipaul is the good realism that Rahman Khan lacks) and the clumsiness he thinks he finds in *Salammbô*. There is nothing that need detain us here, since the florid Orientalism of the later novel has been mocked often enough. The second part of the essay is more intriguing, and finds Naipaul embarking on the reading of a set of Latin texts from the Roman Empire, including Caesar, Cicero, and a poem by the pseudo-Virgil. It turns out that the purpose of this exercise is linked to the purpose of the book as a whole; in the end, we're told, men in the Roman Empire, like those in India or the Caribbean (or indeed anywhere other than the modern West), 'use words to hide from reality' rather than in order to reveal it—as Naipaul believes he himself does. The Roman writers cannot face up to the ugliness of their own world, its violence, slavery, and sordidness, just as most Indians cannot face up to caste and filth. So, 'in this world without balance'— which means Rome or the Third World—'people need more than ever the classical half view, the ability to see and not see.' In sum, Naipaul is reproducing a conceit set out and demolished at length by historians of anthropology such as Johannes Fabian in *Time and the Other*: the rest of the world is still located in the ancient past of the West, the only difference being that the West was able to redeem itself and become modern.

That hope is not entirely given to India. The final essay concludes with particular sourness, affected by the aftertaste of some of Naipaul's recent (post-Nobel) visits to India, where he has sometimes been lionized but also criticized and even heckled. 'India has no autonomous intellectual life', Naipaul declares, and adds: 'India is hard and materialist. What it knows best about Indian writers and books are their advances and their prizes. There is little discussion about the substance of a book or its literary quality or the point of view of the writer.' No writers or critics are mentioned by name, and the one attempt at parody seems more directed at Ved Mehta than at any of the younger crop writing in English. The world beyond English, of course, the world of Vishvanatha Satyanarayana, does not exist for Naipaul. It is predictable that the only writer from the twentieth century he finds worth discussing at length is Nirad Chaudhuri, whose *Autobiography of an Unknown Indian* is carefully dissected and appreciated for its largely positive evaluation of the British Empire. Again, the possibility that Chaudhuri and his Anglophilia might be a mirror held up to

Naipaul is never considered. A book that is as full of certainty as Naipaul's can have no place in it for self-reflection. At the end of the book, India stands pretty much condemned: 'As much as for Gandhi, born in 1869, and for Chaudhuri, born in 1897, India's poverty and colonial past . . . continue to stand in the way of identity and strength and intellectual growth.'

At least that is the way it appears to Naipaul, born in 1932. What would happen if he were to be analysed as an actor in history, the spokesman for a point of view? What does he really represent, and where does he come from? We can do without the materialist presumption that all men are merely creatures of their circumstances, even if Naipaul seems determined to be one. He is a prisoner by choice, and also as a matter of taste. But of what is he a prisoner? Clues can be found in his own writings, including this book, though they are at times obscured by his manner of presentation. Naipaul is, first and foremost, a child of the Indian diaspora, but not the one that exists today of Telugu software engineers and Punjabi fast-food millionaires. The diaspora to which he belongs and by which he is marked is the nineteenth-century diaspora that emerged in the immediate aftermath of the British abolition of slavery in the 1830s. The first Indian indentured migrants to Trinidad (and the Caribbean more generally) arrived shortly thereafter, and the trickle became a flow after the Indian uprising of 1857–8. Between 1845 and 1917, the official statistics suggest, Trinidad received about 144,000 Indian immigrants, and in 1980 they and their descendants formed about 41 per cent of the island's population of more than a million. The Caribbean was only one part of the story; other labouring migrants from India went to Fiji, mainland South East Asia, Sri Lanka, Mauritius, and East Africa. Many parts of India contributed to these flows, and even today Sylhetis (from eastern Bengal) may dominate Indian migration in one part of the world and rural Sikh farmers in another. The two most significant areas of emigration (or 'labour catchment areas') for the late nineteenth century were the east-central Gangetic plain and southern India, and the migrants had significantly different profiles. The latter were often Tamil-speaking, belonged to the middling and lower castes, and carried with them a popular Hindu religiosity that had a very thin overlay of Sanskritic and Brahminized culture. This is what we see today in Malaysia and Singapore, and it is surely no coincidence that they have not produced a Naipaul.

The migrants to the Caribbean—and to an extent Mauritius and Fiji—were of a different order. After an initial phase in which southern India was well represented, it was the Gangetic plain that eventually came to dominate. Whether or not they were truly peasants in their origins—Brahmins and high castes like the Naipauls in fact represented only 14.3 per cent of migrants to Trinidad between 1874 and 1917—these migrants had often felt the impact of the great Hindu reform movements of the nineteenth century, which were themselves a reaction to the claims and insults of Protestant missionaries. Thus, mixed with the residues of pre-colonial religiosity of the type favoured by men like Rahman Khan, there existed a more muscular neo-Hinduism based on a strategic imitation of Protestantism. It was the sort of religiosity and culture eventually made popular in the twentieth century by explicitly reformist groups such as the Arya Samaj, but also—already by 1881 in the case of Trinidad—by rival neo-traditionalists who came to define Hinduism using the disguised neologism of 'Sanatan Dharam'. This was ostensibly a hoary phrase from the Sanskrit epics; it had once meant no more than 'ancient way' or 'age-old custom' but it now came to stand for a stripped-down Hinduism with a distinct preference for ur-texts (which were meant to be read directly, as with the Protestant Bible) and a largely Vaishnava form of expression. It was into this expatriate culture—envious of the West and its superiority, suspicious of Islam and Muslims, often with a healthy contempt for many of the practices and 'superstitions' of the old motherland that had been left behind—that Naipaul was born. It is here that one finds the disgust of India that Naipaul evokes in describing his own mother's visit there, as she nervously hides her Guiana gold, looks at the food with fear, and turns bilious as someone stirs her tea with a grubby finger. By leaving India, the Naipauls had reformed; the old country, it seemed to them, had stayed just as it was.

It is the ghost of this neo-Hinduism of the diaspora that lives on in this book, and which also inhabits hundreds of websites posted by other expatriate Indians who find themselves caught in the trap of in-betweenness. Naipaul is wide of the mark in his claim that most Indians today in the US 'wish to shake India off' and would rather 'make cookies and shovel snow' than deal with their Indian past. On the contrary: these are communities which often greatly admire Naipaul, share his roots in various sorts of neo-Hinduism, claim insistently that Islam is a worldwide threat, agitate over school textbooks in California which state that Hinduism is chaotically polytheistic, and wear surgical masks when they visit India and relatives who stir tea with forefingers. For, ironically, 'Indianness' is the chief element in the cultural capital of such groups, as it is for Naipaul himself. On the distant other side, Protestantism beckons, but most Protestantism does not go together with cultural *métissage*; it is pretty much an all-or-nothing deal. Further, Indians living outside India have, it is well known, been rather racist when it comes to other people of colour, and the anti-black rhetoric that pervades Naipaul's writings (including the first chapter of this book) is once again only symptomatic of a larger malaise that extends from East Africa to New Jersey.

So, in the end, there is a reason why we should be grateful that Naipaul exists. With his clarity of expression and utter lack of self-awareness, he provides a window into a world and its prejudices: he is larger than himself. This book, like his others, should be read together with those of Munshi Rahman Khan for a deeper understanding of the Indian diaspora and its ways of looking, feeling, and suffering.

6

The Booker and 'India Shining'*

Anyone who has read the inside pages of Indian newspapers over the past some decades will be familiar with a variety of stereotypical stories of violent urban crime. Some of these concern 'crimes of passion' and use a peculiar Indian journalistic vocabulary in English, involving such odd terms as 'eve-teasing', 'absconding', 'paramour', and 'nabbed'. Some of these crimes of passion centre on incest or close familial relationships—say, between father-in-law and daughter-in-law—while others are stomach-churning tales of paedophilia and 'child molestation'. Another favourite theme of which citizens and residents of Delhi will be well aware concerns the violent crimes committed by groups nicely termed 'criminal castes', who in the neo-colonial imagination of the city's bourgeoisie are often linked to the villages that have been displaced or are in the process of being gradually asphyxiated by the expansion of Delhi over the erstwhile lands of pastoralists and small farmers. In an urban legend that was a great favourite in the 1990s, it was reported that such crimes often involved needless excesses of violence, including people bludgeoned to death in their houses with blunt instruments even though they had not resisted; and that the perpetrators of such crimes would show

*On *The White Tiger: A Novel* by Aravind Adiga (New York: Free Press, 2008), 277pp.

their contempt for the victims by defecating in their living rooms
before departing into shadowy abodes. Though class elements
were present in the first type of crime of passion—which
the elite naturally associated largely with slum dwellers and
irregular squatters—in the second there was more of a flavour
of something approaching real class warfare. In one set of glib
narratives of the anti-Sikh pogrom of late 1984 in Delhi it
was claimed that the violence took precisely such class lines,
opposing the residents of encircled inner-city villages such as
Kotla Mubarakpur and Lado Sarai to the prosperous bourgeois
residents of Defence Colony and Green Park.

But the dominant story of the past years involves the domestic
servant, an indispensable element but also a source of endless
paranoia in metropolitan households in India. There may already
be excellent sociological studies of the subject, but I myself am
really not aware of any—such as one in Berkeley—that have
proceeded beyond the project stage. These domestic servants
come in differing incarnations. Some commute by public
transport to work, perform tasks serially in several households,
and return home at the end of the day—home being frequently
a slum adjacent to a posh residential area. Many others are
children, or barely into their adolescence, and sleep in the house
where they work without being allowed to use the bathrooms
and toilets of their employers. Some of these child servants are
in fact poor relatives from a collateral and less fortunate branch
of the family. Others are adults from outside the family who
nevertheless live in extreme proximity with the joint or nuclear
families they serve. They have little by way of fixed hours, though
at times they are given a day off every week or every fortnight.
The Indian government recognizes their existence officially by
providing every state employee who has attained high 'officer'
status with a flat or house that has 'servants' quarters', known by
the euphemistic abbreviation 'SQ', attached to it. In these SQs,
which usually open out into the back alleys of the government
residential areas, a parallel world exists to that of the houses and

flats that look out into the streets and gardens. It is a curious form of what the Brazilian sociologist Gilberto Freyre once termed, in the context of slave society, *Casa grande e senzala* (The Manor and the Slave-Quarters); sometimes the children of the masters and those of the servants can be found spinning tops or flying kites together.

Servants are naturally a favourite subject of conversation amongst their Indian employers. 'They are so difficult to get and so hard to keep.' 'They don't know their station in the world any more.' 'It's not like it was in the good old days when they were so loyal that they were really members of the family.' 'They backchat so much!'—this last being indignation at a servant's ability to argue. And so on. Eventually, this can shade into paranoia, especially each time a story breaks in the newspaper of an elderly couple found dead and robbed by their resident domestic servant. At such moments the police place public interest advertisements in the newspapers advising employers to run 'background checks' on their potential employees. Attempts are made from time to time to introduce identity cards for servants, and elite urban Indians sigh wistfully for the arrangements of Singapore, where servants are strictly regimented by the state, have just one day off a month, and where female servants can be kicked out for becoming pregnant. At times, paranoia turns into xenophobia and dark mutterings can be heard from official circles about not hiring people from a 'certain neighbouring country' (which was till recently a monarchy, and the capital of which begins with the letter K). But despite washing machines, vacuum cleaners, microwaves, and other electronic domestic aids, which bourgeois after all can live in a metropolitan Indian city, or even a small town, without a servant or several of them? Every American, European, or Japanese who lives in these cities may arrive there with the best of intentions but succumbs soon enough to the Servant Raj, unless they prefer to be resident in the flea-ridden hotels of the hippie trail.

Some two decades ago a friend of mine had a lavish wedding

in one of these cities. Though he lived and worked in India, his family was spread across a good part of the West and turned up in large numbers accompanied by their Western friends who were not above a bit of freeloading. The wedding was an extended affair and what began cordially enough soon deteriorated into quite a bit of squabbling. Some of this was the usual friction resulting from a false sense of familial proximity, but a part of it also took a curious turn. Some of the relatives from abroad declared that they were appalled by the prevailing state of class relations in India. This extended not just to rickshaw-pullers on the streets but to the place and treatment of the domestic servants who had been mobilized in large numbers for the occasion—to clean up after parties that ended in the early hours of the morning, and to make masala omelettes for the honoured visitors when they rolled out of bed. To the flown-in wedding guests it all smacked of a dreadful form of feudalism, never mind that their own parents had lived in India a bare generation before, surrounded, in all probability, by even larger numbers of servants. It seemed archaic and primitive, unworthy of a democracy, of liberal principles. Eventually, many of those who had come from abroad stormed off in high dudgeon with their moral superiority intact, leaving in their wake a train of bemused Indian relatives.

These sorts of scenarios have not been central to the writings of social scientists reflecting on India. To be sure, class exists as a problem but it is normally treated either in its rural version— relations between landlords, small peasants, and wage labourers; or in its classic urban incarnation of the factory and shop floor; or in terms of what has been termed 'footloose labour', which is to say the labour that is often used on construction sites or for contractual work against wages or piece rates. Even the broad intellectual grouping known as 'Subaltern Studies' has not taken domestic work into account, save for the occasional moment when a conversation with a domestic servant provides the researcher with an anecdote or a factoid to motivate an essay on some suitably profound question. It is hard to define or measure class in a country where data on personal income and assets is extremely difficult to come by. It is even harder to know for certain what has happened over the past two decades since economic liberalization was announced. But impressionistic views certainly exist. There are very rich people now in the cities with fancy imported cars, expensive watches and clothes, and showy lifestyles, and they live side by side with slum-dwellers and those who sleep on pavements. There are urban and suburban developments that boast such names as Malibu Towers, Beverly Hills Residence, and Bel-Air Estate, often involving residential towers so high that no fire engine in the area can reach them; apparently no one in India cares that in Los Angeles streets also bear such names as Baroda Drive, named after the Gaekwad Maharaja of Baroda in Gujarat. This is growth all right, but of a sort that can induce vertigo. This is what Aravind Adiga's recent and much-toasted Man Booker Prize-winning book, *The White Tiger*, is ostensibly about.

It purports to tell the story of a murder committed by its narrator, a certain Balram Halwai (also known for a peculiar reason as 'White Tiger') from the eastern Indian state of Bihar, who moves first to the prosperous suburb of Gurgaon near Delhi to work for a certain Mr Ashok and his wife Pinky Madam, and eventually to the booming city of Bangalore in South India which, together with Hyderabad, is associated in clichés with the great Indian economic transformation of recent times. We learn the fact of this murder some thirty pages into the book, at the end of the first chapter: 'Eight months later, I slit Mr Ashok's throat.' The reader thus knows pretty much from the start where the book is headed; it is then simply a question of Adiga's artfulness in getting us there. The plot has no twists and turns, no real surprises, and no sleights-of-hand. It just rolls on in a linear fashion like an Indian Railways train, from one stop to another, over its seven chapters notionally recounted over seven nights.

Why Bihar? We should be aware that Bihar has a notable set of clichés attached to it. It has some of the lowest economic and developmental indicators in India today, and is also part of a large swathe of territory where 'Naxalite' (or Maoist) groups operate with impunity. Urban Indians, especially from the great metropolitan centres, love to sneer at Bihar as the worst of the so-called 'Cow Belt', a place where banditry, caste warfare, and feudalism are rampant and where the leading politicians include Laloo Prasad Yadav, who provides much hilarity in the salons of Delhi, Mumbai, and Bangalore (and who plays a role even in this novel). This is a part of the world which Balram qualifies in this novel as the world of 'Darkness', a term that appears repeatedly in the book in opposition to 'Light'—which is to say the sophisticated urban destinations to which the protagonist-narrator is headed. People like him do not automatically speak the increasingly standard Hindi of northern India, but rather its eastern Indian versions, such as Maithili and Bhojpuri which were also the dialects spoken by nineteenth-century working-class migrants—such as V.S. Naipaul's forefathers—to Calcutta, Fiji, Mauritius, and Guyana. Even now, they are marked and mocked as rustic in the great Indian metropolitan cities on that account. Still, Balram hates Bihar and his ancestral village of Laxmangarh, which is apparently only a few miles from Bodh Gaya, the pilgrimage site where the Buddha is said to have attained enlightenment. 'I wonder if the Buddha walked through Laxmangarh—some people say he did. My own feeling is that he ran through it—as fast as he could—and got to the other side—and never looked back!' In short, Balram has strong attitudes. He is irreligious and even deeply cynical about Hindu religion, which he views in an entirely instrumental manner. He despises the holy river Ganges which, for him, is nothing more than a large open drain. His own village is a dreadful place which 'a bright strip of sewage splits into two' and where there are 'three more or less identical shops selling more or less identically adulterated and stale items of rice, cooking oil, kerosene, biscuits, cigarettes, and jaggery [a form of molasses]'. This is then what propels him from the anything-but-bucolic world of Laxmangarh to employment in the provincial city and mining centre of Dhanbad.

Here, after a short course of apprenticeship in a motor school, he finds work as a driver with a powerful family that controls much of the power and resources in his natal region. The next sections of the book then take us through Balram's ascension in the household of this master, where, after first being obliged to drive the humble Indo-Japanese Maruti Suzuki, he emerges into a situation of triumph where he can get behind the wheel of the chief car of the family, a luxurious Honda City. In order to do this, Balram must exercise his ruthlessness, developing further the skills that he had honed in an earlier moment when he worked in a teashop doing his job 'with near total dishonesty, lack of dedication, and insincerity'. This involves betraying and blackmailing another driver—a Muslim pretending to be a Hindu called Ram Persad. Balram discovers the secret during the fasting month of Ramadan and manipulates it to his own advantage. By stages, he is eventually redeployed to serve not in Dhanbad, but at a far higher salary in Delhi and Gurgaon, where the family has sent its sons so that they live far from harm's way (on account of the Naxalites) and closer to the real seats of political power. A third of the way into the novel we thus find our way from Darkness into Light, from the rather schematic feudal world of Bihar into the suburban and metropolitan one of Gurgaon and Delhi.

Adiga's may be the first novel in English to attempt to come to terms in any way with the phenomenon that is Gurgaon. It is, to put it mildly, a rather curious place. A bare quarter-century ago this was primarily an agrarian region in the state of Haryana on the fringes of Delhi, inhabited largely by Jat agriculturists and Gujjar pastoralists and farmers. However, as Delhi expanded southwards, it became a frontier of opportunity where the state of Haryana offered advantageous conditions for entrepreneurs to invest under favourable terms. I can remember the first condominiums opening up for sale in the late 1980s, and early Non-Resident Indians (NRIs) buying them. The car firm Maruti Suzuki, one of whose products Balram drives in Dhanbad, opened a factory there with larger spin-offs. Money began to flow in, often in obscene quantities. I clearly recall visiting a bank in Gurgaon in the mid-1990s and meeting its manager in order to make a safe deposit enquiry on behalf of a friend; the manager smugly pointed to a large and freshly cemented patch in the roof where armed robbers had broken in one night, a couple of weeks before, and fought a pitched gun battle with local police. Fortunately my friend's deposit was still intact, but there was a sense in which we were proudly dealing with the local Butch Cassidys and Sundance Kids.

But it has not been all fun and games in Gurgaon since then, really. There are now enormous malls and glass towers that house firms such as Alcatel. Yet it is an insecure world, one where the employees of these high-end firms walk to their parking garages with what I gather is an understandable sense of nervousness. Muggings are frequent, as are kidnappings and carjacking. Some years ago IBM was reported to have issued an advisory to its employees warning them of just how unsafe it was and advising them to take an extended series of precautions. The following story from the *Hindustan Times* of 2 September 2008 gives a flavour of the situation as well as of Indian journalese:

> Yet another incident of carjacking was reported from Gurgaon on Monday. Two armed youths reportedly snatched the keys of a Scorpio (HR 26 AH 8100) that was parked in DLF Cyber City from its driver and drove away with the driver still inside. The incident occurred at 11.15 pm when hundreds of other vehicles were parked in the

area. The SUV belongs to a businessman who lives in Sushant Lok, Phase I. Ashok Kumar, station head officer of DLF City police station said driver Rajeshwar Mandal was sitting in the vehicle and the owner, Vikram Veer, had gone to a restaurant at Infinity Towers. 'Two youths armed with pistols entered into an altercation with the driver saying he had hit their car. The youths then pushed the driver inside and drove the car away,' Kumar said. The robbers snatched Mandal's mobile phone and other belongings and stripped him before dumping him near Palam Vihar.

Police had issued warning

In June this year, the Gurgaon police had issued a word of caution to people driving their cars at odd hours. It had cautioned a motorcycle-borne gang of carjackers was on the prowl in Gurgaon and was snatching cars at gunpoint. In August also, Gurgaon police commissioner Mohinder Lal had said a gang of professional auto-lifters from neighbouring towns as well as from Bihar and West Bengal were active in Gurgaon. As many as 1,100 auto theft cases have been reported till date in Gurgaon as against 950 cases in the corresponding period last year.

In this Wild West atmosphere, which Gurgaon shares to an extent with other prosperous Delhi suburbs such as Noida and Faridabad, nothing is quite what it seems. There can be shootouts in the courthouse. There are swank clinics with five-star decors and marbled floors where the actual medical attention borders on the criminally negligent. Gurgaon is a fragile world, but one into which many NRIs are happy to buy because what we have in it is a series of illusions: the illusion of security, the illusion of gated communities, the illusion of not living in India because one is surrounded by Benetton, Nike, Pizza Hut, TGI Friday, and the like. But it is an illusion that can only be sustained because, as usual, there are the drivers and domestics, the cleaners and sweepers, not to speak of the armed security guards, in order to do the necessary. I imagine that there are now more and more French and German business executives who fly into New Delhi's Indira Gandhi airport business class and return to Paris or Düsseldorf three days later without ever having set foot in any part of India other than Gurgaon. Their experience can only be compared to a rather boring film called *Jet Lag* from 2002, in which Jean Reno and Juliette Binoche do not even make it out of the complex of Roissy-Charles de Gaulle in order to further their romance.

It is this world of Gurgaon that Adiga sets out to dissect in the most ambitious part of the book. Balram lives in the SQ of one of the residences, termed Buckingham Towers B Block. It is, as he describes it, part of a 'warren of interconnected rooms where all the drivers, cooks, sweepers, maids, and chefs of the apartment can rest, sleep, and wait.' By contrast, Balram's master and mistress, who after an intermediate period emerge as Mr Ashok and his wife Pinky Madam—the son and daughter-in-law of his feudal Dhanbad employer—live on the thirteenth floor of the apartment block in a flat that their driver finds cramped after the wide spaces of the Dhanbad house. The plot now quickly finds a way to its resolution. Mr Ashok, it turns out, is a rather wishy-washy liberal who has been educated in the United States, unlike his brother Mukesh who is a far more rooted and vicious representative of the Bihari landlord milieu. Mr Ashok has, however, had the courage to oppose his family in marrying Pinky, presented here less as an NRI than an ABCD (American-Born Confused *Desi*), an Indian-American who is Christian to boot. Balram lusts after Pinky—her fancy perfumes, skirts, and low-cut tops—through the rear-view mirror, but does not dare act on it. For her part Pinky sneers at Balram and his crude elements of English, and at his habit of scratching his crotch while working in the kitchen. We are presented with a series of drives from Gurgaon into the five-star world of Delhi, its hotels and its ministerial bungalows, as the tensions between Mr Ashok and his wife fester.

Eventually, a resolution is reached. In an improbable moment, a drunken Pinky insists on taking the wheel and accidentally runs over the child of a pavement-dweller. There is an attempt to persuade Balram to take the fall and he does indeed sign a statement falsely admitting his guilt in the matter. But the matter is resolved otherwise, because the poor have no rights anyway and no one has sought to register the hit-and-run accident. Still, a disgusted and somewhat remorseful Pinky departs for America and asks for a divorce. Mr Ashok falls into decline and despair, drinking and puking his way through the next few pages. He begins to frequent former girlfriends and even the odd blonde Ukrainian prostitute in seedy hotels in the South Delhi area of Jangpura. Balram is torn between a certain sympathy for his state of existential misery and contempt for his lack of spine and feudal gumption. Eventually, it is the latter sentiment that triumphs. Step by step, he is drawn to contemplate the murder of his employer. When he eventually does so, it is at a moment when Mr Ashok is in possession of a large sum of cash to pay a political bribe. Balram draws his reluctant employer out of the car on a rainy night, claiming that a tyre needs repair, and kills him with an empty bottle of Johnnie Walker Black Label, first smashing it on his head and then cutting his throat. He then leaves for Bangalore, accompanied by his young nephew Dharam who has recently joined him from Bihar. Of course, Balram knows that his employer's family will visit vengeance on his own. But he does not care. His brothers and their children may be slaughtered, the women of the family may be raped, he is largely indifferent to it all. Adiga wants us to see this as emblematic of the new Indian Tough Guy, the ruthless and murderous entrepreneur who will—literally and metaphorically—step over any number of dead bodies to get his own way.

Now, the murder plot has served as a schematic device for many a celebrated novel from Dostoyevsky to Nabokov, from *Crime and Punishment* to *Despair*. The idea of a resentful, socially mobile character murdering his employer and getting away with it in pursuit of his ideal of social mobility also cannot really be considered much of a novelty. The innovation in this novel must be sought at another level, then, something closer to the warp and weft of its execution. This must take us to the construction of the narrative voice in the novel, which in turn draws us to the central personage of Balram Halwai. Before entering into this question, there is a framing device that must be mentioned. This is a conceit: each of the chapters is a message sent by Balram to Wen Jiabao, prime minister of the People's Republic of China, who is about to visit Bangalore. Frankly, this is a rather tedious device that adds nothing to the novel beyond permitting Balram to present himself as some sort of a generalized Third World racist rather than a merely Indian one. Besides, it is one that consciously or otherwise imitates far more amusing and successful examples that are only to Adiga's disadvantage, such as John Barth's celebrated 'Petition' from *Lost in the Funhouse*, addressed to the King of Siam. The idea of the seven nights, and its heavy referential weight, also seems rather unnecessary. Here is an author who one feels has been rather badly advised by his editors, even if too well served by his publicists.

But these are trivial matters when compared to the heart of the issue: what is this novel all about? It is not, contrary to some rather confused assertions in the Indian press, another attempt at a form of Indian magical realism in the distant wake of Salman Rushdie. No one has telepathic or supernatural powers here; time is broadly Newtonian in its flow; no references to García Márquez lurk in the undergrowth. Rather, this is a novel which wishes to be realistic, even if that realism is meant to be understood as ringed with black comedic intent. There may even be the hint of some great moralistic motive here, with the novelist denouncing the greed and corruption of the new Indian society. But the matter must eventually rest on the credibility and verisimilitude of the voice of the narrator and central personage, Balram Halwai. Now, as it turns out, the Halwais are an upper-middling caste of sweetmeat-makers, resident across large swathes of northern India and often using the widespread caste name 'Gupta'. Balram is presented in the novel, though, as impoverished but still possessing an education, even if one that does not give him access to proper English. 'Neither you nor I speak English', he writes to Wen Jiabao at the outset of the novel, and yet the novel is written in English. Is this meant to be another miracle of Babel Fish? Hardly. Rather, we are meant to believe—even within the conventions of the realist novel—that a character who must really function in Maithili or Bhojpuri can now express his thoughts seamlessly in the English language, a language that he does not speak.

This is a problem that takes us back to the roots of the Indian novel in English. These novels can be divided into two broad categories for our purposes, however unconvincing they may seem to the likes of that self-appointed arbiter of modern Indian fiction, Pankaj Mishra. One set contains Indian characters who speak English because they actually have a Western education (as in the work of Vikram Seth). Such novels often involve issues of middle-class angst, urban lust and loss, and satirical views of post-colonial pretension. Some of them are more or less ironic about the tragic fate of anglicized members of India's elite colleges, rotting away in the 1980s in the wilds, in places like Dhanbad, while dreaming of Fleetwood Mac or Supertramp. At its most genteel, and moving into the extra-Indian sphere, this form of expression may be found in the world of an Indian-American writer such as Jhumpa Lahiri, whose powers and spectrum of characters cannot really embrace the subjectivity of a rather crass chauffeur from Bihar who smashes the head of his employer with a whisky bottle in Dhaula Kuan while chewing betel-leaf. However, there is a far larger range of novels which claim to represent, in the English language, speech and verbalized thought which in fact does not take place in English. This is a rather involved piece of jugglery which will repay attention. For how, after all, does one represent speech save in the form in which it occurs? Is this not a basic premise of 'realism' as a novelistic conceit?

The matter has been addressed in various ways by differing authors. Some, like Raja Rao, adopted a sort of elaborate sing-song tone in English, allegedly meant to correspond to the rhythms not merely of the Indian vernaculars but of Indian life itself. Others, including Rushdie, have tried the macaronic solution, sprinkling the English with Hindi or Urdu words, and even inventing words where an Indian verb root ends with an '–ofy'. This produces sentences such as: 'You samjao that baysharram pair that this sort of tamasha is simply not the cheese.' Still others, such as the American Lee Siegel (who navigates between Indology and fiction writing), have attempted for comic effect to have Indians speak in an exaggerated and droll way, by way of the use of odd vowels and diphthongs, and dental and retroflex consonants in English. But none of these come across as a realistic solution, and many seem the analogue of SS officers in World War II films speaking English amongst themselves with a strong accent from *Mitteleuropa*. Rushdie's characters sound like no known Indian who has ever been encountered; they are mere variants of His Master's Voice, but this is not meant to matter because his novels are not realistic. We are far from the ethnographic conceits of a Zola, attempting to capture the nuances of the speech of the Other, notebook in hand—the novelist as a sort of folklorist.

But what of Balram Halwai? What does he sound like? Despite the odd *namaste, daal, paan,* and *ghat,* his vocabulary is not overly sprinkled with North Indian vernacular terms. His sentences are usually short and quite crudely constructed, which is apparently meant to be a reflection of the fact that we are dealing with one of the 'subaltern' classes. (It also must make the novelist's task quite a lot easier.) He engages in no Rushdiean wordplay. But he does use a series of expressions that simply do not add up. His office is described by him as a 'hole in the wall'. He refers to the notion of 'kissing some god's arse', an idiomatic expression that does not exist in any known North Indian language. When he gets more complex, he holds forth about how 'half-formed ideas bugger one another, and make more half-formed ideas'. He advises the Chinese prime minister: 'Don't you ever let that blasphemous idea into your yellow skull.' On another matter he sneers: 'It's so yesterday.' A clever little phrase appears: 'A statutory warning—as they say on cigarette packs—before we begin.' Dogs are referred to as 'mutts'. Yet whose vocabulary and whose expressions are these? They carry no sense of verisimilitude at all. Page after page, one is brought up short by the jangling dissonance of the language and the falsity of the expressions. This is a posh English-educated voice trying to talk down and dirty, but one that is not able to pull it off. This is not Salinger speaking as Holden Caulfield, or Joyce speaking as Molly Bloom. It is certainly not the stuff of Ralph Ellison and James Baldwin, whom Adiga has claimed as his models in speaking for the underdog. What we are dealing with is someone with no sense of the texture of Indian vernaculars claiming to produce a realistic text.

Let us imagine a different experiment, one that anthropologists and folklorists have tried, as have literary scholars. Imagine recording a passage by an interlocutor—say a driver encountered in a Gurgaon car park—in an Indian language and trying to render it not literally but credibly, with some effort at verisimilitude, into English. Let me assure you this is no easy task. We simply cannot have him saying 'it's so yesterday' or sounding like a City banker slumming it in a South London bar. Or, to make matters easier, imagine taking a written text with reported speech in Hindi by Premchand, Rahi Masoom Reza, or Alka Saraogi and setting it into English. In fact, one does not have to imagine it; this has already been done in many cases. The translator is of course always in a dilemma, and can never get it quite 'right'. But we also know what it is to get it disastrously wrong. It is literary catastrophe when the 'autobiography' of an Indian untouchable woman appears in French using expressions from Victor Hugo: a false tone, the wrong set of ambient references, and the wrong sort of musicality take over. But the falsity in Adiga's novel goes much further. His central character cannot read Urdu and certainly has no notion of Persian yet tells us that his favourite poets include Jalaluddin Rumi and Mirza Ghalib. This is like having someone who cannot read English tell us he loves Chaucer, Shakespeare, and Keats.

Where Adiga gets the tone right is when he speaks of the world of the bourgeois. Some of this is quite funny and rings partly true:

> 'Ashok,' she said. 'Now hear this. Balram, what is it we're eating?'
> I knew it was a trap, but what could I do?—I answered. The two of them burst into giggles.
> 'Say it again, Balram.'
> They laughed again.
> 'It's not piJJA. It's piZZa. Say it properly.'
> 'Wait—you're mispronouncing it too. There's a *T* in the middle. *Peet. Zah.*'
> 'Don't correct *my* English, Ashok. There's no *T* in pizza. Look at the box.'

Some two decades ago the controversial literary theorist and Derridean analyst Gayatri Chakravorty Spivak wrote one of her most celebrated essays: 'Can the Subaltern Speak?' At the time, a folklorist is said to have responded: 'More importantly, can the bourgeois listen?' This is the sort of problem that reading this novel brings home. We cannot hear Balram Halwai's voice here because the author seems to have no access to it. The novel has its share of well-meaning anger at the injustices of the new globalized India. This is good to know in the context of a growing chorus of celebratory voices. But its central subaltern character comes across as a badly made ventriloquist's dummy, a caricature, a cardboard cut-out. The curious paradox is that, for many of this novel's readers, this fundamental lack of verisimilitude will not matter because for them India is and will remain an exotic place. It might be said therefore that the book adds another brick to the very patronizing edifice it wants to tear down.

7

Thugs, Thuggee, and Things Thuggish*

I n the early 1980s the Bombay-born film producer Ismail
Merchant, then in his mid-forties and yet to complete his
best-known E.M. Forster-derived work, set out to make
one of his less-known films, *The Deceivers*. He was without his
usual collaborator James Ivory, who was apparently not enthused
by the project. The film eventually appeared in 1988, after *A
Room with a View* (1985) and *Maurice* (1987), and was met by
a near-unanimous lack of critical acclaim. The screenplay was
based on a novel by John Masters (1914–83), who had served
in the British army in India and its neighbourhood before and
during the Second World War. Masters came from a family with
a long relationship with India which apparently stretched back
some five generations; I am told by elderly Indian army officers
who served with him in the Gurkhas that he cut a dashing figure
and had a number of exciting tales to recount, in particular
regarding his participation in the guerrilla called the Chindits,
which had been rendered notorious by the glamorous and
eccentric personage of a Nainital-born Christian Zionist, Orde
Wingate. Masters wrote a three-volume memoir between 1956

*On *Stranglers and Bandits: A Historical Anthology of 'Thuggee'*, edited
by Kim Wagner (New Delhi: Oxford University Press, 2009), xvi+318pp.

and 1971 that continues to be of interest to historians of the British army overseas, but he was for a long time better known for his novels, most of which had an Indian theme. Best known of these was probably *Bhowani Junction*, which was made into a film by George Cukor in 1956 with Ava Gardner and Stewart Granger, and which concerned a torrid love affair in the 1940s between an Anglo-Indian (or Eurasian) woman called Victoria Jones from a railway family and Colonel Rodney Savage, a character who featured in more than one of Masters's novels and who seems to have been loosely autobiographical in inspiration. Masters's Indian novels were in fact a saga of the Savages and their involvement with India dating back to the early seventeenth century, when one of them—a certain Jason Savage—shows up as the hero of the novel *Coromandel!* and eventually spends time at the court of the Mughal emperor Jahangir.

The Deceivers, for its part, is set in the 1820s and features William Savage, played in the film by a distinctly unconvincing (and likely unconvinced) Pierce Brosnan, surrounded by many of the usual suspects from the Merchant–Ivory stable such as Shashi Kapoor and Saeed Jaffrey. Unlike *Bhowani Junction*, which had to be shot in Pakistan because of its unfavourable portrayal of Congress leaders during the Indian freedom movement, Merchant was able to shoot *The Deceivers* in India, in the Rajasthani 'pink city' of Jaipur as well as other western and central Indian locations. He saw it as a swashbuckling tale of derring-do because it focused on one of the early moral triumphs of the British in India, namely the suppression of 'thuggee'. Precisely what 'thuggee' was remains a contentious question, but let us for a moment imagine it just as it appears in Masters's novel, *The Deceivers*: a cult devoted to highway robbery and murder, with distinct religious overtones and involving the worship of a bloodthirsty goddess to whom victims are offered in a form of sacrifice. In short, at the heart of suppressing 'thuggee' is the task of rendering the roads safe, but it also means ridding the

Hindu religion of its more bizarre excesses. One can see why the theme keeps popping up in Hollywood, notably in Spielberg's *Indiana Jones and the Temple of Doom* (1984), where the Indian actor Amrish Puri is Mola Ram, the high priest of Kali, ranting in Hindi as he tears a victim's heart out of his chest.

Merchant eventually wrote a rather dull book about his experiences making the film, which Doubleday published as *Hullabaloo in Old Jeypore* (1989). The book is concerned in good measure with his disagreements and quarrels with his co-producer Tim Van Rellim, and to an extent with the director of the film, Nicholas Meyer. Van Rellim is accused of being 'impertinent and pompous', given to 'politicizing everything . . . and trying to create rival camps'. More interesting is a point to which I will return below, namely the local campaign against the film which eventually culminated in a lawsuit by a social worker by the name of Sunaina Mishra. Merchant himself was mystified by the fact that the subject of his film could generate such controversy. The book from which it was derived was, he notes, 'loosely based on the work of Major-General Sir William Sleeman who, as William Sleeman of the Indian Political Service, discovered, exposed and destroyed thuggee, a secret and widespread religious cult whose members ritually murdered and robbed travellers throughout India, in the name of Kali [. . .] the goddess of destruction, whom they worshipped'. Savage, the hero of the novel who is modelled on Sleeman, 'enters a mysterious world of superstition, ritual and death' but also 'uncovers an unknown side of his [own] personality, a mystic affinity with the blood brotherhood' of the thugs. While Merchant's sometime collaborators, such as Ivory and Ruth Prawer Jhabvala, seem to have winced when faced with the plot's chief premise—that an upper-class Englishman could effortlessly pass himself off as a lower-class Indian—Merchant was convinced that this was 'a matter of record' not only with Sleeman himself but even with Sir Richard Burton, who 'had done exactly that again and again'. Merchant had been educated at St Xavier's College in Bombay before leaving for the US in 1958, and was confident of his knowledge of and grounding in Indian history. From his book it emerges that he was not sceptical about colonial claims of a *mission civilisatrice* in the way that a generation or two of scholars trained in post-colonial studies have learnt to be, both in India and elsewhere. A thug was a thug, and a British hero was a British hero. It was as simple as that. One supposes two centuries of colonial rule in India would have been dreadfully inefficient if the British had not taught at least some members of the Indian elite to think in this fashion.

It is of course notorious that one of the claims that empires and conquerors like to make is that they are bringing order where previously disorder had reigned. An example of this comes to us from late March 1399, when the Central Asian conqueror Timur (or Tamerlane) had his Persian secretary Khwaja Ahmad Simnani draft a 'victory bulletin' (*fath-nama*) describing how and why he had recently conquered and pillaged Delhi. The bulletin was addressed to Timur's grandson, Pir Muhammad-i 'Umar Shaikh in Fars:

> In the year that we decided to leave on a campaign and in a holy war (*ghazw-o-jihad*) to the land of infidels (*dayar-i-kufr*) in certain regions of Hindustan, we were told that since Sultan Firoz Shah had passed from this life to the hereafter, some of the slaves that he had purchased against gold had refused to hand over Delhi and the lands of Islam to his descendants, and that they had taken to tyranny and oppression; they had made rapine and pillage their rallying signs . . . closed the doors to the passage of merchants, and taken brigandage to its height.

These claims were complex acts of propaganda on the part of Timur, and based on a series of manifestly false portrayals: northern India at the time, despite its predominantly Hindu population, could hardly be termed the 'land of the infidels' in such a blanket fashion, nor was Timur really engaged in any sort of jihad. But, as the late French savant Jean Aubin nicely put it, in such texts we see the basis of Timur's own claims of legitimacy, namely the opposition between a sort of *Pax Timurica* on the one hand and 'anarchy, brigandage, and impediments to commercial circulation' on the other. The reality behind Timur's claims was manifestly less favourable than this picture of bringing peace where anarchy had once existed. In fact, the Central Asian conqueror perpetrated massacres around Delhi, notably one at Loni on the banks of the Jamuna river. Many of the great Muslim divines of Delhi fled to the south rather than face his troops, knowing his habit of making pyramids of skulls in the towns he conquered. Then, as now, the omelette of empire needed more than a few eggs to be broken.

The same was undoubtedly true of the empire which that peculiar hybrid animal, the English East India Company, began building in the eighteenth century. The Company belonged to a particular early modern category, namely the national chartered trading company, and had its counterparts in the Netherlands, France, and Denmark. From the outset its commercial character was compromised by the fact that it was also given the legal right by the Crown to sign treaties and wage 'defensive' wars, as well as build fortified settlements wherever these were deemed necessary. For much of the seventeenth century the undercapitalized English East India Company nevertheless proved far less aggressive than its Dutch counterpart, which had a dismal record of blockades, attacks, and even massacres, particularly in South East Asia. To be sure, Sir Josiah Child did attempt briefly in the late 1680s to take on the might of Aurangzeb's Mughal empire, but for the rest the English tended to have limited Asian ambitions until the eighteenth century. All this changed from about 1740. Over the second half of the eighteenth century, the Company built a sizeable territorial state, first in eastern and southern India, and then eventually in northern and western India. The morality of what was being done was, however, constantly under challenge. Indian rulers and other elites often directed sarcastic barbs at Company Bahadur (or the Honourable Company), that rapacious warlord masquerading as a merchant. Other Europeans looked at them with scepticism and disapproval, sometimes tinged with more than a touch of jealousy. In Britain itself the Company was the target of numerous attacks, whether from Edmund Burke or Adam Smith. Seen as combining opportunism and monopolistic greed, it faced a constant moral barrage and eventually turned on its attackers by producing claims to its own moral superiority and right to rule over India, even if only as the ostensible representative of an absent Mughal emperor.

Three elements were key to these claims. The first was the idea that the Company and its servants were restoring a pristine form of government which had existed centuries before (say, under the early Mughals) but had since degenerated. The second was that particular forms of affinity existed between Indians and Englishmen which rendered the latter particularly qualified to carry out this task as opposed, for example, to the French. The third idea, related to the first, was that over the centuries a number of vicious and superstitious notions had come to tarnish Indian cultural norms. These would have to be stripped away, and the underlying institutions reformed.

To make and sustain such difficult-to-reconcile claims was no easy task in view of the Company's many opponents. In the 1770s, for example, when they seized the southern Indian state of Tanjavur (ruled over by a Maratha king), the British Parliament intervened to restore the ruler Tulajaji Bhonsle and rapped the Company on the knuckles for what they saw as an indefensible action. Of course, such reversals usually proved temporary, and in the case of Tanjavur merely delayed matters by about a quarter-century. Nevertheless, what is of importance is the fact that the Company was always on potentially slippery moral ground, not least because its early record of administration was pretty appalling—their mismanagement of the great Bengal famine of the years 1769 to 1773 led to several million deaths. Statistics on the subject are conveniently uncertain, as the Company itself well knew, but there is little doubt that the corporation was poorly equipped to rule a territory like that of Bengal at this stage; and furthermore its employees were too concerned with the primary task of lining their own pockets and returning home as 'nabobs' to bother about their Indian subjects. The loss of the American colonies, the trial of Warren Hastings, and a series of further conflicts in Britain and India eventually led to an attempt to build a more stable ideological basis for colonial rule, and this came into play in the first half of the nineteenth century.

The nature of the transition between the first half-century of Company rule and the next fifty years is thus important to grasp. In the first phase, references to Muslim tyranny and misrule do provide a periodic justification for acts of conquest, as we see in the episode of the so-called Black Hole of Calcutta and the demonization of Nawab Siraj-ud-Daula. This point of view was strengthened by the theme of the Briton not as aggressor but as victim, and in it narratives of captivity (such as those retailed in recent times by Linda Colley) played a significant role. The central figure who emerged in such portrayals was the ruler of Mysore, Tipu Sultan, who was eventually killed at his capital city of Srirangapatna in May 1799 by Company forces. After 1800 there were few such iconic and larger-than-life hate-figures available for the Company's publicists to focus on. The idea of a threat to the Company and its rule became increasingly diffused across population groups rather than focused on tyrannical individuals.

Some years ago I had occasion to read in a leisurely fashion through the extensive papers of a minor but interesting figure who was a participant in this transition. This was the Scotsman

Alexander Walker (or Walker of Bowlands), most of whose manuscript writings—amounting to several hundred volumes—came to be deposited in the National Library of Scotland. Walker (1764–1831) was an amateur savant, and also a collector of texts in Persian and other languages which his son eventually gave to the Bodleian Library. He joined the Company as a cadet in about 1780, and served in the wars against Tipu Sultan, for whom he conceived a lasting hatred. Later, he was sent as a Company administrator to Gujarat and Malabar, before ending his career as governor (and successor to Hudson Lowe) in St Helena in the 1820s.

In this last phase he wrote extensively on such subjects as 'Hindoo Manners, Practices and Customs' and 'Hindoo Castes and Professions'. He also looked back on his earlier collaboration with the likes of Edward Moor on exposing such practices as female infanticide which, he claimed, was particularly common amongst the Jadeja Rajputs of Gujarat. Walker, like Moor and many others, was thus inclined more and more as his career progressed to see Indian society as made up not of individuals but of groups with collective forms of behaviour. It was these forms of behaviour that had first to be studied and then to be reformed where needed. 'The influence of the English in changing the sentiments of the Hindus', he wrote, 'has been considerable but the changes we have effected are cold and philosophical.' To be sure, he added, 'we have taught the natives useful arts and improved them in others. We have instilled into them a more rational use of money by enabling them to spend it in security and by making them better acquainted with the elegancies and conveniences of life.' But this had really not struck at the heart of a number of deplorable practices. Thus, writing of the kingdom of Jaipur (which he, like Ismail Merchant, liked to spell 'Jeypore' or 'Jaypore'), he noted the existence there of specialized hereditary thieves and robbers. 'The Maina caste', he noted, 'is celebrated for its expertness in committing theft. It is customary for them to allow no child to see the light for three days after birth; that its eyes may strengthen themselves in their natural clearness, and by this their sight is better in the night than ours. If they wish any person to be unusually expert, they do not allow him to see a candle for forty days after his birth; and they say that a person who has not seen a candle (or light) for forty days after birth will see as well in the darkest night as at noonday.'

Walker, like his other friends (including the somewhat celebrated Jonathan Duncan), naturally insisted that none of these insights into India was their own invention. Rather, he always held forth on his proximity to Indian informants, such as one Gangadhar Patvardhan Sastri, or, in the case of Jaipur, a certain Nawab Nizam-ud-Din Khan. The thrust of his reflections was decidedly ethnographic if not downright sociological. It is of some significance that his collaboration with Edward Moor on the subject of Indian female infanticide coincided almost exactly with the beginning of persistent mention in Company records of a group called the 'Tugs', described in a report of 1809 as a 'detestable race of monsters . . . who are constantly lurking in jungles and wastes [to] entrap any travellers who may be incautious enough to travel by night.' This was during the governorship of the first Earl of Minto, a Scottish peer better known for his aggressive actions in Java and Mauritius. These were good years for Scots in Company service in India, and many (like the well-known Colin Mackenzie) came to give an institutional basis to an understanding of India firmly rooted in an ethnographic vision. As surveys followed conquests, various Indian groups and their habitats and customs came to be identified.

There was a particular preoccupation with customs that were connected to actual or potential acts of violence. Walker wrote at some length on the Bhats and Charans of Gujarat and their practice of *traga*, where they threatened to mutilate or kill themselves if someone did not do as they wished; the sin for this act would then fall on the head of the intended target. Again, Muharram processions brought out some anxiety in him. 'The processions', he noted, 'are armed and their infuriated zeal is often guilty of dangerous excesses. This has induced precautions in the English settlements to guard against the consequences of their fanatism [*sic*].' Again, Walker, like many of his European contemporaries and predecessors, reflected on more than one occasion on 'suttee', the practice of burning widows upon the funeral pyres of their deceased husbands. However, he seems to have written little or nothing on the subject of 'thugs' or 'thuggee'.

'Thugs' became something of a *cause célèbre* in the 1820s and early 1830s. They were identified as a major and peculiar threat to peace in the domains of the East India Company. Bandits and robbers had long been known to exist in India, as indeed in most other parts of the world. Some were also known to inhabit the penumbra of states, acting as the irregular auxiliaries of rulers, an example being the 'Pindaris' with whom the East India Company was concerned in its campaigns in western and southern India. There were also organized groups that apparently combined violence and ritual activities, such as the *sannyasis* or warrior-ascetics. These groups, deftly juggling a mix of trade, warfare, and sectarian religious organization, had emerged in medieval times and attracted notice in the later sixteenth century—the Mughal emperor Akbar had, in 1567, intervened in a violent conflict between them at Thanesar. In the new political circumstances of the eighteenth century, some of them acquired considerable prominence (they have been the object of study by several generations of scholars). In 1761, at the Third Battle of Panipat, the Afghan ruler Ahmad Shah Abdali is said to have expressed disgust at his Maratha adversaries resorting to ash-smeared men who could not even be bothered to cover their private parts before venturing into combat. Usually, but not always, associated with worship of the god Shiva, these ascetics were rather remarkable characters.

In the first three decades of the nineteenth century, Company officials made a considerable effort to separate from this confusing tumult of bandits, freebooters, and warrior-ascetics a specific group called the 'Thugs'. As Kim Wagner's anthology shows ably enough, they did not invent the term. Wagner has already devoted several essays and a monograph entitled *Thuggee: Banditry and the British in Early Nineteenth-Century India* (2007) to this question; by so doing he joined a veritable industry on the subject which featured such predictable titles as *Thug, or a Million Murders* (1933), *The Yellow Scarf* (1961), *The Strangled Traveler* (2002), and *Thug: The True Story of India's Murderous Religion* (2005), the last a sensational and commercially astute work by the popular historian Mike Dash. Wagner begins his anthology with excerpts from articles by the Indologists Wilhelm Halbfass and Paul Dundas, suggesting that the word *thaka* or *thaga* can be found at least as early as in medieval Jain textual tradition to mean a cheat, swindler, or slippery character. Reading this together with other later Hindi and Persian works, we can easily concur that the British did not invent the word, just as they did not invent the word *sati*. Rather, they transformed and contracted it semantically, giving it a specific meaning but also shifting its larger context by inventing the far larger word and concept 'thuggee'. This became a sort of pseudo-ethnographic term, which meant something quite specific. Elevated to an abstract status, 'thuggee' came to mean a well-organized group of robbers with a specific technique, a secret language, a ritual (or religious) purpose to their activity, and a considerable geographic spread extending from the Gangetic plain well into southern India.

As we can see, early Company officials themselves had considerable doubts on the matter. One of them, Leycester, had actually noted in the 1810s that 'the word Thug is a local cant term, and consequently little understood in any uniform way', while Ernst, the magistrate at Hughli, claimed as early as 1810 that the practices of the thugs 'fall very short of those which are ascribed to them in Mr Wright's letter to the government'. The arrest of the first group of suspected thugs in Etawa in March 1810 did not help. Many of them, such as a certain Ghulam Husain, turned out to be Muslims, as did their victims, whereas later claims were to be that the murders were ritual acts linked to the worship of the goddess Kali or Bhavani. Of course, heterodox popular practices and worship amongst Muslims were not unknown, but the lack of proper evidence eventually led to a situation where the case against Ghulam Husain and the others collapsed. It was only in 1826 that a group of 'thugs' was finally convicted in a colonial court, but by this time the view had become firmly rooted that the phenomenon was widespread. In 1816 R. Sherwood published a description of *phansigars* (or stranglers) operating in southern India, noting that 'though the Phansigars are almost all Mussulmans, they have nevertheless universally adopted, on certain occasions, the idolatrous worship of Hindu deities.' These deities, according to him, centrally involved the smallpox goddess Mariyamman, to whom animal sacrifices were also offered. Sherwood's account was crucial in many ways. It made mention of earlier accounts, such as one by the seventeenth-century French traveller Jean de Thévenot, and also underlined the importance of a secret language, which he termed *pheraseri-ci-bat*, made up of 'signs, and of words and phrases not understood by others as channels of communication.' The fact that the stranglers used stealth and cunning was stressed, as was the notion that 'phansigars never commit robbery unaccompanied by murder, their practice being first to strangle and then to rifle their victims.' These then were a 'distinct class of hereditary murderers and plunderers, settled in various parts of India, and alike remarkable for the singularity of their practice, and the extent of their depredations'. Once 'stranglers' and 'thugs' were made congruent, the picture was complete and the stage set for a campaign to make the roads safe both for the passage of travellers and soldiers (or sepoys), and for the expanded traffic in both cash and key commercial goods such as central Indian opium.

It has been claimed that in the campaigns against 'thuggee' in the 1820s and 1830s, some 4000 people were convicted and hanged. The laws were rather draconian and the definition of 'thugs' and 'thuggee' extremely vague, even in the so-called Act XXX of 1836. The campaign was also the occasion for self-aggrandizement on the part of some Company officials, of whom the most conspicuous example was undoubtedly W.H. Sleeman, who eventually published the so-called 'standard work on thuggee', namely *Ramaseeana, or a vocabulary of the peculiar language used by the Thugs* (1836). According to a report he authored in May 1830, the activities of the thugs 'make almost every road in India between the Jumna and the Indus from the beginning of November until the end of May a dreadful scene of hourly murder.' Sleeman then went on in October of the same year to publish an anonymous account of the thugs in the *Calcutta Literary Gazette*, where he made strenuous efforts to link them to a particular Bhavani temple at Vindhyachal (near Mirzapur in Uttar Pradesh). He also made much of the thugs' ritual practices and their use of the scarf or *rumal* that had been consecrated by a priest in order to strangle their victims; he added that 'the investiture with the romal is knighthood to these monsters.' The religious paradox involved did not escape his attention, and he made a point to insist that these were rather peculiar Muslims who worshipped the goddess, did not eat beef, and 'are not suffered to invoke the name of Mahommud' even though 'the Koran is still their civil code'.

Historians have in general been unable to arrive at a consensus as regards the status of these claims. The fact that the bulk of the thug trials centred on testimonies extracted from 'approvers', which is to say people who testified against others in order to receive reduced sentences, lies at the heart of the matter, as does the relentlessly sensationalist and self-serving character of Sleeman's own account. The discovery of mass graves of victims is another key element, but the forensic techniques of the time were notoriously crude. Nevertheless, we can trace a clear path in terms of historians' understandings of what 'thuggee' was or might have been.

The simplest attitude to take would be to accept Sleeman's account, and a handful of other converging ones from the 1820s and 1830s, as the unvarnished truth. This would, however, involve setting aside the contradictions within the archives of the Company. If we chose this route, the assumption would be that the thugs were an ancient secret society which was 'discovered' by the British and then attacked and eventually disbanded. Such a view pervaded historiography for over a century from the time of the anti-thuggee campaigns, and is still the standard view in popular histories and cinematic representations (including that of Ismail Merchant).

A second position was that taken by a group of historians beginning with Hiralal Gupta in the late 1950s. Gupta argued that thugs did indeed exist but were not at all a 'religious fraternity'. Rather, the peculiar circumstances created by Company expansion in the later eighteenth and early nineteenth centuries led to forms of banditry that were quite secular in character, and their community logic was simply one of 'reciprocity of interest'. This approach, initially a part of Indian nationalist historiography, came to be generalized in the writings of American historians in the 1960s and 1970s. These historians emphasized the pragmatic aims of the 'thugs', their alliance with local magnates, and their attacks on couriers and bankers' agents.

From an interest in questions of political economy that surrounded and rendered comprehensible the rise of forms of banditry, the question then arose of whether all this was no

more than 'colonial myth-making', as even the relatively staid
Sir Christopher Bayly put it by the 1990s. With Hobsbawm
and Ranger's celebrated 1983 formula of 'the invention of
tradition' in mind, it became common to accuse the British
of having 'discovered' nothing and 'invented' everything in
their encounter with India. Reviewing an old-fashioned and
rather inconsistent work on thugs by Martine van Woerkens, a
young historian, Satadru Sen, could write: 'Over the course of
the 1830s British administrators in India invented, unearthed,
pursued and popularized the "thug" as a particularly horrifying
category of colonial criminal and native subject.'

Eventually, and inevitably, scholars of literature entered the
scene *en masse*, abandoning any hope of recovering 'facts' and
instead shifting the focus to the representation of thugs and
'thuggee'. One of them, cited in Wagner's anthology, pointed to
how 'the discourse on and around thuggee can be instrumental
in opening up our present understanding of the theorization of
colonial mimicry.' Finally, Tom Lloyd, a writer with vaulting
epistemological ambitions writing in 2006 (who is given the
last word in Wagner's compendium) notes that 'a historical
account of "thuggee" can only study its representations', because
'as historians, dealing with documents from the past, we can
assess the discursive constitution of "thugs", not their *actual*
behaviour.' It was the same old story in short: the thug could
perhaps strangle, but he could certainly not speak.

All of this may be somewhat disheartening, because we could
easily substitute the words 'thugs' and 'thuggee' with many others
(such as, let us say, 'cricket') and still come up with precisely the
same debates and conflicted diagnoses based on *a priori* positions.
We would thus get: 'the discourse on and around cricket can
be instrumental in opening up our present understanding of
the theorization of colonial mimicry', or again that 'a historical
account of "cricket" can only study its representations', because
'as historians, dealing with documents from the past, we can

assess the discursive constitution of "cricketers", not their *actual* behaviour.' Central to these debates are several questions, some of which are alarmingly simple-minded. Was colonial know-ledge-making a simple act of conspiracy? Or was it a series of small misunderstandings and misrecognitions which eventually cohered to form a pattern? It is clear that whatever the gulf between different groups of scholars working on India, it is dwarfed by the far greater chasm that seperates popular histo-ries and fictions from them, taken as a whole.

It is of some significance here to compare the problem of 'thuggee' with that of 'suttee'. Unlike the word 'thug', the abstract and systemic concept of 'thuggee' was—it has been noted above—probably invented by the British. In the case of 'suttee', on the other hand, a semantic displacement was effected by which the word *sati*, which meant a true or virtuous woman, was understood to mean not a person but an act, that of self-immolation. Did 'suttee' (in the British sense) exist in a pervasive way before Company rule? The accounts of numerous European and even Muslim travellers can be summoned up in favour of this view, even if it is likely that a certain number of them invented their accounts of widow self-immolation since no travel account worth its salt could fail to mention and describe it. It is thus no coincidence that a parallel compendium to that of Wagner, edited by Andrea Major, is entitled *Sati: A Historical Anthology* (2007). The two—'thuggee' and 'suttee'—were the major preoccupations of the governorship of William Bentinck (1828–35), and part of a significant occupation of the moral high ground by British and Indian reformers against their traditionalist opponents of varying stripes. But what is highly uncertain is the extent to which widow self-immolation was practised. Was it restricted to certain castes and regions, or, as British official writings sometimes implied, a practice that one encountered up and down Indian society, and in all corners of the subcontinent?

Unlike 'suttee', which has been glorified and defended by some as a glorious part of traditional Indian culture, we are yet to find Indian social activists or postcolonial theorists defending 'thuggee' on quite the same terms. Yet, the travails of Ismail Merchant and *The Deceivers* are not without interest in this regard. A first lawsuit filed against the film argued that by taking Sleeman's (and Masters's) view of the matter, the film projected a 'wrong picture of our Hindu culture, religion and mythology', notably the place therein of the goddess Kali; Merchant's response, which astonishingly won the day in court, was simply to the effect that 'thuggee is a well-documented part of Indian history'. A second lawsuit by the same parties was then significantly on the very issue of 'suttee' which is also featured in the film. William Savage, the hero, not content with ridding India of thugs, also takes time in the film as in the novel to rescue a beautiful widow (played by Neena Gupta) from self-immolation. In view of recent incidents of those years, notably the infamous Roop Kanwar immolation at Deorala on 4 September 1987, it was suggested that Merchant and his crew were in fact glorifying such dreadful acts. Once again, Merchant is categorical in his book. 'Sleeman and his exploits, on which the novel is based, were not fiction. Neither is sati, which is one of the film's sub-plots.' However, he posed himself as a defender of women's rights, and noted that this was another instance in which the British had helped improve India. Besides, he notes, *The Far Pavilions* too had had its obligatory 'suttee' scene and no one had objected.

Here, the longer trajectory of 'suttee' may be said to depart somewhat from that of 'thuggee'. For the latter in fact had a considerable institutional afterlife. Much after Sleeman's campaigns of the 1830s, the idea that criminality in India was hereditary, ritually handed down, and enshrined in the caste system (in its broader acception), continued to play a significant role in colonial administrative thinking, even after the transition from Company to Crown. It eventually led to the definition, through the Criminal Tribes Acts of the 1870s and 1920s, of a series of groups who were defined by default as criminal. Sleeman's own early interest in phrenology in some senses pointed the way in this direction. These Acts were eventually repealed, but the stigma associated with them remained in place even after they were no longer on the books and may not have disappeared even today.

The Indonesian historian Onghokham once wrote (with tongue somewhat in cheek) of colonialism that it was the encounter between 'the inscrutable and the paranoid'. If that diagnosis is correct, it may explain the history of 'thuggee' as part of a larger problem of mistrust, misperception, and misrecognition. But the end of colonial rule did not provide us with a happy ending either. What remains troubling is the legacy of the 'thuggee' campaign even for the post-colonial polity. In the late 1980s and early 1990s the Indian state undertook a set of draconian campaigns to exterminate what was described as Sikh 'terrorism' in the Punjab. The chief of police, Kanwar Pal Singh Gill, was given powers equalling or exceeding those handed out to Sleeman, and the number of those summarily killed certainly exceeded those who were hanged in the thug trials of the 1830s. As in the 1830s, some of those who died may have been implicated in various crimes and acts of violence while others surely were not. Like 'thuggee' in the 1830s, 'terrorism' in the 1980s and early 1990s was a sufficiently vague and capacious category to cover much that was done merely for reasons of state. In his defence Gill wrote, 'Truth does not triumph; unless it has champions to propound it, unless it has armies to defend it.' The same could be said, one supposes, of falsehood, and neither the champions nor the armies are necessarily constituted to tell the difference.

8

What, Exactly, is an Empire?*

In the year 1283 of the Hegiran era, or 1866 of the Common
Era, the Ottoman traveller 'Abdur Rahman bin 'Abdullah
al-Baghdadi al-Dimashqi arrived in Brazil on the imperial
corvette *Bursa* to begin a three-year-long visit in the Land of
the Holy Cross (*Terra de Santa Cruz*). A first-person account in
Arabic of his experiences, entitled *Maslihat al-gharib bi-kull-i
amr 'ajib* (The delight of the traveller concerning all that is
marvellous) has recently been published in the original from
Rio de Janeiro, together with excellent translations into Spanish
and Portuguese—indispensable for those like myself who can do
no more than merely read the Arabic script. It is an important
text for a number of reasons, including the light it sheds on
the status of Islam amongst slaves of West African origin in
nineteenth-century Brazil, but it is also one that permits us to
reflect on what empires exactly are and were. For on the face
of it, Al-Baghdadi, a man of high religion and culture (in his
own terms, an *imam* and an *adib*), who had been educated in
Damascus, was the representative of one empire in another. But
were these two empires in fact creatures of the same species or
is it just an arbitrary convention of ours that places them under
the same rubric? How indeed does one compare the Brazilian

*On *After Tamerlane: The Global History of Empire Since 1405* by John
Darwin (New York: Bloomsbury Press, 2008), xiv+575pp.

'empire' of the long-reigning monarch Dom Pedro II (1831–89) with the Ottoman empire of Sultan Abdülaziz (1861–76)?

The two monarchs certainly had something in common. Both were travellers not in the usual early modern mode, when rulers toured their own lands incessantly (to cure scrofula or to ensure loyalty) and sometimes led armies into battle across land or maritime frontiers, but rather in the typical later nineteenth-century mode of long-distance royal diplomatic tourism. The Ottoman sultan was in fact the first of his line to engage in such travels, and paid an official visit to Napoleon III in 1867, besides sojourning in London, Berlin, and Vienna. He thus had occasion to inspect the centres of other empires and would-be empires closely, and to visit museums that collected imperial loot and treasures. Nine years later, in 1876, Pedro II visited the United States for the Philadelphia Exposition, where a partly apocryphal anecdote connects him with Alexander Graham Bell and the early use of the telephone. The emperor, in an anecdote retailed by the historian Samuel Eliot Morison, either recited some celebrated lines from *Hamlet* into the instrument or heard them recited by Bell, and was mightily impressed one way or another. To be or not to be an emperor might already have been on his mind; about a decade later, in 1889, he was eventually deposed by a military *coup* and replaced by the oligarchic *café-com-leite* (coffee-with-milk) republican regime that endured until the 1930s. As for the Ottomans, their own version of imperial rule continued into the early 1920s, ending after the First World War in chaos, massacres, and the broken dreams of pan-Islamic revival that accompanied the painful formation of the Turkish republic.

Our traveller Al-Baghdadi was certainly interested in giving his Ottoman readers some sense of Brazil, even if political economy was not his primary interest. He writes of the great Amazon river, 'the largest river in the world', of Brazil's population of eight and a half million, and the fact that the ruler had armed forces comprising some 85 steam-powered vessels and 40,000 men. However, this description occurs in the context of a section entitled 'location of the state of Brazil' (*iqlim dawlat Berazilya*) where he refrains from identifying Brazil specifically as anything like an 'empire'. The term *dawlat* would for Al-Baghdadi and his readers have meant simply a state, though on one occasion he does term Rio de Janeiro with the somewhat higher-sounding title of 'the foot of the throne of the state of Brazil' (*pa'i takht dawlat Berazilya*) which was usually reserved for important capital cities. Yet, nowhere does he state or even imply that Brazil as an empire could be placed on a similar footing in terms of political vocabulary to the Ottomans. Clearly, this was quite different from the manner in which the Ottomans had once treated the Habsburgs or even the Mughals, the former a Christian state and the latter a Muslim one.

This is not merely an arcane point of debate. After all, one of the questions to ask after reading nearly 600 pages on the 'global history of empire since 1405' is what exactly the author means by empire. John Darwin does not address this question directly. But we can reflect on it by asking two related questions. First, what is not empire (and hence left out of this work)? Second, what are the other terms that empire comes paired with, in the usual complementary oppositions that historians and other social scientists are so fond of, such as empire versus nation-state?

It may be useful to start, though, by taking a slightly different tack, namely a consideration of the issues that this book explicitly claims to address. It does so by setting out three broad themes, and four basic assumptions. The themes are: first, the move from 'global connectedness' to 'globalization'; second, the role of Europe and European empires in such long-term transformations; and third, the 'resilience'—or perhaps we should say residual agency—of non-European states and other actors in these processes. These themes are in turn linked to what Darwin chooses to term 'the four basic assumptions' set out early in the work, which are as follows.

- That the historical change produced by and through empires after 1400 was conjunctural and reversible, instead of being linear, cumulative, and teleological.
- That Europe in these six centuries should constantly be placed within its larger setting of Eurasia in order to escape the trap of European exceptionalism.
- That the idea of 'Europe' itself should be subject to constant interrogation to separate its distinct uses as 'a geographical space; a socio-political community; and a cultural programme.'
- That empire was a widespread practice and not merely a European one, indeed 'the default mode of political organization throughout most of history' rather than 'the original sin of European peoples.'

Whether the first three of these are in fact 'assumptions' as opposed to hypotheses or speculations is not immediately clear. Taken together they do, however, give us a relatively clear location for Darwin in a fraught historiographical field: he is neither one of those with a triumphalist view of Europe's worldwide mission (still dashingly espoused by some recent authors like John Headley), nor a votary of a certain style of post-colonial studies; and thus he is neither a cringing devotee of the politically correct nor rudely politically incorrect in his readings. The book is an attempt in short at some sort of judicious balance, the sort that often may win one enemies all around. Before looking in some detail into his work, it may be worth locating, even if briefly, this book in a quite extended career of continuous academic production on the subject of empire.

It is over a quarter-century since John Darwin published *Britain, Egypt and the Middle East: Imperial Policy in the Aftermath of War, 1918–1922* (1980), and in the intervening period he has published at least two other works on the last days of the British empire. Empire has been at the heart of his research and publishing career, as indeed of his teaching. The work under review here departs markedly, however, from the earlier ones in three ways: in terms of its conception as a popular work, in its far larger (even global) geographical scope, and in its embrace of both the early modern and the modern periods. In his preface Darwin suggests that there are sound English, even Oxbridge, precedents for his work: he notes that his 'first introduction to the fascination of viewing world history as a connected whole came as a pupil of the late Jack Gallagher, whose historical imagination was boundless.' Elsewhere in the same prefatory text he relates his work to earlier literature on the rise of the West and European expansion, while acknowledging his debt to 'the huge volume of new writing in the last twenty years (. . .) on global history.' He adds thereafter that 'it is not only recently that historians have insisted on a global view of the past: that tradition, after all, goes back to Herodotus.' Did Herodotus ever speak or even reflect on a 'global view of the past' when he was presumably not aware of the earth as a globe? I rather doubt it. This may be a little generous, but probably not as generous as the reference to Gallagher, whose vision remained entirely confined so far as anyone can see to the later British empire of the nineteenth and twentieth centuries and its vicissitudes. This version of boundless imagination is possibly, like that of the placid dreams of the Empress of Blandings, based on the exuberant semiosis of a few enigmatic grunts.

There is, all the same, every reason to applaud the courage of this work, which begins in the early fifteenth century and proceeds in nine chronologically organized chapters through five and a half centuries of world history in an imperial mode. Described in the blurb as 'one of Britain's leading scholars of global history', John Darwin is in fact one of a mere handful of scholars in Britain and the British tradition who can even pretend to practise any form of global history. Notable amongst other practitioners of the genre (if genre it is) are Christopher Bayly for the modern period; the remarkable early modern master–disciple pairing of John Elliott and Geoffrey Parker, of whom the latter is not by chance a long-time exile from the shores of Blighty; and finally the entirely *sui generis* figure of Felipe Fernández-Armesto, whom no one has yet dared to classify. Darwin joins my UCLA colleague Anthony Pagden as a relatively recent entrant into this field, and does not possess the obvious resources that Pagden has, namely a comparative perspective on the Iberian and British worlds and a deep background in classical materials from Greece and Rome. Instead, he has a strong drive towards a social and institutional history (as opposed to a history of ideas), and a clear commitment to a balanced geographical view to the extent that the materials he has at his disposal will allow. This is thus a work of courage and more; I would even call it a work of *chutzpah*, coming as it does from the confines of Oxbridge.

The breadth of vision is already on display in an opening chapter entitled 'Orientations'. We begin with the celebrated anecdote of the meeting between Amir Timur and Ibn Khaldun at the walls of Damascus in 1401, but the great Central Asian conqueror is given relatively short shrift thereafter, as a mere 'transitional figure in Eurasian history'. Instead Darwin points us in the direction of the great interpretative debates of the nineteenth and twentieth centuries regarding the long sweep of history, from Marx and Weber, to the more obscure Halford Mackinder and J.C. van Leur, to more culturally-oriented recent readings such as those of Edward Said. In a few brief pages he thus efficiently summarizes the large and complex debate on the idea of modernity, concluding against the forceful advice of the Africanist Frederick Cooper that 'it is too useful an idea to be thrown away', but adding that 'it may be wise to accept it as a fuzzy abstraction'. Using the idea of 'three great civilizational zones', namely China, Islamdom, and Europe, as his starting point, he then proceeds to sketch a broad comparative framework, drawing amongst others on the classic work of Mark Elvin from the early 1970s. The tone is thus set in this first chapter: narrative history is leavened by regular references to social science debates, and the presentation is always argumentative but never contentious. The endnotes to the first chapter are also telling in the pattern they set: they reflect recent literature as well as classic references, but are almost all in English, with a bare sprinkling in French. The other European-language historiographies and primary materials simply do not make the cut, let alone those in more 'exotic' languages. Here we see a characteristic weakness of 'global history' in its Anglo-American incarnation, namely its default assumption of a monolingual world of debate and discussion. If you write about empires in Spanish, you are apparently provincial and not worthy of notice.

The second and third chapters take on the early modern period, with the centuries after 1750 then accounting for the lion's share of what remains. I shall return to a few elements of these early modern chapters presently; they are transparently entitled 'Eurasia and the Age of Discovery' and 'The Early Modern Equilibrium'. The fourth chapter is in some respects crucial: entitled 'The Eurasian Revolution', it describes the transition between the aforementioned early modern equilibrium of older imperial formations and the new balance that emerged in the nineteenth century. Darwin takes a firm stance here, arguing that the changes of the period from 1750 to 1830 involved three revolutions in one, 'in geopolitics, in culture and in economics'; however, he is confident that it was the geopolitical shift that in many ways drove the other two. This is an important argument, and will be harshly received by those who wish to see the changes of the period as driven primarily by European cultural, scientific, and technological supremacy. It does sit well with Kenneth Pomeranz's view of the 'great divergence', which Darwin refers to approvingly in spite of its tensions with Mark Elvin's viewpoint that he has earlier espoused. But Darwin is at times still prone to returning to blunt-edged culturalistic explanations, sometimes in quite mistaken terms, such as when he writes confidently of an 'Ottoman indifference to the Americas' as typical of a lack of curiosity in the non-Western world. On the contrary, the work of Thomas Goodrich shows us quite clearly that the extent of Ottoman Americana—such as the *Tarih-i Hind-i Garbi*—was not to be sneezed at even in the sixteenth century. Two centuries before 'Abdur Rahman al-Baghdadi we have the Arabic travel account of Ilyas al-Mawsuli to Spanish America, of which not one but two recent translations into English exist. We ignore these works, and take Bernard Lewis as our infallible guide, at our own peril.

Once the divide into the nineteenth century has been crossed, the book's narrative takes on a more traditional form: 'a race against time' and modernizing push that is driven largely by Europeans, until in the late nineteenth century the 'limits of empire' are reached largely in the context of the scramble for Africa. Darwin is careful however not to centre the whole narrative on the European empires, and devotes time and space to the Ottomans, China, and Japan. This takes us to the extended world crisis that runs in Darwin's account from 1914 to 1942 (the latter the year of Midway and Alamein), leading in turn in the penultimate chapter to decolonization, the Cold War, and eventually the fall of the Soviet Union. The two main protagonists of the Cold War are both treated explicitly here as empires, and after 1990, Darwin emphatically claims, America became 'the only world empire'. Yet, he argues that those who compare the present-day US to Victorian Britain 'betray a staggering ignorance of the history of both', since American financial and cultural dominance vastly exceeds that which Britain possessed. There are no prizes for guessing the target of that particular barb. The combination of empire and globalization is thus seen as a mixture far more potent than just the existence of empire.

There are a number of stimulating claims and hypotheses

here which will undoubtedly make the book a standard point of departure for essays and reflections on global history in the next decade, alongside the works of Bayly, Pagden, and others. However, there are also some troubling conceptual issues. Let us begin by taking the term 'empire', which, as we have seen, Darwin more or less refuses to address or define, perhaps taking it as an article of common sense or something one could look up in the *Oxford English Dictionary*. Leaving the dictionary aside, since it is never really helpful in such matters, let us look to what might be a broad consensus or *sens commun* amongst historians. Clearly, empires must be distinguished from other political forms that exist in space, such as city-states, compact kingdoms, republics, and nation-states, some of which have in fact had a relatively short history, even if they cast a long shadow on current discussion. This is, on the face of it, a mere matter of scale; but matters are not quite so simple. Some of today's nation-states such as India, China, and the United States, are as large as many past empires, and further Darwin would have us believe that the United States is both a nation-state and an empire. So an argument from the idea of exclusion ('What is not an empire because it is something else?') is not entirely persuasive. Nor do Darwin's rather eclectic empirical examples persuade us that matters are clear even in his own mind. Take the case of Japan, where it is noted by him that an 'emperor' existed from at least the twelfth century. But what does this really mean? The most commonly used Japanese word in this context is *tennō*, which I gather simply means a heavenly ruler. The term *kōtei* is a loan word from the Chinese (the Chinese term is *huangdi*) used to designate imperial rulers outside Japan, but not in Japan itself. Now the decision to term the ruler of Japan an emperor is a modern one. There is little reason to see the domains they ruled from the twelfth to the nineteenth centuries as empires, if one sets aside the aberration of Hideyoshi's brief invasions of Korea in the 1590s, and the complex but limited dealings with the

Ryukyu Islands from the seventeenth century. Japan's imperial moment obviously dates to the years after 1890, and lasted a bare half-century, and it is important to limit the use of the term 'empire' to that period.

The reasoning for this must be made explicit. Empire implies political complexity, and cultural as well as—more often than not—ethnic and linguistic diversity amongst the subject populations. The form that political complexity typically takes is a variety of heterogeneous political and administrative arrangements across space, often featuring notions of layered sovereignty. The Ottoman empire in the sixteenth and seventeenth centuries is an excellent example of this. Some of its territories were ruled directly and fell into the category of the *has* (or *khass*); in some others, existing dynasties were incorporated as tribute-paying entities; in still others a variety of other fiscal and administrative arrangements could be found. The situations in Wallachia, in Anatolia, and the Hijaz were thus remarkably diverse and remained so even as they changed. Furthermore, the three major Religions of the Book were to be found in the Ottoman domains, as well as a variety of other 'heterodox' religious practices that were more or less tolerated (with the exception of certain forms of Shi'ism). If Ottoman Turkish was the chief language of administration, a vast number of other Semitic, Slavic, and other languages were practised within the sultan's territories.

The brief description that I have presented already demonstrates to us why empire is not merely seen as a form of 'original sin' (in Darwin's terms) but is also a possible object of nostalgia. Faced with the situation in Kosovo in the 1990s, one can see why a gilded legend of the Ottomans could emerge. In India, if right-wing Hindu nationalists have transformed the Mughals into a veritable object of hatred, many others, including the likes of Amartya Sen, have made their empire appear to be a near-utopian political arrangement created by the genius of a happy few like the emperor Akbar (1556–1605). Empire here comes to stand for diversity, tolerance, and difference, as distinct from the nation-state with its inherent drive towards homogeneity in linguistic, religious, and other terms. On the other hand, to many nationalists, empires stand for archaism and hidebound tradition, as we see in the frequent Turkish nationalist depiction of the Ottomans as bigoted and backward-looking Sunnis. If this is what Turkish nationalists have to say, we may only imagine with a shudder what the Greek or the Bulgarian nationalists have in mind when they evoke the House of Osman.

This takes us to the heart of the problem. Even if it is a single word, with a traceable history taking us back to the Roman *imperium*, empire is not one thing but many. Here, it seems to me that Darwin's position radically simplifies issues, as we see in the following passage where he compares empire-building as an impulse to Adam Smith's notion of the universal drive to 'truck, barter and exchange'. He writes: 'a second propensity in human communities has been the accumulation of power on an extensive scale: the building of empires. Indeed, the difficulty of forming autonomous states on an ethnic basis, against the gravitational pull of cultural or economic attraction (as well as disparities of military force), has been so great that empire (where different ethnic communities fall under a common ruler) has been the default mode of political organization throughout most of history. Imperial power has usually been the rule of the road.' The problem however is that empires could be radically different from one another. We may provisionally set out a loose taxonomy of empires for the post-1400 period, even if it is in a somewhat Borgesian vein.

1. Empires that think they are empires use explicitly imperial terminology, and link themselves to a recognizable imperial tradition (such as Alexander, Rome, the Achaemenids, the Sasanians, the Caliphate) by thinking in the logic of *translatio imperii*. This is the most obvious category

and would include the Ottomans, the Habsburgs, the Mughals, and so on.

2. States that pretend to be empires, though there are good reasons to doubt their pretensions. The Danes in the seventeenth century are a suitably obscure example, but perhaps we could classify nineteenth-century Brazil into this slot too.

3. Empires that deny that they are empires. The English East India Company comes to mind, as does the Dutch East India Company in certain of its incarnations. If we accept Darwin's classification, this is where the United States would fall.

4. Cases where the jury is still out, such as Safavid Iran or (if one is to credit Darwin's former Oxford colleague Timothy Brook) Ming—as opposed to Qing—China, because they had only some rather weak imperial traits.

5. Contiguous land empires, as distinct from empires with elements separated by large stretches of water.

6. Empires made up of tiny territories stretched over a vast expanse, such as the sixteenth-century Portuguese empire.

We can see the difficulty now with manipulating the category 'empire', and the necessity of coming to terms with this difficulty rather than denying its existence. To be sure, 'empire' is an easier category to work with than, say, 'globalization' or 'modernity', in that it is far more than an abstract noun and is also both 'etic' and 'emic' in some respects. What further confounds matters is the fact that, in the fifteenth or sixteenth century, the unit that was typically opposed to empire was the autonomous kingdom (which may or may not have had an 'ethnic' basis), whereas in the twentieth century it was the nation-state (whose citizens were all to have a common 'nationality').

These are not particularly original reflections. They form

the staple of a number of conference volumes, as well as some single- or dual-authored texts on the subject of empire that have been published in recent years. What they all come together to suggest is that empire (like market) is a useful but loose descriptive category (and metaphor) using the cover of which certain analytical operations may be carried out, but it is not a tight analytical or operational category using which historical hypotheses can be rigorously examined. In other words, it is one thing to write a history of the world after 1400 focusing on issues of political economy and state power. In such a history, the term 'empire' will undoubtedly figure many times, as it has in John Darwin's magisterial survey. Whether empire itself explains anything of what transpired, to my mind at least, is a different issue. At the end of this thought-provoking book, I am uncertain whether John Darwin believes it does either. It would be quite another matter if inter-imperial rivalry were to be made a motor for historical change, either through a Gerschenkronian strategy of playing 'catch-up' or some other game-theoretic procedure. But that would make for a quite different approach and a quite different book. In any event, it would mean that the category 'empire' would then turn out to be no more than an occasion for the staging of a predictable model of inter-state competition.

This may explain why our traveller Al-Baghdadi was so indifferent to the question of whether Brazil was an empire or not. It was abundantly clear to him that, although it had been conquered and settled, this process was not particularly similar to Ottoman conquest; he does not refer to the transfer of the court from Lisbon to Rio in 1808 but would have found it even more bizarre had he known about it. Instead, the presence of a very extensive, racially distinct, and culturally alienated slave population that formed the basis of the economy and society struck him time and again, though he was hardly unfamiliar with the institution of slavery in the Ottoman domains. In contrast to this Ilyas al-Mawsuli, writing some two centuries earlier, had seen far greater likenesses between Ottoman institutions and those in Habsburg Spanish America. This was perhaps logical, for the Ottomans and the Habsburgs were at that time still imperial rivals, vying for pre-eminent status in a competition that was recognized by contemporary writers such as Erasmus. Lacking this connection, the worlds of the Iberian South Atlantic and Ottoman Damascus had drifted apart by the nineteenth century. It would take another century, and a quite different set of waves of migration, to bring the two worlds together through the likes of Carlos Menem and Shakira. This is perhaps a story of 'globalization'; whether it has much to do with empire is doubtful.

9

Márquez, Hemingway, and the Cult of Power*

When Luis Miguel Dominguín, the celebrated *torero* or bullfighter, died at the age of 69 in early May 1996, the obituaries were many and typically rather generous. They recalled his curious and somewhat hostile relationship to Ernest Hemingway, his love affairs with the likes of Ava Gardner, and the fact that he was the father of the celebrated singer Miguel Bosé. They also wrote at length of his close friendship with Pablo Picasso, and the obituary in *Le Monde* quoted an extract from his brief work *Pour Pablo*, written for the painter in 1960. Dominguín had written there: 'Every famous man must be careful not to destroy his own legend, which accompanies him throughout his life, from birth until celebrity. The life of a man is never long enough to destroy one legend and create another. And without a legend, it is impossible to enter into History.' This reflection was either manufactured by Dominguín, or a version of something he had heard and liked. It is a striking and assertive claim regarding a sort of 'self-fashioning', to the point of almost being embarrassing. It tells us that there is a marked difference between famous men

*On *Gabriel García Márquez: A Life* by Gerald Martin (London, Bloomsbury, 2008), xxiii+664pp.

and others. It is only the celebrities who have a legend which accompanies them all through their lives, like a sort of invisible twin, or *hamzad* as the Persians might have it. One can either tend this legend or destroy it. If one chooses the latter option, it is impossible to start over; and if that is the case, it is impossible to become a part of History with a capital H. These are rather pretentious words one might think for a man whose profession consisted of a rather primitive if stylized form of public combat against animals. Yet they help us reflect on the problem not merely of celebrity, but of how celebrities think about celebrity; they also take us back by a complex route to chivalric terms like *fama* and *leyenda*, which Cervantes was already being ironical about some four hundred years ago.

This is a natural reflection at the end of a massive 664-page tome on the life of one of the twentieth century's great creative writers who has also been an unceasing and relentless manipulator of his own image. At the very end of it, Gerald Martin—emeritus professor at the University of Edinburgh and authority on modern Latin American fiction—writes of his subject Gabriel García Márquez: 'Literature and politics have been the two most effective ways of achieving immortality in the transient world that Western civilization has created for the planet; few would hold that political glory is more enduring than the glory that comes from writing famous books.' Not good books, we note, but famous ones. Martin has just described a huge public celebration, one of several which the book revels in. This one was held in Cartagena at the Convention Centre on 26 March 2007 and involved a large number of political actors, including a president and four ex-presidents of Colombia and the king of Spain. In the midst of the events, meant to honour the life and achievements of the 79-year-old García Márquez, Martin describes a melodramatic moment when the arrival of Bill Clinton was announced: 'The crowd rose as the most famous man on earth made his way down to the front of the hall.' Only

Fidel Castro and the Pope, he remarks, were missing from the potential 'superstars' who might have been there.

How did a novelist, even a Nobel Prize-winning and best-selling one, come to occupy such a position? Was it mere coincidence, or a testimony to the power of Spanish itself, one of the few languages (together with Chinese) determinedly and massively to resist in some form at least the advance of English in the twentieth century? How can one relate the undeniable literary quality of Márquez's work to his own curious worship of power and the cult of celebrity in which his biographer also seems willy-nilly to participate? Even if the writer-as-celebrity may have existed in some form before the twentieth century, there is no denying the fact that various forms of media—glossy magazines and television above all—have done much in the past century or so to promote it. But so have writers themselves, and a key figure in this respect is a man who features on more than one occasion in Martin's book, Ernest Hemingway.

Martin recounts an anecdote, for example, regarding Hemingway's suicide in July 1961, when Márquez had just arrived in Mexico City. In one version of the story, he was apparently woken up by his Mexican friend Juan García Ponce, who said to him: 'Listen to this, that bastard Hemingway has blown his head off with a shotgun.' In another less dramatic account, he was informed by journalists of the suicide. At any rate, Márquez hastened to write a long essay in homage, entitled 'A Man has Died a Natural Death' ('*Un hombre ha muerto de muerte natural*'), and published it in the literary supplement to the newspaper *Novedades* on 9 July. In it he praised Hemingway as an underestimated writer who would 'eat up many a great writer through his knowledge of men's motives and the secrets of his trade', but also noted that 'a new era' had begun in literature, perhaps hinting at a passing of the literary baton. Twenty years later he returned to Hemingway in an essay in Spanish in *El Espectador* which was also translated and published in the *New York Times* of 26 July 1981. The account here centred on a sort of meeting between the two, an episode that forms the closing vignette of Martin's chapter entitled 'Hungry in Paris: *La Bohème*, 1956–1957'. Here is Márquez's own version.

> I recognized him immediately, passing with his wife Mary Welsh on the Boulevard St Michel in Paris one rainy spring day in 1957. He walked on the other side of the street, in the direction of the Luxembourg Gardens, wearing a very worn pair of cowboy pants, a plaid shirt and a ballplayer's cap. The only thing that didn't look as if it belonged to him was a pair of metal-rimmed glasses, tiny and round, which gave him a prematurely grandfatherly air. He had turned 59, and he was large and almost too visible, but he didn't give the impression of brutal strength that he undoubtedly wished to, because his hips were narrow and his legs looked a little emaciated above his coarse lumberjack shoes.

At this time Márquez would have been 30 (though he states he was 28), and, as he describes himself, 'with a published novel and a literary prize in Colombia, but [. . .] adrift and without direction in Paris.' He claims that at the time his two great masters were not Latin American or even Spanish-language writers, but rather Faulkner and Hemingway. Of the two, he continues, 'Faulkner is a writer who has had much to do with my soul, but Hemingway is the one who had the most to do with my craft—not simply for his books, but for his astounding knowledge of the aspect of craftsmanship in the science of writing.' This is a slightly unexpected claim, meant perhaps to defend himself against the frequent accusation of owing too much to Faulkner. At any rate, Márquez claims to have been thoroughly star-struck at the sight of Hemingway across the street, surrounded and at the same time left anonymous by a 'youthful torrent' of students from the Sorbonne.

> I didn't know whether to ask him for an interview or cross the avenue to express my unqualified admiration for him. But with either proposition, I faced the same great inconvenience. At the time, I spoke the same rudimentary English that I still speak now, and I wasn't very

sure about his bullfighter's Spanish. [Apparently, French did not strike him as an option.] And so I didn't do either of the things that could have spoiled that moment, but instead cupped both hands over my mouth and, like Tarzan in the jungle, yelled from one sidewalk to the other: 'Maaaeeestro!' Ernest Hemingway understood that there could be no other master amid the multitude of students, and he turned, raised his hand, and shouted to me in Castilian in a very childish voice, 'Adiooos, amigo!' It was the only time I saw him.

In Martin's account, this rainy day in May somewhat inexplicably becomes a 'bright day early in 1957', but it is also somewhat puzzling that he does not make more of the rather obvious fact that Márquez saw Hemingway as a sort of role model as much as a literary figure to emulate.

The life story of Gabriel García Márquez has been told so often, and in so many versions, that its outlines are surely familiar to anyone who has a serious interest in twentieth-century literature. He was born in March 1927 and grew up, we all know, in a small town called Aracataca near the Caribbean coast of Colombia, by the Sierra Nevada mountains and the border with Venezuela. This was banana country, and a boom had allowed the population of the town to expand to about 10,000 at the time of the novelist's birth. The central character here was a somewhat shady American by the name of Minor Cooper Keith (1848–1929) who, together with Andrew Preston, had founded the United Fruit Company in 1899 and proceeded to buy up huge tracts of fruit-producing land in the Caribbean. By the time Márquez was born, this company apparently exported some ten million bunches of bananas a year from Santa Marta, the railhead that lay at the other end of the tracks from Fundación and Aracataca. By 1928, however, the shine was already off the banana trade. The year after Márquez's birth saw bloody struggles between workers and management in the banana country, presaging the great crash that would occur the next year in New York. Márquez's childhood thus coincided with the Great Depression, and therefore with the precipitous fall in the prices of primary commodities like fruit that was a characteristic of those times. It was this childhood, of a time in an increasingly dilapidated setting that looked back at a glorious if somewhat illusory past, that would become a more-or-less inexhaustible mine of memories and materials from which Márquez would draw for his novels.

We learn again from Martin that a major influence on Márquez while he was growing up was that of his maternal grandfather, Colonel Nicolás Márquez, who died when the novelist was 10. The colonel was a curious man who fathered three children (including Márquez's mother) with his wife, and at least nine other children with six other women. He was also probably a murderer who in 1908 bushwhacked a former companion after ensuring that he was unarmed—for fear that the latter, a skilled marksman, would challenge him to a duel over his sexual shenanigans. Márquez clearly hero-worshipped the older man, who seems to have served as a surrogate father in view of the novelist's rather difficult relationship with his own father, Gabriel Eligio García: even years later, we find the grandson in denial about what had happened, claiming simply that the colonel 'had to kill a man when he was very young.' García *père*, it is reported, saw his son not as an imaginative boy but as a born liar who would 'go somewhere, see something and come home telling something completely different.' This being the very talent later exploited by the son in forging his particular brand of fiction, the observation seems with hindsight to say as much about the father's lack of prescience in relation to his child as about the desire to magnify everything that was already brewing within the boy. For all the paternal lack of empathy, it was with his father that Márquez had to move, first to Sincé, then to Barranquilla closer to the coast, and eventually to Sucre. By the age of 15 he had begun to frequent brothels with his illegitimate half-brother, and then embarked on a series of

precocious love affairs. By the age of 19 his literary talents had
been recognized by some of his teachers; he had published some
poetry and done very well in his school-leaving examination.
The path seemed paved for a young man of modest means from
the backwoods to find his way into a respectable middle-class
professional existence, as a doctor or lawyer. This was certainly
what García, himself hardly an epitome of stability, desired for
his son. And this was what took the son in 1957 away from the
coast and into the highlands, to the Universidad Nacional in
Bogotá, for a degree in law.

But the next years brought something quite different. It is
at this point that Márquez begins his autobiography, *Vivir para
contarla*, translated into English by Edith Grossman as *Living to
Tell the Tale*. He recalls how in February 1950, soon after he had
dropped out of university, returned to the coast, and become
a journalist for the newspaper *El Heraldo*, his mother came to
fetch him at the Librería Mundo, the bookshop in Barranquilla
where he spent a good part of his time. Her purpose was twofold:
first, to sell or raise money on the old family house where he
had been born; and second, to have him render some form of
explanation for his erratic behaviour to the still-absent but ever-
disapproving father. What follows is a narrative tour de force as
García Márquez takes us from the coast via the Ciénaga Grande,
the great swamp, down the old banana railway that ran to
Aracataca. On the way we pass 'the only banana plantation along
the route that had its name written over the gate: *Macondo*.' This
is one of the difficulties which one faces with the first part of
Martin's book. While it is meticulous and carefully documented,
its initial pages must in an odd way compete with Márquez's
own far more compelling narrative. It is only in 1955, when
Vivir para contarla ends with Márquez's arrival in Geneva, that
Martin is inadvertently liberated—but that has already taken us
nearly a third into his book.

Márquez's autobiography is an extraordinary book which, as

has often been remarked, stands comparison with many of his novels while also giving us a real sense of where he stands—and already stood by his late twenties—at the crossroads of fiction, journalism, and politics. Its title has a slightly ungrammatical feel about it, and may have been chosen because the Spanish poet José Manuel Caballero Bonald (who was for a time in exile in Colombia and knew Márquez) had published a collection of verse called *Vivir para contarlo* (1969). (We may note that 'lo' rather than 'la' is the normal form that 'it' would take here.) Gerald Martin sometimes confuses the two titles, and one supposes a lesser writer than Márquez might not have taken the liberty. At any rate, the autobiography also announces his tastes and literary affinities in no uncertain terms, and it is not a coincidence that on the trip across the great swamp with his mother he carries a copy of Faulkner's *Light in August*, the writer whom he there terms 'the most faithful of my tutelary demons'. Márquez has been known in interviews to compare his childhood milieu quite directly with the American South, the affinity with Faulkner ensuing as much from the 'guts' of a lived experience as from anything more literary. He has even noted that when he visited parts of the South on a road trip from New York to Mexico City in the early 1960s, he found the built environment there somewhat familiar because the Americans who managed the fruit company had tended to build in the same style in Colombia.

In any event, this is an ongoing question that recurs time and again in Martin's account: what is the extent to which we can comprehend Márquez in some exclusively Latin American tradition of the novel? If not, what are the alternatives? We are reminded by Luis Villar Borda, one of his classmates at the Universidad Nacional in Bogotá in the late 1940s, that when he first met Márquez the latter's central references were 'Dos Passos, Hemingway, Faulkner, Hesse, Mann and the Russians [and] Colombian literature hardly at all, just a few poets.' Should one think of Márquez the novelist more as American in a general sense than Latin American? Is he Latin American to any great degree, given what appears to be his indifference to Brazilian writing, even to Machado de Assis? At the same time, there is little doubt that Márquez, perhaps more than many of his major contemporary writers in Spanish, remains deeply monolingual. One listens to his spoken Spanish with the clarity and music of its limpid Colombian pronunciation with pleasure, but also with the knowledge of his pride in the fact that he speaks practically no English or any other language (with the possible exception of French). The world thus came to him through translation, and it was through translation that he gained access to Kafka and Dostoyevsky (two influences he readily acknowledges), as well as the writers Borda lists.

So it is tempting in this as in other respects to compare him with his great contemporary from neighbouring Peru, Mario Vargas Llosa, and not only because the two were good friends for a time before a celebrated falling-out. Martin has some interesting passages pointing to the parallels between their lives: difficulties with their fathers and a close proximity to their maternal grandfathers; an early experience of brothels; a good deal of time spent as journalists; their support in the 1960s to the Cuban Revolution. Indeed, Vargas Llosa, also an accomplished literary critic, published an interesting work on Márquez as early as 1971 entitled *García Márquez: Historia de un deicidio*. This book was put out just four years after what is generally acknowledged as Márquez's most successful novel, *Cien años de soledad* (*One Hundred Years of Solitude*), and in it Vargas Llosa looks at the relationship between the 'real reality' from which Márquez draws and the 'fictitious reality' that he produces both in this novel and his earlier writings. It contains not only a close reading of Márquez's principal works at that time, but draws on a series of conversations that the two had had over the preceding years to suggest a complex series of possible influences on Márquez ranging from Defoe and the Arabian Nights to

Rabelais and Virginia Woolf. Vargas Llosa also criticizes him, probably justly, for an excessively teleological vision of his own work, seeing what he wrote before *Cien años de soledad* only as forms of preparation for the 'great novel'.

Vargas Llosa's book may comprise one of the most generous tributes paid by a novelist of importance to one of his contemporaries, but it also underlines several major distinctions between the two writers—other than the fact that, in their politics, they have over the years drifted considerably apart. Vargas Llosa has long been more attracted to Europe and its culture in general than García Márquez, whose obligatory stay in Paris as a young man does not seem to have brought him great intellectual sustenance. Indeed, the Peruvian novelist shares with Borges the fact that he is something of an Anglophile who has been known to speak fluent and idiomatic (if strongly accented) English when interviewed by the likes of David Frost. We also see from the equal ease with which he deploys Barthes and writes brilliant comic novels such as *Aunt Julia and the Scriptwriter* that Vargas Llosa is one of those exceptional novelists who are comfortable in the world of high literary theory. With Márquez, by contrast, we are more in the world of the autodidact, more in the presence of an instinctive writer than one who moves between abstract concepts and the business of narrative in fiction and journalism. His reaction to Vargas Llosa's book about his work, which he has steadfastly refused to read, is testimony to this: 'if someone showed me all the secret mechanisms of my work, the sources, what it is that makes me write, if someone told me all that, I think it would paralyse me.'

To put the matter somewhat differently, we might say that there has always been a certain interesting naïveté about Márquez which has served him well most of the time. But there have been exceptions, even if one leaves aside his very odd and continuing devotion to Fidel Castro, whom he has described as 'a man of austere ways and insatiable illusions [. . .] and incapable of conceiving any idea which is not out of the ordinary'. Martin also recalls the strange moment in December 1982 when Márquez appeared in Stockholm to receive the Nobel Prize wearing black boots and a *liqui-liqui*, a linen suit with working-class connotations which he never really wore in his normal life. More recently, we have his rather peculiar appearances with and endorsements of the pop singer Shakira. Some may wish to ascribe his adoration of celebrities and desire to rub shoulders with them to something like naïveté, and this brings us back to our point of departure. Martin's work is meticulously documented and painstakingly written, but it is also a deeply conventional biography which takes us step by step through the chronological sequence of a rather long life. Its three parts carry us along in the following fashion: the first to 1955 (where *Vivir para contarla* also ends); the second from 1955 to 1967, which is to say the twelve years of wanderings in Europe, South America, and eventually Mexico, where *One Hundred Years of Solitude* would be finished; and a third (entitled 'Man of the World: Celebrity and Politics'), carrying us from 1967 to 2005 and also discussing the writing and reception of many of the successful later books such as *The Autumn of the Patriarch* (1975) and *Love in the Time of Cholera* (1985).

For García Márquez the Nobel Prize was not the end of a literary career but a point of inflection, and he has continued to write at a regular and even astonishing rhythm since 1982. However, while considering his late works, Martin, though an accomplished literary scholar, has for the most part decided to leave the analytical edge out, preferring a rather flat, at times even adulatory, tone. One of the questions he does not confront is precisely that of celebrity and its meaning in the literary world of the late twentieth century. To be sure, the matter can depend on one's geographical location, and as Martin astutely remarks: 'If an American or an English man or woman wins the honour [the Nobel Prize] it barely makes the news [. . .] but this was [. . .] an award to a man from Colombia', a country which has won no Nobel Prize before or since. But Márquez also apparently wished to open up a larger space, namely a claim regarding his status as the leading writer of his time in Spanish, as we can see from his bitter feud with the Guatemalan Miguel Angel Asturias, who had won the Nobel Prize for Literature in 1967. One encounters here the view that the accumulation of symbolic capital in the shape of fame is a zero-sum game; the more one author has of it, the less another can get. This is a quite distinct view from that which had met the publication of *Cien años de soledad* in 1967, when a wide swathe of quite different writers—from Carlos Fuentes and Vargas Llosa to Borges—greeted it in a dithyrambic fashion. Márquez's own response corresponded rather with the view of literature as blood competition espoused by none other than Hemingway, who once wrote (and he was not being ironical) that he 'would be glad at any time, if in training, to go twenty [rounds] with Mr Cervantes in his own home town (Alcalá de Henares) and beat the shit out of him.'

When one has finished reading Martin's massive work it becomes clear that García Márquez is far too intelligent to lack all ironic distance from his own celebrity. We see this in the discussion of *The Autumn of the Patriarch*, which is ostensibly about an unnamed dictator in an unknown Latin American country. This 'poem on the solitude of power', as Márquez called it, is also, as Martin perspicaciously remarks, a novel that 'confronted the pitfalls of fame and power before they had even fully engulfed him [Márquez].' Still, in the end, it is hard to escape the feeling that through his peculiar relationship to the fact of celebrity, Márquez, like Hemingway, fell victim to a twisted version of what Pierre Bourdieu once termed the 'biographical illusion'. Perhaps it takes a biography like this one for us to understand that; and, in any event, it does not diminish Márquez in the slightest as one of the great novelists of the last half-century. But it does leave me wishing, sometimes, for the sake of preserving my own illusions of such a writer, that I had done no more than read his brilliant novels.

10

Do Civilizations Suffer from Altitude Sickness?*

The central trick in the social sciences, and in social science inflected history-writing, has been to transform the local and particular into some form of the universal. The researcher starts out with fieldwork data from a village or set of villages, or material from a set of archives, or even a set of conversations with friends in a pub (what some economists tactfully like to call 'stylized facts'), and then proceeds to weave these into a convincing set of hypotheses that will hopefully stand the test either of vertical transformations in scale or of horizontal movement in space. But what is a good place from which to start? There is a particular difficulty having to do with location here, because not all places are equally seductive for the purposes of generating hypotheses in the minds of readers. Many more such processes seem to begin, say, in Provence, Central Mexico, the Amazonian jungle, the South Seas, Vienna, and the Yangtze delta than in locations less favoured than these. South East Asia, in particular, has had a problem in this respect, because it has so often found itself marginal in relation to its neighbours to the

*On *The Art of Not Being Governed: An Anarchist History of Upland Southeast Asia* by James C. Scott (New Haven and London: Yale University Press, 2009), xviii+442pp.

west and east, the so-called 'Great Civilizations' of India and China. Still, there have been major interventions in the social sciences over the last fifty years which have begun life from a location there.

Three quite different figures in the Western academy can be associated with these: Clifford Geertz, Benedict Anderson, and James C. Scott. Geertz, whose many talents included the superbly perfidious book review, was the master of the catchy phrase: he gave us 'theatre state', 'agricultural involution', and quite a few others which then travelled from their initial South East Asian lodgings to distant *résidences secondaires* the world over. Anderson, who has worked in Indonesia, the Philippines, and Thailand, has also successfully prodded readers and listeners to venture into parts of the tropical South East Asian world where they might otherwise never have set foot, literally or metaphorically. Scott, the youngest of the three by a bare few months, has equally been tireless in using South East Asia as his laboratory, and also as his point of departure for very broad claims that have stimulated, provoked, and even irritated over the past three or four decades.

Though sometimes presented as a marginal or contrarian figure, he has in fact published a steady and influential stream of books over the years, successfully directed the Agrarian Studies programme at Yale University, and is the editor of the Yale Agrarian Studies Series (in which the book under review appears). His major publications began modestly, over forty years ago, with *Political Ideology in Malaysia* (1968), which was followed by the far more celebrated *The Moral Economy of the Peasant* (1976)—a book vigorously and simplistically attacked for its logical and empirical basis by neo-classical proponents of peasant rationality such as Samuel Popkin. Popkin argued that if peasants were properly and individualistically rational (in the sense of Milton Friedman), they would not have the forms of collective solidarity that Scott suggested because they would prefer to be 'free riders'; this was of course just the point Scott was making. A decade later, there came *Weapons of the Weak* (1985), and then a widely cited and controversial work entitled *Domination and the Arts of Resistance: Hidden Transcripts* (1990), which sealed the split between Scott and many on the traditional left who saw him as abandoning the gritty tenets of class struggle for a more romantic vision of what 'resistance' was. Most recently, Scott has written *Seeing Like a State* (1998), a work that can in fact be paired for certain purposes with *The Art of Not Being Governed*. Many of these later works have been concerned to elaborate the dialectic between an oppressive, modernizing state on the one hand, and various 'everyday forms' of resistance to it on the other. In this manner, Scott's work has run parallel to, and at times intersected, the strand known as Subaltern Studies, which, before it became a global brand, had its origins not in writings on South East Asia but in those on South Asia. Both have drawn in a manner on Foucault, and in the late 1980s two lines, 'Scottism' and 'Subalternism', were at times posed as different but complementary; but over the years the latter has evolved through its gingerly embrace of postcolonial doxa while Scott has trodden his own quite distinctive path, in a mode he likes to term 'anarchist'.

At the heart of this book is the political theorist's rediscovery of geography, not the new-fangled cultural variety of the past two decades, but, rather, old-fashioned physical geography. Now, geographers have had a good deal to say about state-formation processes in South East Asia over the years. A common enough conceptual framework when one writes about state formation in maritime South East Asia (and especially the Malay-speaking world) is the creative opposition or tension between *hulu* (or *ulu*) and *hilir*, that is the upstream and downstream centres in polities organized on riverine axes. This idea was set out as a schematic 'functional model' of coastal state-making some years ago by the archaeologist Bennet Bronson. It has since served as the starting point for a number of discussions, especially regarding Sumatra (Palembang, Barus, and so on), but also for western Java, the Philippines, and other areas. While seductive, and based on what appears to be an 'indigenously rooted' analytical opposition, the chief problem the model poses to some analysts is its lack of historicity.

The central idea of *The Art of Not Being Governed* is also driven by geography, and is given away by its author early on in the game. Scott wishes to argue that, once we move away from a preoccupation with the coasts, much can be gained by thinking simply in terms of altitude. His focus is thus on the area known as the South East Asian mainland massif, recently rechristened 'Zomia' by the Dutch scholar Willem van Schendel. This is a huge area, currently populated by over a hundred million 'minority peoples' (such as the Akha, Chin, Hmong, Kachin, Karen, Khmu, Lahu, Miao, Wa, and Yao), and occupies some 2.5 million square kilometres, between western China, north-eastern India, and the upland sections of five mainland South East Asian countries: Burma, Thailand, Laos, Vietnam, and Cambodia. Scott has a 'simple, suggestive, and controversial' thesis regarding this area. Hitherto, he suggests, most of these minority populations have been seen by anthropologists as well as policy-makers as archaic vestiges, survivors from another time. He argues that, on the contrary, 'hill peoples are best understood as runaway, fugitive, maroon communities who have, over the course of two millennia, been fleeing the oppressions of state-making projects in the valleys—slavery, conscription, taxes, corvée labor, epidemics, and warfare.' At the heart of the book lies the title of the lecture that Scott has widely delivered in anticipation of its publication: 'Why Civilizations Can't Climb Hills'.

There is an evident continuity between this book and Scott's work of the past decades, perhaps even the entire body of his work. But there are also some shifts, a few highly visible, a couple rather more subtle, in his manner of reasoning. To begin with, this work is heavily and explicitly influenced by the work of the French political anthropologist (described in some quarters as a 'Nietzschean') Pierre Clastres (1934–77). While Clastres broke to an extent from his master Claude Lévi-Strauss (and famously became associated for a time with Gilles Deleuze and Félix Guattari), he nevertheless remained true to Lévi-Strauss's fieldwork techniques, structuralist orientation, and geographical preference for Latin America. After a long series of essays and fieldwork reports in the journal *L'Homme* (published from about 1962 on), his first substantial monographic work, *Chronique des Indiens Guayaki* (1972), appeared in the celebrated 'Terre humaine' series of Jean Malaurie and concerned a Native American group in Paraguay on whom he had done fieldwork since 1963. Two shorter works then followed in rapid succession before his untimely death in a car accident: *Le grand parler: Mythes et chants sacrés des Indiens guarani* (1974), which was soon translated into Portuguese; and most significantly *La société contre l'État: Recherches d'anthropologie politique* (1974; English translation 1977). A posthumous work was also published nearly two decades later: *Mythologie des Indiens Chulupi* (1992). Clastres, writing in the early 1960s, was inclined himself to see the Guayaki as vestiges of a lost world, a small group (250 to 300 people in his estimation) which would shed light on the origins of the far larger grouping of Guarani Indians. Later he changed his mind radically and proceeded to mount a ferocious polemical attack on those who saw matters in such an evolutionary (and thus, he argued, ethnocentric) light. This may have had something to do with his experiences in the barricades of the Left Bank in Paris as a *soixante-huitard*. It became progressively evident to him that such groups chose deliberately to avoid certain institutions, and remained 'savage' by preference (it is here that one sees the Nietzschean referrent most clearly, one supposes, as well as the growing distance from Lévi-Strauss).

It is from *La société contre l'État* that Scott draws, time and again, in his work, beginning with his rather curious epigraph: 'It is said that the history of peoples who have a history is the history of class struggles. It might be said with at least as much truthfulness, that the history of peoples without history is a history of their struggle against the state.' In Zomia, rather than a history of class struggle, then, Scott wishes to present us with the history of a 'struggle against the state', therefore an 'anarchist history'. So, Scott's work is based on a neat and radical opposition, which some will find seductive. It is his claim that large-scale state-making in his chosen region is and has always been the business of plains and lowland people, with relatively high population densities and a proclivity to rice (or padi) cultivation requiring a good deal of labour. These lowland polities have an inbuilt logic of expansion, which also causes them to deploy the usual technologies of the state, including military mobilization, cadasters, generalized record-keeping, ethnography, and chronicling in written form (here we return to some of the themes of *Seeing Like a State*). Inevitably, they come up against physical limits to their processes of expansion, because there are also elevated territories which are intrinsically less accessible to their technologies and not so interesting in terms of their revenue-yield. It is these elevated lands which have for long centuries, Scott argues, defined the limits of 'civilizations', whether for states in Vietnam, Thailand, and Burma, or for the Chinese imperial state stretching to its south-western limits. Scott states his position bluntly enough: 'Political control sweeps readily across a flat terrain. Once it confronts the friction of distance, abrupt changes in altitude, ruggedness of terrain, and the political obstacle of population dispersion and mixed cultivation, it runs out of political breath.' In sum, lowland-based polities and their associated 'civilizations' suffer from altitude sickness.

In putting forward this thesis, Scott is naturally aware of two problems. One is of falling into a sort of mechanistic geographical determinism where altitude becomes a ready predictor of state centralization and reach. On quite a few occasions he comes close to this position, but is then careful to draw back from the precipice. A second issue is that altitude in and of itself may not be significant; rather, it is merely one of many natural obstacles to the deploying of state technologies. In some circumstances, marshlands, deserts, and even large water-bodies can defeat the expansionary ambitions of states for a time, sometimes for centuries. Indeed, as Clastres was well aware, tropical forests too can perform this function rather well. Yet, Scott is still quite enamoured of his altitude-based 'friction-of-distance' model of state-building, which he comes at in varied ways (and with a certain degree of repetitiveness) in the early chapters of the book. At one point he proposes a mental experiment involving a rigid white map with altitudes marked on it in high relief and 'each rice-growing core [with] . . . a reservoir of red paint filled to the very brim.' Tilting the map this way and that, and laying it flat again, the spread and concentration of the red ink would mark the strength of the state, while the white blotches of high altitude would be 'rarely if ever directly ruled' by lowland, rice-based states.

It therefore follows, as the chapters in the second half of the book then seek to demonstrate, that those who wish to 'keep the state at a distance' would naturally congregate in these less accessible, high-altitude zones. These then are deliberate strategies of 'state evasion' and 'state prevention', not chance locations for different peoples. In such areas we would find groups defining first subsistence strategies and then the agricultural patterns that are their direct consequence, which are 'designed to escape detection and maximize their physical mobility should they be forced to flee again at a moment's notice.' This part of the thesis is summed up by Scott:

The techniques of evasion practiced by desperate Karen villagers represent an extreme instance of strategies that characterize much of the history and social organization of Zomia as a whole. A good deal of what we have come to consider 'hill' agriculture, 'hill' social structure, and 'hill' location itself is, I would argue, largely defined by patterns of state evasion (and prevention). Such strategies have been devised and elaborated over many centuries in constant 'dialogue' with lowland padi states, including the colonial regime. This dialogue is, in important respects, constitutive of both hill societies and their padi-state interlocutors. Each represents an alternative pattern of subsistence, social organization, and power; each 'shadows' the other in a complex relationship of mimicry and contradiction. Hill societies operate in the shadow of lowland states. By the same token, the lowland states of Southeast Asia have been surrounded, for the whole of their existence, by relatively free communities in the hills, swamps, and labyrinthine waterways that represent, simultaneously, a threat, a zone of 'barbarism', a temptation, a refuge, and a source of valuable products.

I will return to this set of rather abstract propositions; here it is worth noting that Scott draws again upon Clastres to make an imporant argument, this time an anti-teleological one, noting that many Native American groups 'adapted to a more mobile life as a means of escaping the servitude and disease that civilization has to offer', as 'nomadic subsistence strategies to stay out of harm's way.' This might refer to agricultural and material life, but Scott also insists that many of these groups that are characterized as pre-literate are in fact 'postliterate', and have deliberately given up literacy in order to disengage with certain state forms and technologies. Once more, there is the portentuous epigraph from Clastres: 'For, in its severity, the law is at the same time writing. Writing is on the side of the law; the law lives in writing.' Those who wish to escape the law will naturally want to escape writing as well. They may become 'barbarians' by virtue of this, but with the form of barbarism being constructed and produced rather than the result of being in a state-of-nature. While the thrust of the argument may be anti-teleological, there is a strong whiff of functionalism that nevertheless hangs over the intellectual enterprise as a whole.

The intriguing Chapter 7, devoted to the subject of 'ethnogenesis', develops what Scott terms a 'radical constructionist' point of view, and in so doing departs significantly from his own past work. The extensive writings on resistance, as well as on the 'moral economy', had always had a touch of the romantic about them, and were, more significantly, highly communitarian in their logic. The bounds of the moral economy were often the same as those of a primordial community of some sort, to which were opposed the twin external forces of state and market. Neither state nor market were ever really explained, but rather appeared in the role of *deus ex machina*. In this chapter, however, Scott proposes a quite different reading from his earlier one. Community and ethnicity now become constructions and inventions, some of them imposed by states (which 'fabricate tribes in several ways'), some created in the mêlée of constant movement and reshuffling that characterizes these processes of 'state evasion'. Scott agrees that 'named tribes with self-consciousness of their identities do most certainly exist', but adds that 'rather than existing in nature, they are a creative human construction—a political project—in dialogue and competition with other "tribes" and states.' Here he draws on the vast and growing general literature on the 'invention of tradition', but also once more makes explicit use of materials on Latin America after the Iberian conquest. Interestingly, this includes the work of Frank Salomon and Stuart Schwartz in the *Cambridge History of the Native Peoples of the Americas*, vol. 3 (1999), regarding forms of adaptation, ethnic reinvention (or ethnogenesis), and *mestizaje* in the aftermath of the conquest. These writings famously brought upon the two American historians the Olympian wrath of Claude Lévi-Strauss and a signed denunciation by him in the journal *L'Homme* in 2001. Salomon and Schwartz, to the extent one can discern, did not share Clastres's Nietzschean stance, and were less inclined to pose historical change in the language of resistance and radical agency. Lévi-Strauss's complaint, nevertheless, was that their version of the story of conquest was inadequately tragic in its emplotment and thus tantamount to a form of 'holocaust denial'. Scott's narrative, on the other hand, is still broadly tragic, but it is a tragedy long and slow in its unfolding, leaving time for adaptation and ethnogenesis in the medium term. In his view, after three previous eras (a 'stateless' one, one of 'small-scale states', and one of the 'expansion of state power'), we are now finally entering 'an era in which virtually the entire globe is "administered space" and the periphery is not much more than a folkloric remnant'; he adds that 'about the long-run trend there can be not a shred of doubt.' For him, then, the Zomia he describes over the book is now largely in the past tense, and it is in this form that the Zomians appear in the 'Conclusion', as against the other tenses in which they inhabit earlier chapters. This will perhaps confirm the view of those who have regularly demanded why Scott does not produce 'optimistic stories of resistance and protest'.

That discussion regarding the normative status of narratives of resistance and protest is in the last analysis a political one. My own ensuing remarks will, however, mostly be of a more simple and methodological nature. How in fact does James Scott arrive at his conclusions? What are the materials he uses, and how does he deploy them to persuade us? Where does this book stand in terms of the social sciences today? Intriguingly (and modestly), Scott tells us in his preface that to his 'mild astonishment' he has 'become a kind of historian—not a particularly good one, perhaps, but a historian nonetheless.' The mild astonishment might befit his readers rather more: Scott is professor of political science and anthropology at Yale University.

The book for the most part rests on two pillars: a massive (and sometimes difficult to digest) sweep of secondary literature relating to South East Asia but also to the world at large; and some ethnography, principally conducted in Burma. Covering as it does a huge territory and many centuries (indeed more than a millennium), it proceeds in a manner that will not always be persuasive to empirically rigorous historians. Few individual actors appear, and those that do have some importance as— somewhat disconcertingly—colonial ethnographers whose work is used, analysed, and reframed. It is therefore difficult to grasp how exactly we are to know that we are witnessing 'state evasion' and 'state prevention' on the part of groups. The difficulties are twofold and have to do, on the one hand, with functional explanations, and on the other with issues of tracking intention. Let us suppose we could indeed demonstrate that certain social institutions, crop-patterns, and physical locations make state penetration and tax-demands difficult. Yet this does not prove they have arisen for that very reason; to assume so is an elementary functionalist fallacy. As regards intention, we have seen that Scott allies himself with a growing trend amongst anthropologists of South East Asia (but also prevalent elsewhere in the world) which asserts that 'states, in effect, create tribes'. He cites the work of Geoffrey Benjamin to this effect: 'all historically and ethnologically reported tribal societies are secondary formations, characterized by the positive steps they have taken to hold themselves apart from incorporation into the state apparatus (or its more remote tentacles), while often attempting to suppress the knowledge that their way of life has been shaped by the presence of the state.' These are strong claims regarding 'strategy' and 'choice' (Benjamin has argued, for example, that 'tribality has resulted largely from choice'), which it is naturally hard to demonstrate if one simultaneously claims that those who make these choices suffer from amnesia regarding them.

There is a further uncomfortable idea here. Much contemporary discussion regarding the rights of these 'minority' or 'tribal' peoples rests precisely on the fact that they are somehow the 'original' or 'authentic' occupiers of lands, victims of yesterday's railways and today's mining companies. One sees this time and again in writings regarding the Maoist insurgency in Central India, for example, from the pens of both Ramachandra Guha and Arundhati Roy—otherwise not the closest of intellectual allies. The Malay term *orang asli* (often translated as 'aboriginal') exemplifies this claim well, as it derives from *orang* ('man') and *asli* (itself a loan-word from Arabo-Persian meaning 'rooted', 'authentic', or 'original'). It is devilishly difficult to make a case for radical ethnogenesis on the one hand, and for deep aboriginal rights on the other (as Lévi-Strauss was surely aware). Ideas of choice and agency thus come into rude and constant conflict with notions of victimhood and the rights of victims of 'displacement'. Further muddying the waters is the fact that such analyses usually place the origins of all historical processes outside such groups, which are essentially seen to react to pressures rather than initiating actions. This makes it difficult to account for a number of varied historical situations that we can find. For example, there are clear instances when groups from the less productive uplands (or hills) expanded into the more productive lowlands rather than the other way around; this was the case of the incorporation of the Mon kingdom of Pegu into the larger Burmese state in the course of the sixteenth century. Further, it seems to fly in the face of a good deal of accumulated evidence to suggest that the narrative of collective resistance by groups to the state can substitute for a study of internal tensions within groups, which often provide a reasonable explanation of dynamic processes without having to take constant resort to the state as *deus ex machina*. One can see why a historian of state formation in South East Asia such as Victor Lieberman should be rendered so uncomfortable by Scott's analysis (as we see from his lengthy review of it in the *Journal of Global History*). For Lieberman, state formation is something to be explained and not taken for granted; for Scott, states in general can now be treated as colonial states have usually been treated in the past, namely as violent intrusions from an external sphere, without a corresponding dimension of 'capillary action' (to borrow the celebrated phrase of Foucault).

In sum, the brush that Scott uses here is very broad, and his conception anything but Popperian; no alternative hypothesis or contrary body of evidence is allowed much oxygen. One may also suspect that this is because Scott's method is usually to choose his examples once his hypothesis has been defined, and, even if he is 'mistaken in some particulars', it is never clear that these particulars will modify the overall thesis. By taking such a stance, Scott is as far distant from the mainstream of political science and anthropology as he is from that of history, which is why this work presents such great difficulties to reviewers like myself and Lieberman. In line with the work of Clastres, one imagines it may well become a cult classic, transcending the disciplines and their order. But, equally, it runs the risk of leaving readers scratching their heads, not because it is obscure or incomprehensible, nor because its claims are bold, but because its epistemological foundations are so unclear. Then again, perhaps it should not be read with the head but with the heart. If this is indeed the case, we would only be confirming the view that the work of James Scott remains above all that of a pessimistic romantic.

11

Churchill and the
Great Man Theory of History*

O ne of the greatest weaknesses of the discipline of history—
sometimes paradoxically turned by practitioners of
intellectual ju-jitsu into a strength—is its epistemological fuzziness. Ask six historians what sort of training should be
given in common to all budding historians and you risk getting
six or more different answers. If you pose the same question
to half a dozen practising economists, the matter would very
quickly be resolved. It turns out then that the 'methods' of
history are notoriously hard to pin down, and what often passes
for training in history is not in history itself but in matters
auxiliary to history, such as palaeography, statistics, kinship
theory, narratology, or even language-acquisition. Historians
are thus often trained by the use of *exempla*, that is, by reading
a fair sample of texts from the past couple of generations, such
texts also serving to illustrate where the profession is at the
moment.

However, most professional historians today would agree that
the one thing they would not hand down to their university

*On *Churchill's Empire: The World that Made Him and the World He Made*
by Richard Toye (London: Macmillan, 2010), xviii+423pp., and *Churchill's
Secret War: The British Empire and the Ravaging of India during World War II*
by Madhusree Mukerjee (New York: Basic Books, 2010), xxxvi+332pp.

students is the 'great man' view of history. Most, but not all, for a few in fields that have only recently been allowed a respectable seat at the historian's table continue to foreground their own heroes and heroines, adding them to an existing pantheon or suggesting them as replacements. Some US historians still doggedly pursue the path of endless volumes on their 'founding fathers', for which there is apparently a more or less infinitely elastic market, and a handful of other figures from the twentieth century remain central to the matter of 'great man history'. These characters are largely the same as those that one might find, let us say, in *Time* magazine's 1999 list of the greatest 'persons of the twentieth century': names like Gandhi, Mao, Stalin, Hitler, and Churchill, each of whom has spawned an industry of vast proportions. Less certain is the professional historian's interest in the actual winner of *Time*'s poll, namely Einstein. I cannot see any of my colleagues in the history of science undertaking to write a study of Einstein as 'great man', but perhaps things are different elsewhere.

Time's list was, curiously enough, meant as morally neutral, a fact that caused much controversy at the time it appeared. The editors claimed it was meant to measure influence, not whether that influence was positive or negative. Had the moral judgement been put to readers, it seems likely that Churchill would have crept up the list a bit, though he would not have attained the heights he did in 1949–50, when *Time* declared him the 'man of the half century'. This choice had not met then with universal approbation. One reader, Mary Stuart of New Jersey, declared that she was not renewing her subscription to the magazine on account of her 'anger and disbelief' at the choice; a certain J. Gardner called the editors 'damn fools'; Fred Rice from New York termed the choice 'preposterous'. Most eloquent was a certain Martin Kranick from Oregon: 'He may have lived in the 20th century, fought in the 20th century, and had a lot of bloody words to say about it, but his political and social philosophy definitely belonged to the 19ᵗʰ.' This is a theme to return to, the trope of Churchill as a Victorian and ideological *passéiste* who lived outside his time. Some of those incensed were, naturally, supporters of FDR's candidacy, but at least one noted that there were several 'men who will outlive the memory of Churchill. On this list, to name only a few, will be Albert Schweitzer, Albert Einstein, Mohandas Gandhi and Woodrow Wilson.' In reality, Einstein and Gandhi have fared rather better so far than Schweitzer and Wilson; as for Churchill, his reputation today cannot match those exalted heights of the early 1950s when, with astonishing chutzpah, the Nobel Prize committee awarded him the 1953 Prize for Literature 'for his mastery of historical and biographical description as well as for brilliant oratory in defending exalted human values.' Still, Churchill retains his extraordinarily exalted status in certain circles, both in Britain and the US, particularly among conservatives and former Cold Warriors. He was greatly admired, of course, both by Margaret Thatcher and George W. Bush.

A large part of Churchill's retrospective persona and continuing myth centres precisely on the fact that he 'had a lot of bloody words to say'. *The Collected Works of Sir Winston Churchill* in the 'Library of Imperial History' edition run to thirty-four volumes; his listed writings in the Library of Congress catalogue begin with *The Story of the Malakand Field Force* (1898) and *River War* (1899), the latter in two volumes, both written when Churchill was in his mid-twenties. They encompass a variety of genres: war memoirs, travelogues, pamphlets, histories, even some thinly disguised fictions. To add to this there is the official biography in eight volumes begun by his son Randolph Churchill and continued by Martin Gilbert, as well as the many companion volumes that go with it. Of all his competitors mentioned above, only Gandhi—who was five years older than Churchill and lived twelve fewer years—can match him pound for pound in sheer weight of output. Since Churchill prided himself, moreover, on his wit and capacity for the *bon mot*, this oeuvre is an almost endless trove of quotable quotes. It is also an uncommon record for a man without a university education, whose father sent him from Harrow to military training in Sandhurst because he did not have a particularly exalted opinion of the son's intelligence. Psychologically-minded historians have often pointed to the oppressive presence of his father in Churchill's early career and political choices, long after Lord Randolph Churchill's premature death (most likely from syphilis) in 1895. Not even the two-volume biography he wrote of his father in 1906 seems quite to have exorcized the ghost. It was first and foremost to his father that Churchill owed his view of the British imperial *mission civilisatrice* as 'a sheet of oil spread out over a surface of, and keeping calm and quiet and unruffled by storms, an immense and profound sea of humanity'—the words being Lord Randolph's. Were that imperial 'sheet' to disappear, both father and son believed, the world would return to a barbaric state, and the savage nature of the bulk of humanity would once again assert itself.

Empire figured prominently in the life of every British politician of the first half of the twentieth century, but more prominently in Churchill. This has prompted Richard Toye, in *Churchill's Empire*, to write a conventional and chronologically-organized history of Churchill's engagement with imperial questions, a history which deals largely (but not exclusively) with Africa and India. His chronological segments are 1874–97, 1897–9, 1899–1901, 1901–8, 1908–22, 1922–39, 1939–42, 1942–5, and 1945–55. Where the action comes thick and fast, the chronological segments become shorter, and where the action is slow (often the moments when Churchill exercises little or no power, as in Chapter 6), the segments can be as long as seventeen years. Toye is a professional historian who teaches at the University of Exeter, and has earlier authored *Lloyd George and Churchill* (2007). His investment in Churchill is thus more than a passing fancy. Toye is also relatively young (in his late thirties), which makes his persistence in writing a history focused on 'great men' a little puzzling. Even if his technique is remarkably old-fashioned, his politics seem to be moderate. Large conceptual questions are kept resolutely at bay, the history being written in the narrative mode, the narrative being built on the back of quotations from Churchill and his contemporaries, some worn to the point of cliché, others less so. It is meant above all as an exercise in fairness, in measuring the positive with the negative, in order to come up with something like a balance-sheet. In the end, we learn, Churchill was a victim of the law of unintended consequences. 'The spirit of freedom, which he articulated so eloquently on so many occasions, escaped the bounds he would have set upon it. The decline of Churchill's Empire, much as the man himself regretted it, can be seen in part as a tribute to the power of beliefs that he himself prized dearly.' This seems in some ways a more devious and slightly less intelligent formulation of a statement by Zhou Enlai, in a conversation with Kissinger in 1971, which Toye himself cites as his epigraph. Zhou is reported to have said: 'Although he didn't like to do so, Mr Churchill ended the stage of the British Empire. This was not his subjective will. He said that to President Roosevelt. But objectively he ended the British Empire.'

Though Churchill was a prolific writer even before he began to employ ghosts, a powerful manipulator of rhetoric, and an old-fashioned but highly effective stylist, what has never been clear is his status as a thinker. This is as true on political matters in general as on empire in particular. His devoted biographer Martin Gilbert is also the author of a short work entitled *Churchill's Political Philosophy* (1981), but the book is not particularly enlightening. In one of the many reviews that the *London Review of Books* has devoted to Churchilliana, Bernard Porter says: 'His whole political philosophy—if it can be called that—derived from a romantic ideal of noblesse oblige, working class gratitude, British goodness, and English speaking loyalty.' There are two unspoken ideas here. British goodness must constantly be contrasted with the actual (or potential) lack of goodness in other people, a form of nationalism that frequently crossed the border into chauvinism and jingoism. As for English-speaking loyalty, it explains the one exception that Churchill made in his quite generalized xenophobia, namely the Americans. This was also of course crudely self-serving, since his mother was American. (One is also here tempted to wonder if a xenophobe and royalist as diehard as Churchill might not have thought of American English as a language only slightly less foreign than Swahili.)

Though Churchill was in general not noted for his consistency in either politics or thought, it may nevertheless be worth asking how and from whom he learnt 'to think imperially' (to borrow Toye's phrase). Some of his central attitudes came from his particular aristocratic background, he being a member of the cadet branch of descendants of the seventh Duke of Marlborough (which also, so the genealogists assure us, made him a sixth cousin of the eighth Earl Spencer, Princess Diana's father). His desire to be seen as a 'free trader' and fascination with Africa and India both stemmed in part from his father, Lord Randolph Churchill, whose rather ludicrous flirtation with mining in South Africa is described with some humour by Toye. Some of his attitudes also came from Harrow and its headmaster James Welldon, later to be Bishop of Calcutta (Kolkata), though, as Toye sagely remarks, even Harrow—whose pupils included Jawaharlal Nehru—'did not turn out identikit imperialists'.

But we must go beyond Churchill's schoolboy reading of Rider Haggard and Kipling to grasp his political thinking. Here, Toye suggests an important phase was that of his first real army posting in Bangalore in 1896–7, when in a moment of luxurious idleness, partly subsidized by his mother, he read such works as his father's favourite Gibbon, Macaulay, Plato, the

Duc de Saint-Simon, Adam Smith's *Wealth of Nations* (which it is fairly clear he did not absorb for the most part), and also a now obscure but once celebrated Victorian author of Scottish birth, William Winwood Reade (1838–75). Of these, Gibbon and Macaulay are particularly significant for their stylistic and rhetorical impact on him, while Winwood Reade is worthy of some attention on account of what Toye terms 'Reade's impact on his thinking about Empire and human development.'

However eccentric he may appear to us today, Reade was an influential figure over his short life and immediately after, being read, cited, and admired by H.G. Wells, Cecil Rhodes (a particular devotee), and Conan Doyle—who even has Holmes recommend Reade's work to Watson in one of his India-related stories, 'The Sign of Four'. Reade had travelled in South and West Africa, endured a period of captivity in Sierra Leone, and was best known for what he termed a 'universal history' entitled *The Martyrdom of Man* (1872). Although claiming to restore the place of Africa in universal history, this short work was in fact a very curious confection based on a rather haphazard reading of everything from Portuguese overseas expansion to Chinese culture and social norms. One of its significant passages runs:

> The great Turkish and Chinese Empires, the lands of Morocco, Abyssinia and Tibet, will be eventually filled with free, industrious, and educated populations. But those people will never begin to advance until their property is rendered secure, until they enjoy the rights of man; and these they will never obtain except by means of European conquest. In British India, the peasant reaps the rice which he has sown; and the merchant has no need to hide his gold beneath the ground. The young men of the new generation are looking forward to the time when the civil appointments of their country will be held by them. The Indian Mutiny was a mutiny only, and not a rebellion; the industrial and mercantile classes were on the English side. There is a sickly school of politicians who declare that all countries belong to their inhabitants, and that to take them is a crime. If any country

in Asia did belong to its inhabitants, there might be some force to this objection. But Asia is possessed by a few kings and by their soldiers; these rulers are usually foreigners; the masses of the people are invariably slaves. The conquest of Asia by European Powers is therefore in reality emancipation, and is the first step towards the establishment of Oriental nationality. It is needless to say that Europe will never engage in crusades to liberate servile populations; but the pride and ignorance of military despots will provoke foreign wars, which will prove fatal to their rule. Thus war will, for long years yet to come, be required to prepare the way for freedom and progress in the East; and in Europe itself, it is not probable that war will ever absolutely cease until science discovers some destroying force, so simple in its administration, so horrible in its effects, that all art, all gallantry, will be at an end, and battles will be massacres which the feelings of mankind will be unable to endure.

Conquest in Asia was thus really emancipation, holding out a vague but unspecified promise of some form of political freedom once the conquered populations were deserving of it. H.G. Wells would eventually take a step back from this position, notably in his essay 'The Future of the British Empire' published in the *Empire Review* of 1923, suggesting instead something like a federated form of world-government to replace empire. But Churchill never resiled from this view, perhaps because he had far stronger views on the innate and insuperable nature of both racial and religious differences than either Reade or Wells. From Reade, Churchill admitted, he learnt to doubt the conventional Christianity in which he had been brought up, and exchanged it for a loosely defined version of Social Darwinism. But he retained the militant Protestant's overt contempt for all other religions, first Islam which he encountered on the Indian North-West Frontier and in Mahdist Sudan, and later Hinduism which, in the 1920s and 1930s, he constantly fulminated against.

So where does this leave us with regard to Churchill's broad views on empire? To be sure, on relatively small, tactical matters, his views could change, even rapidly. Kipling, who did not reciprocate Churchill's admiration of him, once remarked of his floor-crossing and political opportunism that 'it is impossible to cure a political prostitute from whoring', and this applied to imperial politics in the short term as well. But Churchill's whoring did not extend to all customers. Adherence to the empire and opposition to decolonization (even in its relatively weak forms) run like a red thread through the many decades of his political career. This was even after he had taken, in the inter-war years, to claiming that the imperial bargain was one where the Indian industrial capitalists and the detestable *baboos* were exploiting the poor English working class. The only exception was Ireland, where Toye shows him for once subordinating imperial ideology to realpolitik, although with a certain duplicity on the Ulster question.

Yet this bracketing of Ireland only opens up the vexed question once more of the extent to which Churchill's understanding of empire was tied up with race. To an extent, his view of Africans was marked by pure paternalism; the Kikuyu, he stated as late as 1954, had been a 'happy, naked and charming people' when he had known them decades earlier, but were now 'savages armed with ideas—much more difficult to deal with.' His real *bêtes noires* were Indians, whose malignant place in the colonial world he even frequently emphasized when speaking of East and South Africa. This is what rendered him largely impervious to the changing circumstances of the 1920s and 1930s, as the Indian nationalist movement gained force and popular support. It also made him an admirer of virulent tracts such as *Verdict on India* (1944), whose author, Beverley Nichols, claimed that the Indian National Congress was 'the only 100 percent, full-blooded, uncompromising example of undiluted Fascism in the modern world.' The affinity is scarcely puzzling when one sees Churchill's own crude attempts, for example, to equate Gandhi with Hitler.

Churchill's Empire is a well-written and engaging book but not necessarily one which points us in the direction of deeper answers. While it assiduously tracks Churchill's travels, writings, and conversations, as well as his tactical negotiations on imperial matters, there is often no big picture here. Its author admits it is of little use to fall back for explanation on time-honoured clichés such as that Churchill was really a Victorian who some-how managed to live into the reign of Victoria's great-great-granddaughter. We must seek to explain Churchill's arrested mental development, if that is what it was.

Whatever one thinks of the Nobel Prize of 1953, there is no doubt of Churchill's abilities as a prose writer and rhetorician in a certain mode. Equally, there is little doubt of his cunning and relentless self-promotion from the earliest days of his career as militaryman and journalist at Malakand and Omdurman. His retrospective emplotment of his life in a teleological mode in the early 1950s, as if the first sixty-five years had been a mere preparation for the glory years from 1940 to 1945, bespeaks a messiah complex rather than any great lucidity. Here one begins to suspect that his intelligence may have been vastly overestimated, especially by interlocutors in awe of him. A small incident recounted by Toye is significant; in 1900, Churchill was vigorously attacked while in New York by Mark Twain, who was obviously not in awe of him, for his bellicose views on the Boer War, from which Churchill had recently returned, and by Churchill's own admission he was soon reduced to the chauvinistic position of 'my country right or wrong'.

But the Churchill myth, even if it has receded in the four decades and more since his death, persists and has even been replaced in some circles by the 'Churchill Litmus Test'. This is due to none other than Sir Geoffrey Elton, who in his *Political History* wrote: 'When I meet a historian who cannot think that there have been great men, great men moreover in politics, I feel myself in the presence of a bad historian. And there are times when I incline to judge all historians by their opinion of Winston Churchill—whether they can see that, no matter how much better the details, often damaging, of the man and his career become known, he still remains, quite simply, a great man.' Now, I freely admit to failing Elton's Churchill Litmus Test, and am pleased to find that this is equally true of almost all other reviewers of Churchilliana in the past three decades. Further, while I can comprehend how Elton's own history may have awoken in him an inordinate admiration for Churchill as the scourge of Nazism, this sort of provocation means that one is bound to get another sort of history, one in which Churchill is still larger than life but now amongst the Forces of Darkness.

Something of this impulse seems to underpin Madhusree Mukerjee's book, *Churchill's Secret War*, beginning with its controversial title. Mukerjee is avowedly an Indian nationalist: she dedicates her book 'to those who fell so that I could be born free'. Yet, despite its dedication and controversy-seeking title, the work's overall tone is quite sober, though periodically lapsing into some strange prose, as when the partition of India and Pakistan is compared to the hacking apart of Siamese twins; or into displays of exaggerated sarcasm, as when Indian hunger is contrasted to Churchill's own lavish dinner menus.

Mukerjee, by her own admission, is not a historian but a journalist with a training in science who disarmingly notes that in order to write this book she had to 'learn the basics of world history'. Her task, on the other hand, is strikingly complex for an amateur historian, namely to provide as panoramic an account as any that has been given so far of the causes, consequences, and experience of the great Bengal famine of 1943–4. This famine has attracted a great deal of attention among scholars, particularly economists and demographers, in part because it was the only major famine to occur in British India within the twentieth century—in contrast to a whole host of famines in the previous century. Much debate has focused on the extent to which the famine was caused in a proximate sense by actual food shortages due to inclement weather and crop failure, as opposed to the imperfect working of market forces in a climate of wartime speculation. In the aftermath of her book, Mukerjee has entered into a somewhat sterile controversy with Amartya Sen and others on this matter in the pages of the *New York Review of Books*; however, Sen had always noted that whether the famine resulted fundamentally from 'food availability decline' or a problem of 'exchange entitlements', its effects could have been mitigated and even averted by the same policy—namely, an improvement in food supplies in Bengal. His work thus suggests that there was a signal failure of famine policy on the part of the British colonial government.

But Mukerjee demands a story with a clearer plot in which heroes and villains have real faces and names. In her version, then, the villains are a handful of British political and technical actors who cynically deprived Bengal of necessary supplies in 1943–4 by a variety of means: by diverting crucial shipping from the Indian Ocean, by stockpiling food elsewhere rather than sending it to Bengal, and even by refusing some unexpected offers of help from such quarters as the maverick nationalist leader and Japanese ally Subhas Chandra Bose. At first sight, the central villain appears to be Churchill himself, and Mukerjee goes over some of the same ground as Toye (though the two writers are apparently not aware of each other's work), citing many of the same sources to give us a sense of Churchill's racial consciousness through his upbringing and sojourn in India as a subaltern, and his particular loathing for Hindus. Churchill is quoted in 1945 telling his private secretary John Colwell that the Hindus were a foul race 'protected by their mere pullulation from the doom that is their due', and that he only wished that he could order Air Chief Marshal Arthur 'Bomber' (or less kindly 'Butcher') Harris to 'send some of his surplus bombers to destroy them.' But presently it turns out that her real villain is Churchill's scientific adviser, the physicist F.A. Lindemann, who had been given the title 'Lord Cherwell'. Cherwell, a social-climbing Oxford don with 'a German accent and aristocratic tastes', a confirmed anti-Semite with 'a distaste of dark-skinned foreigners and working-class Britons', appears here like a gift from Central Casting. In this, Mukerjee returns to the claims of a line of Cherwell's detractors, most notably C.P. Snow, who had argued that Cherwell had a broadly disastrous impact on British policy during the war. The minor difficulty with this portrayal is the fact that Cherwell was the target of British xenophobia, besides being the object of some mistrust among many members of the top brass during the war. He had consistently to prove himself more royalist than the king lest suspicion fall on him. This picture is muddied a bit by the recent work of David Edgerton, who has done some damage to Snow's rather caricaturing (and sometimes plainly inaccurate) version of debates in which Cherwell was a protagonist.

If Mukerjee's plot has two villains on the British side (or three, if one counts the shipping czar Frederick Leathers), it also has a sort of hero, even if he is one cast in a tragic hue. This is Leopold Amery, Churchill's slightly older contemporary from Harrow, who also served during the war as Secretary for India. Amery is Mukerjee's chief source for much of what she writes about Churchill and Cherwell, and her views appear very dependent on his; she eventually concludes, somewhat unsurprisingly, that 'one person who emerges from the [Bengal] famine with remarkably clean hands is Leopold Amery.' She concedes that Amery too supported a scorched-earth policy, practised procrastination, and eventually 'orchestrated a cover-up', but still sees him as a forlorn figure 'whose willingness to endure opprobrium for the Bengal famine may have been a form of atonement for the actions of his son', John Amery, a collaborator with the Nazis who was hanged in December 1945. It is unclear what this inference regarding guilt and atonement is actually based on.

Are Mukerjee's claims on British governmental responsibility
for the Bengal famine so novel? Toye notes that in late 1947
Churchill reproached the Labour government for the violence
of the Partition, 'hideous massacres, the like of which have
never stained the British Empire in all its history', and that
some months later a Labour MP retaliated by accusing him
of responsibility in the Bengal famine. Toye's own quite brief
remarks on the famine state that 'maladministration made
the consequences worse than they need have been, and that
Churchill's own reaction was grossly inept and, it is tempting
to add, callous.' The difference lies perhaps in Mukerjee's sense
that this act lay somehow at the heart of Churchill's persona,
and so constituted pretty much a war crime, in contrast to Toye's
view that though Churchill 'displayed genuine callousness, and
shortsightedness to boot [in regard to the famine, it] . . . must,
however, be viewed alongside the many positive aspects of his
war leadership.'

This said, one must also wonder whether Mukerjee's book
title, and even the longer description that appears on its cover,
do not do her work a genuine disservice. For, contrary to what
we might infer from all the above, the story of Churchill and
Cherwell and the duo's impact on the Bengal famine is only one
part of Mukerjee's book. This part is in fact a 'history from the
top', based on memoirs, diaries, and records in places such as
Oxford, Cambridge, Kew, and London—the same sort of records
that Toye has used. But there is quite another part of the book
which is in fact a 'history from below'—of the lived experience
of the famine, and of its concrete local and regional context.
With the possible exception of the American historian Paul
Greenough, in his important *Prosperity and Misery in Modern
Bengal* (1982), it has been rare to approach this famine (or
almost any other in British India) from this angle. That Mukerjee
has been able to do this is the result of two significant facts: her
access to published materials in Bengali, such as the works of

contemporaries like Radhakrishna Bari and Sushil Kumar Dhara; and her direct access to survivors of the famine, who sometimes lived to a ripe old age. These included rural inhabitants, but also prostitutes from Kolkata's Sonagachi quarter, some of whom were sold into the sex trade in the context of the famine. Moreover, Mukerjee has been able to link the famine to the curious and important episode of the insurgent Tamluk National Government that arose in Midnapore district of western Bengal in December 1942, which, besides publishing its own *Biplabi* ('Revolutionary') newsletter, resisted colonial occupation for nearly two years until it was instructed to surrender by Gandhi. By listening carefully to these 'small voices' of history in over a third of her chapters, Mukerjee accomplishes several tasks. First, she moves from the high political history of elites, once beloved of academic historians, to a real social history involving a more varied cast of characters. Second, like much of the best new work on British imperial history, she moves beyond the imperial archive (usually in English) to a more diverse body of materials in languages such as Bengali (other authors have similarly made use of Swahili or Malay). Third, although she does not cite such notable historians in the 'subaltern studies' mode as David Arnold (on famines) or Ranajit Guha (on Bengali peasants), this part of Mukerjee's work can indeed be understood as partaking of some of the same inspiration. Searching for a concrete link between this work and that historiographical strand, we may well be led to the celebrated Bengali writer Mahasweta Devi, one of Mukerjee's avowed 'sources of inspiration and information'.

Yet, most reviewers of the book, its own publicists, as well as the author herself have shown a marked tendency to sell this aspect of the book short. In an interview to the Kolkata newspaper, *The Telegraph*, Mukerjee even compared her attempt to centre the book, as well as the chains of causality in the argument, on Churchill as the equivalent of hunting 'big game'. And so, at the end of the day, the prejudices of academic historians of yesteryear may still be found in histories written outside the academy. For a history book to be worthwhile, even in its author's own eyes, it must really be about a great man—greatly good or greatly evil. I hope I am not the only one who believes that this cannot be the future of history, whether inside the academy or outside it.

12

Fiction, Islam, and *The Satanic Verses*

I n the autumn and early winter of 1988 I spent some months
in England. I was an assiduous reader of the British press,
taking in three or four newspapers a day in the common
room of a modest Cambridge college, Clare Hall. Scarcely
a week seemed to pass when Salman Rushdie was not in the
news. A documentary film on India, *The Riddle of Midnight*,
had just been made for Channel 4 by Geoff Dunlop with
Rushdie as narrator, and there was some discussion of it as
well as of Rushdie's vision of India's future as a democracy.
But Rushdie-bashing was also a low form of journalistic sport,
including unpleasant puns on his name ('Salmonella' Rushdie
and so on). Weekend newspaper supplements retailed gossipy
accounts of how *The Satanic Verses* had failed to win the Booker
Prize, with malicious claims regarding Rushdie's tantrums when
this happened. (Suspiciously similar stories had circulated with
regard to *Shame*, which had also been shortlisted.)

I recall a dinner at an Italian restaurant in London with
journalist friends at which Rushdie occupied a good part of the
conversation—he had appeared on TV a night or two before
and made a series of acid remarks against racism in Britain. The
argument grew so vigorous that some of the restaurant staff, who
as it turned out were mostly Portuguese from Madeira, joined
in. Several of those at the table declared that, even as liberals,

they had found Rushdie's remarks 'over the top'. One of the British journalists was of South Asian origin and became deeply annoyed because the Portuguese waiters refused to accept his claim that he, like me, was 'Indian'. 'Just listen to his accent: more English than that and you'll die', was their judgement. It seemed that whether we liked it or not the predicaments of some of Rushdie's protagonists were ours, too.

This meal took place sometime between 5 October, when *The Satanic Verses* was banned by the Indian government under its Customs Act, and 19 October, when Rushdie wrote his celebrated open letter to the prime minister of India at the time, Rajiv Gandhi, declaring that 'your government has become unable or unwilling to resist pressure from more or less any extremist religious grouping.' But the ban was not lifted and the protests spread to Britain. In mid-February Ayatollah Khomeini issued his infamous fatwa against the book and its author, and Rushdie went into hiding. It is now over twenty years since that Valentine's Day message from the imam to the writer, and today there are literally dozens of books and thousands of essays and articles that deal with *The Satanic Verses*. No postcolonial literary critic can seemingly make a career without a comment on the matter. Even Rushdie has returned at length to the scene of the crime with a memoir entitled *Joseph Anton* (from the name he assumed at the time); and this rather self-indulgent book has provided more grist to the mill for the professional Rushdie-baiters amongst Indian critics and novelists, who feel it is definitely time to expunge him from the literary scene to make more space for themselves.

The Satanic Verses weighs in at a little under 600 pages and is no easy read. The wordplay, involving two and sometimes three languages, is relentless, and it sometimes feels like reading a particularly cryptic crossword puzzle. There are in-jokes too, many of which need to be glossed for those who have not grown up in South Asia. These—as the critic Srinivas Aravamudan has noted—include the flight number (420: an Indian shorthand for 'con-man') of the Air India jet whose mid-air detonation by bungling Sikh terrorists, called Dara Singh, Buta Singh, Man Singh, and Tavleen (whose names are also complicated in-jokes), opens the book. But the intertextual references also take us to nineteenth-century romantic authors and the Elizabethan dramatists, leaving one feeling that Rushdie would have done well to follow the example of T.S. Eliot, who had added explanatory notes to *The Wasteland*.

It seems futile to sum up the plot, but here goes: *The Satanic Verses* is constructed around a pair of South Asian Muslims—Gibreel Farishta (meaning the Angel Gabriel), born into poverty as Ismail Najmuddin in Poona 'at the empire's fag-end', but who takes up his other name as part of his transformation into a Bollywood star; and Saladin Chamcha (meaning Saladin the Toady), born Salahuddin Chamchawala to a rich and somewhat crass Bombay-based industrialist and his delicate wife. Chamcha, whose trajectory is apparently meant to be an arch commentary on the circumstances of Rushdie's own life, migrates to Britain young, becomes an actor, and marries an Englishwoman called Pamela Lovelace. However, since racism will not allow him to appear as a face (save in Peter Sellers-type roles), his fortune is made through his voice, first on the radio and later wearing a mask in a children's programme called *The Aliens Show*. The fates and stories of Farishta and Chamcha are intertwined through the novel as they delve into their pasts. After they both miraculously survive the explosion on board the hijacked Air India jet, Farishta seems to acquire angelic characteristics and Chamcha devilish ones, but this is just an illusion. In reality, it is Chamcha who is destined to survive at the book's end, along with his Bombayite lover Zeenat Vakil, while Farishta eventually commits suicide by blowing his brains out in Chamcha's recently deceased father's Bombay mansion. He has already caused a series of gory deaths from the outset of the book, and is wanted for multiple murders by its end. There is a clear paradox here. Chamcha, the inauthentic, uptight, and elitist migrant to London, constantly mocked for these qualities while in Bombay, is allowed to redeem himself, while the indigenously rooted and social-climbing villain cannot escape the deserts of his villainy.

At one level this novel is indeed, as Rushdie defensively claimed, 'about migration, metamorphosis, divided selves, love, death, London and Bombay.' It is stylistically closer to the sprawling masterpiece that is *Midnight's Children* than to the briefer and more tightly written *Shame*, but it can also fruitfully be read in relation to one of my favourites among Rushdie's books, *The Moor's Last Sigh* (1995), after which he seems to have largely fallen out of critical favour. In that novel, which might as well have been called *Rushdie's Last Sigh*, the author plays happily with history and historical characters, including some from the (Vasco da) Gama family with whom I have—for my sins—dealt closely over the years. But it is in *The Satanic Verses* that his brilliant talents for pastiche and gaudy and garrulous characters, at times bordering on cruelty, are in full evidence. We also find echoes of other genres, including juvenile ones, which is not surprising from an author who has recently described himself as the 'world expert on superhero comics'.

Had this been solely what the novel was about, it might never have been the object of great controversy. The problematic sections appear within this external frame, in the form of a parallel, but also at times intertwined, narrative concerning a place called Jahilia where a prophet called Mahound has arisen. This second narrative is a sort of dream sequence in two equal parts, and was defended by Rushdie as such. It was, he stated in his letter to Rajiv Gandhi, 'the fictional dream of a fictional character, an Indian movie star [Farishta], and one who is losing his mind, at that. How much further from history could one get?' But were these sections and their construction so far from 'history' after all? It is evident that in order to construct

Jahilia and its prophet Rushdie drew on medieval and early modern European polemics regarding Islam, including in the very use of the term 'Mahound'. It would be my surmise that while a student at King's College, Cambridge, between 1965 and 1968, he was exposed to some of these materials in some fashion. Several late medieval traditions of this sort existed, some of which were simply anti-Islamic; Dante's *Inferno*, dating to about 1300, for example, portrays Muhammad and Ali in the eighth circle of Hell, amongst the sowers of discord, suffering greviously for their sins and errors. A fifteenth-century fresco by the painter Giovanni da Modena in the San Petronio church in Bologna gives a visual form to this sort of verbal depiction, which can also be found in some manuscript paintings. Such polemics treated Muhammad as a charlatan or a trickster who had concocted a spurious text for his own ends and then misled a whole people into following him in a devastating project of conquest. As a charter of Alfonso VI, king of Castile, put it in 1086, the Muslims (or Moors) were not only 'blasphemers of the Christian name', but a 'perfidious race under their faithless leader Muhammad'. Some late medieval Christian texts even mocked the Muslim injunction against the consumption of wine by making out that the prophet Muhammad had served it up as an act of repentance for his own habitual drunkenness.

These materials were eventually given an interesting new twist in Western Europe in the context of the radical Enlightenment of the seventeenth and early eighteenth centuries. The central text here was the so-called *Treatise on the Three Impostors*, which was first published in The Hague in 1719, with a sly attempt to associate it with the thought of the seventeenth-century philosopher Spinoza. We still cannot know for certain who wrote it, and it is possible that it was really the product of collective authorship. Rumours regarding the existence of such a text had been afloat for centuries in Europe, and some had even made out that it was originally written by some prominent Muslim or

Jewish intellectual, such as the great twelfth-century polymath Averroes (or Ibn Rushd). When it eventually came out in print in 1719, it was quickly translated from French into several other languages, and reprinted as well as copied in manuscript, often with huge variations.

Basically, this work was a crude polemic made up of fragments and quotations from a variety of other sources and authors. It argued that the three great monotheistic prophets, Moses, Jesus, and Muhammad, were all 'great masters in the art of deceiving'. Moses, it stated, was not only 'a trickster and an impostor' but also 'reigned as an absolute Despot' over the Jews. Jesus, for his part, was a mere 'magician' who produced bogus miracles; and the Bible, it stated, was 'a tissue of fragments stitched together at different times, collected by different persons, and published on the authority of the Rabbis.' This contemptible book was so poorly put together that it had 'no more order than in the Alcoran of Mahomet; a book, I say, which no one understands, it is so obscure and ill conceived.' One can see why the *Treatise* at once delighted an irreverent mind like that of Voltaire, and made many European states and governments of the eighteenth century deeply nervous, to the point that they banned it. It was a sort of equal-opportunity offender, calculated to annoy almost all religious and believing peoples around Europe and the Mediterranean world. It also stood in a form of complementary opposition to a quite distinct view which had circulated since at least the sixteenth century in Europe and Spanish and Portuguese America, namely that 'everyone could save himself within his own faith', and which was actually a quite extreme form of relativist toleration.

In October 1988 Rushdie defined himself as a 'secular man for whom Islamic culture has been of central importance all his life', but it is clear that his secularism was marked by certain strands of the Enlightenment and its attitude of irreverence towards religion, even if he did not go anywhere near the extremes laid out in the *Treatise*. This is evident not only in the sections regarding Jahilia but in a scene of comical intent in which Farishta visits the Taj Mahal Hotel in Bombay after a near-fatal illness in order to stuff his mouth with all sorts of pork products, including 'the gammon steaks of unbelief and the pig's trotters of secularism'. There is a sense here in which the two words 'unbelief' and 'secularism' are brought into too close a proximity by their presence on the same buffet table. We all know what the first means, and the fact is that the second word, 'secularism', is not at all its equivalent either in the thesaurus or in the world at large.

Reading the book myself, also in 1988, I confess that I found my attention flagging periodically, but I could not put my finger on the cause. Was it the language, and a certain carelessness and self-indulgence in its use? Was it sheer fatigue at having to keep up with endless twists and turns? Rereading the novel now, I have some serious doubts regarding its structure. Are the sections regarding Jahilia, which account for a bit more than seventy pages, really that essential? Rushdie also claimed, in his open letter to Rajiv Gandhi, that in these pages he 'tried to offer [his] view of the phenomenon of revelation and the birth of a great world religion', but was this novel really the appropriate location for what looks more like the title of a dissertation that Rushdie might have done had he only stayed on in Cambridge, rather than (briefly) entering the advertising world, before finally becoming a successful novelist? To be sure, these pages echo with other sections in the book, including the names of characters which mirror those in the dream; this is an effect that folklorists have sometimes termed the 'braided frame'.

Still, my impression is that, just as with the dream sequences of Bollywood cinema, the pages describing the dreams of Farishta regarding Jahilia and its prophet are some of the weakest and most schematic in the book and considerably enfeeble its effect. The pastiche of the early Islamic narrative tradition—for that is what it is—is surprisingly literal-minded and uncomfortably close to what it is seeking to be ironic about. Also, it is here that one finds the references to the 'satanic verses' that produce the title of the book. Rushdie draws here not only on the textual tradition of Islam, but on the sort of oral materials that circulate within households, what one might have heard from one's mother or older siblings while growing up in South Asia. For my part, I can remember hearing stories about the Hindu gods in a similar fashion, though I sometimes cannot actually find them in the 'critical editions' of the *Ramayana* or *Bhagavata Purana* that colonial and post-colonial knowledge have produced for us.

Inevitably, by mid-1989, and with the atmosphere of terror let loose by the fatwa, these seventy pages, rather than the remaining 500-odd, had become what the novel was 'really' about. In Rushdie's view, those who criticized *The Satanic Verses* in India and elsewhere had never read it at all; but I know a good number of people who read only those pages and not the rest of the book. Such readers included many Indian Muslim intellectuals who would be shocked to hear themselves described as 'extremists, even fundamentalists', as Rushdie termed two Indian Muslim politicians who asked for the ban, Syed Shahabuddin and Khurshid Alam Khan. The latter was in fact a middle-of-the-road politician with many close relatives in the Indian communist parties, and his backing of the ban was more significant than Rushdie seems to have realized at the time. Even the historian Mushirul Hasan, who defended Rushdie's right to express his artistic views (and was physically attacked in his own university for this), agreed that he was personally offended by the pages in question. The pastiche was perceived by such figures as much too close to the real thing, despite the author's claim that 'the book isn't actually about Islam'.

As a consequence, it has over the years become well-nigh impossible to discuss *The Satanic Verses* in terms other than those of politics. Edward Said put it acutely: 'the debate about

Salman Rushdie was never really about the literary attributes of *The Satanic Verses* but rather about whether there could be a literary treatment of a religious topic that did not also touch on religious passions in a very, indeed in an exacerbated, public way.' Said, who was apparently a friend of Rushdie, went on to add in the same essay, 'The Public Role of Writers and Intellectuals', that 'even to assert that Rushdie's freedom of expression as a novelist could not be abridged . . . was in fact to debate the issue of the literary freedom to write within a discourse that had already swallowed up and occupied (in the geographical sense) literature's apartness entirely.'

It is here that we come to the heart of the matter: it is not clear to me that many of those who have supported Rushdie any more than those who attacked him have a clear sense of what Said terms 'literature's apartness'. After all, those who give the Booker Prize, the French Prix Goncourt, and other such awards frequently defend the winning books by using all sorts of instrumentalist social and political arguments rather than ones that centre on literary merit. It is no mystery that literary production as a commercial enterprise has little place for a discussion of literary quality as such. It would therefore be mistaken to imagine that this lack of autonomy granted to literary space is some peculiar attribute of the Islamic world, as right-wing Hindu fundamentalists have usually claimed in India, using *The Satanic Verses* as evidence. It may also arise, as the Telugu critic and poet 'Nara' recently wrote, 'If a poet has the delusion that his poetry is meant to change society [when] the business of a poet is to write poetry.'

Still, it may be worthwhile to return to Rushdie's own view that he was attempting on this occasion not only to write a novel, but also to present his 'view of the phenomenon of revelation and the birth of a great world religion.' The 1960s and 1970s in England were the moment when a significant intellectual movement arose that had precisely the same objective with regard to the birth of Islam, but which expressed itself through the academic monograph rather than the novel. Its key institutional centre was the School of Oriental and African Studies, a former nest of spies in London's Bloomsbury district, and its central figure was an American historian and Islamologist from Illinois called John Wansbrough, who began his career by working on the commercial relations between Egypt and Venice in the late fifteenth and early sixteenth centuries, and even published several valuable articles on that subject. A gifted linguist and philologist (especially in regard to diplomatics), Wansbrough then moved to studying the early centuries of Islam, and eventually published a work called *Quranic Studies* in 1977. This work, along with a collaborative book from the same year entitled *Hagarism*, written by two younger scholars, Michael Cook and Patricia Crone, is often thought to stand at the heart of a profound revision of early Islamic history. Wansbrough argued here that the Qur'an as a text was made up 'almost exclusively of elements adopted from the Judaeo-Christian' tradition, and was also 'the product of an organic development from originally independent traditions during a long period of transmission.' Doubts were equally cast on whether the Qur'an in fact originated in the Hijaz itself, or elsewhere, such as the eastern Mediterranean. Such claims drew ripostes, not only from the obvious quarters of orthodox Muslims but also from scholars of Islam and the Arabian world, like R.B. Serjeant, who had been Wansbrough's colleague at the School of Oriental and African Studies before being named Professor of Arabic at Cambridge. In a very sharply worded review of both works, Serjeant noted that while Wansbrough's 'range of reading is praiseworthy', his obvious intention was 'to fit the process by which the canon of the Hebrew Bible was established, on to the Qur'an.' He found in the work 'a disguised polemic seeking to strip Islam and the Prophet of all but the minimum of originality', and, in some cruelly dismissive passages, accused Cook and Crone of going even further and writing a work that was so 'ridiculous' that it seemed a mere 'spoof' or a 'leg-pull'. '*Hagarism*, foaled in the same stable' as Wansbrough's work, scoffed Serjeant, 'is not only bitterly anti-Islamic in tone but anti-Arabian.'

Whether or not these works were intended in such a spirit by their authors, they were taken in that way both by many fervent Muslims and a number of assertive anti-Muslims (including both radical Christians and Jews, and most recently even some supporters of Hindutva). These public polemics were already very much in place in 1988, when *The Satanic Verses* appeared. Over time, Cook—who coincidentally like Wansbrough had begun his career as an economic historian, albeit of the Ottoman empire—came to adopt a far more conciliatory position with regard to the critics of his early work, and today has become a quite traditional scholar of the Islamic textual tradition. Wansbrough appears to have been somewhat shaken by the violence of attacks on his views, and moved to studying other subjects, eventually withdrawing into a somewhat secluded life in France where he died in 2002. The Danish-born Patricia Crone, on the other hand, is generally known for the courage of her convictions; a senior Cambridge don once described her, after an interview for a post of tutor, as being 'as cuddly as an open razor blade'. Predictably, she has remained quite steadfast in her early views, as we see from her recent review of a book by the Chicago professor Fred Donner, *Muhammad and the Believers* (2010). In this book, Donner sets himself the unenviable task of mediating and effecting a compromise between 'revisionists' and 'traditionalists' regarding early Islamic history. For Crone, in her review, the revisionists are those who use 'authentic evidence', while the traditionalists simply and blindly follow a 'master narrative' that was put into place 120 to 150 years after the rise of Islam, that is, sometime in the late eighth century. In the process of reconciling the irreconcilable, she tells us, Donner not only contradicts his own earlier work (which was more in the splendidly 'revisionist' mode), but also tries to sustain the—certainly for her—improbable thesis that for the first hundred years Islam was 'an ecumenical movement' in which Christians and Jews (these are Donner's words) were 'fully integrated, as such, into the early community of Believers.' All this, suggests Crone, is merely some sort of bland political correctness for the consumption of a liberal American audience.

Several points in these seemingly arcane debates are actually of direct relevance for a continuing reflection on *The Satanic Verses*. The first of these concerns the status of the Qur'an itself. Obviously, for believers, it is a revealed text from the Angel Gabriel to the Prophet, whose currently accepted version has been perfectly stable from the very outset. This idea of revelation is in turn indissociably related to the prophethood of Muhammad, who is the last of the prophets, or the 'Seal of Prophecy' in the mainstream Muslim tradition. As we know from public debates (or *munazara*) that confronted Muslims and Christians between the sixteenth and the nineteenth centuries, this was always one of the key points that separated them. Christians refused to give to Muhammad the status of prophet and also denied that the Qur'an was a revealed text, insisting that it was instead a purely fabricated one. Muslims for their part denied the divinity of Jesus but accepted his status as a prophet, and saw the Gospel as not a revealed text but one that—like all histories—was just written by human beings. This contrast in positions was in large part the simple consequence of chronology and the fact that the figure of Jesus (and thus the faith around him) preceded the figure of Muhammad (and the faith around him) by several centuries.

For those who refused and even today refuse the idea of prophethood as such, in any tradition at all, all these points are simply irrelevant save as curiosities. Prophets to them are either simple charlatans, or deluded individuals. This would be the position of someone like Richard Dawkins today, and may have been—though here we are less certain—the view taken by certain 'rationalists' in even the medieval Islamic world. There is thus no point in debating whether the Qur'an is or is not a revealed text, since revelation itself does not and cannot exist. The feigned surprise of some Western scholars of Islam when, in 1972, they found parchment pages of the Qur'an dating from the first two centuries of Islam at the great mosque in Sana'a (in Yemen), and were thus able to show through small textual variants that the work was somewhat variable at the time (and thus not a product of revelation!), is really an attempt to create a false polemic. Rather, the scholarly question for non-believing historians and intellectuals is one of whether one imagines that the Qur'an emerged gradually like the Hebrew Bible (and if so, over what time frame, and in which space), or whether it emerged—as was claimed by Serjeant and before him by John Burton—in the Hijaz in a stable form as 'a canonical consonantal text' during the Prophet Muhammad's own lifetime, and that it may even have been his 'own recension'.

All this may seem a bit pedantic to those who read novels, not debates. But that is what scholarship about the distant past all too often is, rather than some version of *Gunfight at the OK Corral*, where every matter of importance or significance is resolved when the gunsmoke has dispersed. If indeed Salman Rushdie intended to enter the discussion 'of the phenomenon of revelation and the birth of a great world religion', he could have done so either as a believer in prophethood or not. It is clear that he chose the second option, even though he was eventually obliged to deny this fact for a time. It seems to me that Rushdie in 1988 had a very playful and distinctly irreverent view of the Islamic tradition, which may in part have been the consequence of the fact that he believed in a way it also 'belonged' to him. But this was also where the core of the problem lay. The writings of Wansbrough, Cook, and Crone, whether we agree with them or not, were in many senses far more radical than those of the

Egyptian scholar Nasr Abu Zayd (1943–2010), and yet have
received a very different response because they have been read
as an anti-Islamic polemic mounted by Christians from outside
the fold. Zayd and his wife were cruelly punished just because he
proposed a more flexible reading of core Islamic texts, or a new
hermeneutics. As for the others, most of their opponents in the
Islamic world have seen them—however appalling it may seem
to be to these Western scholars—as continuations of the old
public debate, or *munazara*. Let's do it one more time: Is Jesus's
divinity more defensible than Muhammad's prophethood?

In 1988–9 Rushdie faced two important issues in this
regard: first, he was ostensibly (though not really) a Muslim;
and, second, he had written a novel and not a monograph.
Whatever historians and scholars may like to think, it seems
that there was a broad view 'out there' that real and important
truths were articulated not in their works but in works of fiction.
Whatever offence Rushdie had given was thus measured out in
proportion with his apparent capacity to speak either the truth
or its opposite.

Ten years after those events, I happened to spend some time
at a research institute in Germany which had a working group
on Islamic Studies in its midst. The members of the group
were so diverse that the ambience was often very tense. Besides
my old friend Muzaffar Alam, himself a man with a complex
personal history and relationship to the received tradition, four
major figures were present. One was an elderly Belgian scholar,
who was all for understanding between cultures and religious
traditions, but to a point where it was impossible for him to
say anything of interest because it generally interfered with his
political correctness radar. The second was a middle-aged but
still brash American academic from a liberal arts college on the
east coast who was torn between his personal loyalty to friends
in Morocco and Tunisia, where he usually did his fieldwork,
and his sense of proximity with his own Jewish-American milieu.

The last two members were, on the face of it, the most complex and difficult. One was a charming Iranian-German, brilliant and multi-talented, whose main obsession was rock music from the late 1960s and early 1970s. Yet he had done a thesis on Islamic studies in Germany and was working at that time on the problem of 'unbelief' amongst medieval thinkers in the Islamic world. By virtue of the fact that he was not only rather dapper but also a quite brilliant orator and writer in German, he had become a sort of poster-boy for multiculturalism. And, finally, the fourth was a French textual scholar who specialized precisely in early Qur'anic manuscripts of the sort that had been found in Sana'a in the early 1970s. Ironically, we would sometimes come together at the institute's events over a drink; all of us quite fancied a glass of wine or beer at the end of a hard day's work. It was there that we understood after some time that our French colleague, though officially working for a university, was in fact an active member of a Catholic religious order and also that he always voted for the right-wing *Front National*. Nothing of any consequence could be discussed, let alone resolved, by us (I say 'us', though I was hardly a part of the group). It might be said then that we were just comforted in our prejudices and that everyone lived up to his role. In other words, what was meant to be scholarship dissolved all too often into simple ideology; and what in one case was supposed to be objective Qur'anic criticism turned out at the end of the day to be mere religious polemic. It was the Iranian-German who stood up not only for *kölsch*, the light beer from Cologne, but for the 'freethinkers' Omar Khayyam and Fariduddin Attar. It can be hard, after all that, for any of us to claim the right to pass a simple judgement on *The Satanic Verses*.

13

The Global Market for Indian History

Shallow. Give me pardon, sir: if, sir, you come with news from the
   court, I take it there is but two ways: either to utter them, or to
   conceal them. I am, sir, under the King, in some authority.
Pistol. Under which king, Bezonian? Speak, or die.
Shallow. Under King Harry.
Pistol. Harry the Fourth? or Fifth?
Shallow. Harry the Fourth.
Pistol. A foutra for thine office!

—Shakespeare, *Henry IV, Part 2,* V.iii

Let me begin with an extended anecdote that will serve here
as a form of casual ethnography. Some years ago, while at
an American university, I attended a 'job-talk', a lecture
which, though intended above all for members of a department
recruiting a professor, is open to the public at large. These talks
are peculiar affairs, largely unknown on the other side of the
Atlantic, although they have on the rare occasion now begun to
penetrate England, in places like Brighton. They are still unheard
of, though, for the most part, in Paris, Oxford, and Lisbon, or
for that matter in Delhi and Chennai. At the risk of producing
ennui among those who have sat through some of these lectures,
let me briefly summarize my sense of how they work.

The American (and Canadian) job-talk is normally a part
of a larger ritual. It can broadly take two forms. The first,

and statistically less common, is when there is a 'target-of-opportunity' search, which is when the host university is courting the candidate. On such occasions the job-talk is largely a formality and will often be quite poorly attended because its outcome is already known—unless of course the candidate manages to disgrace himself beyond all measure. The talk itself is surrounded by all sorts of other rituals: breakfast, lunch, and dinner meetings with individuals or small groups (the Quadrangle Club at the University of Chicago is fascinating as an ethnographic site from this point of view, suggesting that David Lodge was more reporter than satirist); short conversations with graduate students *en brochette*; appointments for the candidate with deans and provosts; a reception or two with wine and cheese; and a dinner the quality of which will often depend on the perceived importance of the candidate. I was once present when, on account of the candidate's alleged status, the chief host was the president of the university himself and the usual budgetary restrictions were thrown to the winds. But the case I am about to describe belonged to the other, more common, category. The candidate was a younger man, trained in the United Kingdom. There was a certain amount of scepticism in the air about him: it was clear that even a good performance might not suffice to get him through. For an outsider it was hard even to gauge the depth of the waters.

In the event, the actual performance was very polished. There was proper shamanistic ritual in the use of PowerPoint. The speaker stood at a podium as he spoke and used a text to read from, which Americans often prefer not to do as it suggests they have not quite mastered their materials. This, as much as his accent, marked him out not only as someone who came from the other side of the Atlantic, but as one who had been wholly trained there. (British academics who wish to show their familiarity with the US after having spent some time in the country will often make gratuitous references to baseball, or

use what they imagine are deep American expressions such as:
'That's the way the cookie crumbles', or 'That's the good news;
now here's the bad news'.) But in this case the use of the written
text was deft, eye-contact with the audience surprisingly good,
and the applause generous. When the time eventually came for
questions and answers the candidate, sipping water and relieved
at his own performance, was somewhat off-guard. A smoker, he
had clearly not read what a standard guide to job-talks suggests:
'Try to be in good physical condition; long-distance running or
some other types of stamina-development would probably be
good preparation for this challenging stage of the search.'

The questions began, and it was immediately apparent that
they were entirely different from those in a British seminar room.
No empirical materials were discussed. Archives and documents
were not even mentioned. The subject was colonial India and
British rule there, and it was manifest that the most pressing
question that bothered people in the room was the candidate's
own 'subject position', his intellectual genealogy, in short his
scholarly identity. Finally, a questioner from outside the history
department, but one self-professedly linked to the current
known as 'post-colonial studies', raised his/her hand. 'There are
now two schools in Indian history', s/he declared confidently,
'Subaltern Studies, and the Cambridge School. I would like to
know where you are located in relation to these two.'

The candidate was nonplussed. He had some degrees—
though not his doctorate—from Cambridge, but his work
was extensively based on vernacular materials from India, not
normally the case in Cambridge; his perspective was very much
that of a sort of classic social historian, the type that historians
of Europe readily identify with. He therefore attempted to
evade the question by stating that he did not believe in such
self-identifications. The pursuit then grew hotter, the visitor
more uneasy. Eventually, with the man seeming cornered and
squirming, a real cloud settled over the room. The next day,

in the corridors, all the talk was about how the candidate had failed adequately to identify himself. This was unacceptable. Pistol, Shallow, and especially Falstaff in *Henry IV*, would have understood.

I often wonder how—sense of improvisation or *esprit de l'escalier* aside—I myself would have responded in such a situation. A brief history of how the circumstances described came to arise may be worthwhile. The two key oppositional terms in use above were 'Cambridge School' and 'Subaltern Studies', and in a sense they do together comprise a transatlantic mirror of sorts. But such was not always the case. It is simply that the status of the third party in the equation, namely India, has diminished radically and almost disappeared. Now the 'Cambridge School' in relation to the historiography of India and South Asia is a notoriously slippery object. It should not be confounded with at least two other 'Cambridge Schools': that associated with Quentin Skinner, John Dunn, and the analysis of the history of political ideas (or 'ideas in context'); and that associated with Joan Robinson and a form of leftist political economy. The India-related Cambridge School is variously associated in its foundation with figures such as John (Jack) Gallagher and Eric Stokes, continuing through Anil Seal, and encompassing a whole host of others such as Gordon Johnson, B.R. Tomlinson, and Christopher Baker, who often published both essays and acerbic book reviews in *Modern Asian Studies*, a journal created in the mid-1960s.

The 'school' never wanted to identify itself as such. It was instead identified in those terms by its targets and primary opponents, namely nationalist Indian historians who had written in the 1950s and 1960s of matters concerning the Indian national movement. The purpose of the Cambridge historians was seen as demystifying Indian nationalism, cutting the heroic mythical figures of the national movement down to size, and stressing the extensive collaboration of 'native' elites in the running of the British empire in India. A part of this was Lewis B. Namier's notion of politics as really the affair of men in smoke-filled rooms, but the thrust was to stress the importance of interests over ideologies. In this process, British official papers and documents were diligently mined, but none of the historians trained in Cambridge (or Oxford) in the 1960s paid much attention to sources other than those in English.

'Subaltern Studies' on the other hand did identify itself as a project and was self-consciously run somewhat like a journal by a collective of Indian and a few British historians, initially based (to 1988) in India, the United Kingdom, and Australia. It emerged in the late 1970s and was linked in its early stage with Maoist student politics in India. It appears to have crystallized when a number of key figures, such as Ranajit Guha (born in 1923, and a clear generation older than the others, who were really his disciples), Gyanendra Pandey, and Shahid Amin found themselves together in, first, Delhi, and then England. At this point there was nothing transatlantic at all about it, apart from the paradox that Guha was funded for a time by the Ford Foundation in India. There were no American passport-holders or even academics who taught in the United States in the founding collective. In the 1970s, in the context of the Vietnam War, their entry into such a collective would probably have been quite unacceptable.

In its primary incarnation Subaltern Studies targeted both Indian nationalist historiography and the Cambridge School, alleging that both were profoundly elitist in their bias. The experience of common folk—peasants, workers, tribals—had been neglected by them in favour of a narrative where the high politics of the British–Indian encounter was the focus. There was no emphasis by Guha and others, though, on using vernacular sources; it was simply pointed out that even official British sources could be read in a manner sympathetic to the 'subaltern' classes. This enabled historians who worked solely with English-language materials, such as David Arnold, to participate in the project, a shared anti-elitist stance being sufficient for membership. It was a question of having your heart in the right place with regard to class politics; such thorny issues as gender had not yet entered the picture.

The rapid, enormous, and somewhat astonishing success that Subaltern Studies enjoyed in the first half of the 1980s—its first volume came out in 1982—meant that it came almost immediately to attract the attention of established historians based in America who, up to that point, had largely been left out of an argument organized on a Britain–India axis. At this time the leading Indian history figure by far in the US was the Chicago-based Bernard Cohn, a left-leaning professor more comfortable with the essay than the monograph as his form of expression, and who had long proposed a meeting ground between anthropology and history in the context of South Asia. Cohn's rivals for intellectual leadership in the matter of Indian history in the US were few: the chief one was Burton Stein, a Marxisant radical who sometimes described himself mock-seriously as an 'anarcho-syndicalist'. After teaching in Minnesota and Hawaii, Stein had decided in the 1980s to retire early to London, where he claimed he found the radical politics more to his taste than in his native United States. Other prominent figures included Robert Eric Frykenberg at Wisconsin, a conservative figure with a missionary background; and those far more elusive and difficult to pigeonhole, such as Thomas Metcalf at Berkeley, and Ainslee Embree, a Canadian-born American who taught at Columbia. But it was Cohn who, at the prestigious University of Chicago, had the most loyal following and who had trained the largest number of subsequently noteworthy students. Both Cohn and Stein were initially attracted to Subaltern Studies, but only one essay by the former eventually appeared within the project ('The Command of Language and the Language of Command'). It appeared at a moment when

American universities were beginning to emerge as alternatives to Oxford, Cambridge, and London, as destinations for young Indian students wishing to do a doctorate. Stein's essay of the time, on 'peasant insurgency' in Mysore, published in a far more obscure place in the same year as that by Cohn, took a much more critical tone with regard to Guha and Subaltern Studies. It concluded: 'Guha's purpose of bringing events and processes relating to peasant insurgency under serious historical analysis is correctly conceived and defended; I suggest here that his method is not.' Stein's essay was quickly forgotten while Cohn's came to acquire a certain prestige. I can remember the sense of pleasure and pride with which some members of the Subaltern Collective told me—I was then a doctoral student in Delhi—that even the heavyweights of the American academy were now negotiating with them, and that while some of their essays were being accepted, others were being summarily rejected. It was a heady post-colonial moment of sorts, I suppose.

The reaction to Subaltern Studies by the mainstream Indian nationalist historians, whether those attached to the centre-left Congress or the more Stalinist CPI (M), was immediate and violent. One can see this in the pages of *Social Scientist*, in effect the literary mouthpiece of the Indian communists, and in the acid comments of iconic Marxist-nationalist historians like Irfan Habib. This rejection continues in many respects and consists in the main of accusing Subaltern Studies historians either of shallow romanticism, or of a radical culturalism that shares many traits with the far right-wing Hindu trend in Indian politics. (Later Subaltern Studies' devotion to the figures of Nietzsche and Heidegger has really not helped matters in this respect.)

The reaction from Cambridge was more complex. The early figures of prestige, Gallagher and Stokes, were not active by this point in the 1980s, and Anil Seal and Gordon Johnson did not respond. A concrete rejoinder eventually came from C.A. Bayly who, having spent years as a marginal, often unshaven, somewhat cynical figure in a leather jacket claiming discomfort with the 'Cambridge School' label, had by the late 1980s slowly and suavely emerged in a proper jacket, tie, and patent leather shoes as the dominant figure in Cambridge. Initially, like most of his contemporaries, Bayly had worked on the Indian national movement—his focus having been colonial Allahabad; but from the late 1970s he had decided to shift his attention to a far earlier phase, that of early colonial rule under the East India Company beginning in about 1770. This move, in which he was soon to be followed by his close colleague David Washbrook, meant that Bayly was by 1985 not really a central participant in debates on Indian nationalism and the critique thereof. So his response to Subaltern Studies was muted, consisting of a brief essay which pointed out that much of what Subaltern historians claimed to innovate in had already been accomplished by the best-known British radical historians such as Eric Hobsbawm and E.P. Thompson. It was really a dismissive reaction rather than any deep form of intellectual engagement.

By contrast, in the same year, 1988, Rosalind O'Hanlon, a social historian at Cambridge who had in no way been identified with the erstwhile 'Cambridge School' and who worked on lower-caste movements in western India, emerged with a wide-ranging but broadly appreciative critique, pointing to conceptual blind-spots and lacunae in Subaltern Studies. Rather than a bi-polar field defined by a Subaltern–Cambridge axis of tension, what appeared to have emerged in about 1990 was an interesting form of fragmentation, with Subaltern Studies being the centre of attention where late colonial questions were concerned, but largely absent in regard to studies of pre-1900 India. Many debates of the time centred on quite distinct questions: there was for example a rather violent set of exchanges between historians of India on the one hand, and Immanuel Wallerstein and his disciples on the other, on the matter of 'world-systems theory' and its applicability to India (when had India entered the 'periphery' of the capitalist world-system being their grand question); while another central figure was the British Marxist historian Frank Perlin, who, in a series of exciting essays, proposed a radical reconsideration of the political economy of the eighteenth century. So, 'Under which king, Bezonian? Speak, or die' was hardly the issue then.

It was at this point however that transatlantic geopolitics came to play a decisive role. It is usual to identify this with the so-called 'Phase Two' of Subaltern Studies, dated to about 1988, when the supposed engagement of the Subalternists with postmodernism began. Dipesh Chakrabarty, who in recent times has become something like the official historian of Subaltern Studies, describes these matters blandly:

> [Ranajit] Guha retired from the editorial team of *Subaltern Studies* in 1988. In the same year, an anthology entitled *Selected Subaltern Studies* published in New York launched the global career of the project. Edward Said wrote a foreword to the volume describing Guha's statement regarding the aims of *Subaltern Studies* as 'intellectually insurrectionary'. Gayatri Spivak's essay 'Deconstructing Historiography' (1988), published earlier in the sixth volume under Guha's editorship in 1986, served as the introduction to this selection. This essay of Spivak's and a review essay by Rosalind O'Hanlon (1988) published about the same time made two important criticisms of *Subaltern Studies* that had a serious impact on the later intellectual trajectory of the project. Both Spivak and O'Hanlon pointed to the absence of gender questions in *Subaltern Studies*. They also made a more fundamental criticism of the theoretical orientation of the project. They pointed out, in effect, that *Subaltern Studies* historiography operated with an idea of the subject—'to make the subaltern the maker of his own destiny'—that had not wrestled at all with the critique of the very idea of the subject itself that had been mounted by poststructuralist thinkers. Spivak's famous essay 'Can the Subaltern Speak?' (1994), a critical and challenging reading of a conversation between Michel Foucault and Gilles Deleuze, forcefully raised these and related questions by mounting deconstructive and philosophical objections to any straightforward program of 'letting the subaltern speak'.

This is a rather peculiar and narrow framing of a history of ideas shorn of any institutional or other context. It is as if the critiques that Roland Barthes had laid out much earlier, in the late 1960s, suddenly appeared full-blown two decades later on the consciousness of Subaltern Studies historians; the death of the sovereign subject, the death of the authorial voice, and of agency itself—issues that historians in France had grappled with and also come to terms with—ostensibly became the occasion for an extended bout of hand-wringing. Had such self-doubt about the future of history and historical practice been the real basis of a programme, it could hardly have been charged with as much self-confidence as it had.

This makes one wonder: what might the real context be that led from the diverse and dispersed field of 1988 to an imagined landscape where only two strong and self-assertive poles existed, Subaltern Studies and the Cambridge School? We must turn to the debates of the early 1990s and their larger framing to comprehend what really transpired. The central debate is undoubtedly that which took place in the pages of the Ann Arbor-based journal *Comparative Studies in Society and History* between Gyan Prakash on the one hand, and Rosalind O'Hanlon and David Washbrook on the other. It is here that one finds the origins of the imagined Cambridge–Subaltern duopoly.

This is how the debate ran. Prakash had, not long before, finished his doctoral dissertation on landless labour in Bihar, and the spirit cults associated with those who had died a 'bad death' at the hands of a landlord. The work was much admired; it was also less in the spirit of Subaltern Studies than of James C. Scott, the historian and political scientist at Yale who celebrated 'everyday forms' of resistance. However, in the late 1980s Prakash became the central figure in nudging Subaltern Studies into an initially post-structuralist (and then increasingly post-modernist) mode, or what would by 1994 be termed 'postcolonial studies' or 'postcolonial criticism'. This meant weaning Subaltern

Studies away, once and for all, from the social-history tradition
of Thompson and Hobsbawm to which Bayly had insistently
claimed they belonged. It also meant largely abandoning the
fading field of economic history. Henceforth, 'culture' would
lie at the heart of matters. In other words, for Subaltern
Studies to enter the United States academy in force, it had in
effect to take the 'cultural turn', and in no half-hearted way. If
not, it would be indistinguishable from run-of-the-mill Latin
American peasant studies: there being peasant rebellions aplenty
between Nicaragua and Bolivia, a few additions from Bihar
or Andhra would not change matters. Product differentiation
was now of the essence; Ranajit Guha could not be confused
with Subcomandante Marcos. In other words, as oral tradition
would have it, if Gayatri Spivak can be likened to Ry Cooder,
Subaltern Studies at this time should be compared to the Buena
Vista Social Club.

This was the moment, let us recall, of a global reorientation
in Indian Studies. The 'old powers' were beginning to fade
somewhat. The shine had definitely gone off Indology in
France and Germany, and Indian Studies in England was also
in some disarray. In India, the early 1990s saw the first major
attack on university funding. This led under liberalization to
the progressive collapse of major departments in the social
sciences that has gone on ever since. In Pakistan the situation
was by then truly disastrous in history and the social sciences;
the Sri Lankan universities, such as Peradeniya, which had once
enjoyed an excellent reputation, were also in some difficulty. On
the other hand the market for India in the United States was
on the upswing. The 'heritage' students, those of Indian origin,
were just beginning to emerge as a force. Liberalization in terms
of foreign exchange availability would eventually permit more
and more Indians to send their children to universities abroad.
The big American universities and liberal arts colleges were
beginning to wake up to this new market, leading to the veritable

explosion in Indian Studies positions that has resulted since. (In 2006–7 alone, by my count, there were at least fifteen new positions in Indian history in consequential US universities and colleges; the numbers for 2007–8 seem comparable.) Once, in the 1960s and 1970s, India had been the monopoly of a small cartel: Pennsylvania, Berkeley, Chicago, Virginia, Austin, and Columbia. The new context by the late 1980s saw an interest for the first time from the three great Ivy League institutions: Harvard, Princeton, and Yale. None of these had employed a historian of India. This would be the next step.

The problem however lay in the persistent Anglophilia of these institutions, as well as the richer liberal arts colleges. Their natural reflex was to recruit historians of India in Oxford and Cambridge, which they imagined as their transatlantic counterparts. This American demand was to give a new lease of life to the 'Cambridge School', rendering it a form of branding for export. The exception was Princeton, which—possibly on account of the 'culturalist' preferences of scholars there such as Robert Darnton and Natalie Zemon Davis—came to settle for the newly reminted version of Subaltern Studies. The foundation for a duopoly had been laid, and the argument was played out in public.

In effect, then, the Princeton-based Gyan Prakash argued that the future of Indian Studies in the United States and, implicitly, the world, was with Subaltern Studies. This meant a series of things. First, it meant accepting Edward Said's critique of institutionalized Orientalism in the study of the non-West, and since it was assumed that such Orientalism was above all to be found in the study of classical and medieval cultures, it implied focusing exclusively on the colonial and post-colonial periods. Second, it meant embracing the neo-Derridean language that Spivak had popularized with vigour and enthusiasm after her translations of the French philosopher. Third, it increasingly meant coming to terms with the radical cultural critiques of the

West that were emerging in India from outside the universities, and associated with problematic—or shall we say 'complex'?— figures such as Ashis Nandy, himself a viscerally anti-Marxist cultural analyst and psychologist whose early career success had been largely based precisely on his determined opposition to Marxism in India.

In contrast, the O'Hanlon–Washbrook critique attempted to defend what they portrayed as the solid values of British radical history, as yet untainted by post-structuralism and even less by post-modernism. There was no need, in their view, to resort to ideas of radical cultural difference; rather, the old programme of the founders of *Past and Present* and the *History Workshop Journal* would do. Washbrook had begun to define himself in the 1980s as a Marxist social historian, and it was in this guise that he was offered a prestigious position to initiate the teaching of Indian history in Harvard in the late 1980s (a position which he turned down for personal reasons, and which was then later taken up by another Cambridge historian, Sugata Bose).

The Prakash *vs* O'Hanlon-Washbrook debate of 1990–2 rehearsed familiar themes: from Prakash's point of view, there was the hegemony and the disdain of the Oxbridge establishment for all sorts of colonial subjects, as well as the characteristic and empiricist British suspicion of 'theory'; from the O'Hanlon– Washbrook viewpoint, there were solid Old World (and espe- cially European) Marxist universalist values as opposed to an America that had become totally depoliticized (their tone here reminds one of Terry Eagleton), and where 'identity' was the only remaining form of politics—in view of 'the well-known hostility of American political culture to any kind of materialist or class analysis'. It may be worth noting the irony in this, for O'Hanlon and Washbrook were undoubtedly pressed to radi- calize their critique and sharpen their polemic by none other than an American exile in London, Burton Stein.

But a still larger irony should not be lost: in the final analysis the Atlantic did not really act as a divide, it functioned rather like a distorting mirror. On the one hand Subaltern Studies found its way back across the ocean in ways that are subtle and interesting, often through departments of English literature or programmes of post-colonial studies in places as diverse as Portugal and Denmark. On the other hand the reinvented 'Cambridge School' found purchase enough to define a minority, but still constituting an appreciable market-share, in the United States.

This was for two reasons. First, the logic of teaching courses required 'debates' and polemics, however artificial they might be, as forms of orientation for students. Where once the debate was between 'apologists' and 'nationalists', it was now habitually organized into the Cambridge *vs* Subaltern scheme. These two names are 'facts' that even one's colleagues in the most distant fields may now have heard of. And they have the same status that the names Fernand Braudel and Charles Tilly might have had some decades ago for a historian of medieval Japan seeking desperately to make conversation with his counterpart in French history. With each year, one may add names to each side of the list: some years ago the grand American historian Nicholas Dirks, in his book *Castes of Mind*, launched a violent polemic against Washbrook and Bayly, accusing them in effect of being direct descendants of the robber barons of the East India Company, and so found himself at once enshrined in the Subaltern pantheon. However, the problem remains that younger historians are not amenable to such easy classification. It is as if we impoverished drinkers of wines from Saint-Emilion and Lalande-de-Pomerol were constantly asked to declare our preferences between Coca-Cola and Pepsi.

How does this work out in concrete terms? An example may be found from the world of academic journal publication for Indian history in the United States, which is still vastly different from what one finds on the other side of the Atlantic. In the United Kingdom, a prestigious historical review such as *Past and Present* almost never sends out papers to referees; its board of editors is omniscient. The result is that the vast majority of papers on India in the last decade and a half has been written by those closely associated with Bayly, who serves on the editorial board; in other words, this is now pretty much the preserve of the 'Cambridge School'. In the United States the situation is even more peculiar if one looks at a journal such as the *American Historical Review*, to publish in which can be quite crucial for a young and aspiring historian seeking tenure. This journal tends to obtain a vast number of external reports, at times as many as six or seven. It is here that branding is crucial. For if an essay is identified at the outset as belonging to Subaltern Studies—through its acknowledgements and the contents of its first three or four footnotes—it is already placed in a market niche, making it very unlikely that potentially hostile referees will be contacted. However, American academic culture also prides itself on its 'pluralism'. Thus, the editors of such a journal might imagine that if Subaltern Studies has 70 per cent of the market-share, Cambridge must still have 30 per cent. It is those who are not branded that are likely to face a thorny problem with publication, and it is thus inevitable that they will seek anxiously to find some way of worming their way into the Subaltern–Cambridge duopolistic axis, helping it along in the direction of being a self-fulfilling prophecy.

I was recently asked to comment on a book about peasant insurgency in colonial Gujarat by Vinayak Chaturvedi, an American historian of Indian origin. Chaturvedi had initially been greatly influenced by the Marxist intellectual Robert Brenner and his work on agrarian history; he had then gone on to work in Cambridge with Bayly, whom he thanks in his preface for 'his generosity and his belief in an ethos of intellectual pluralism'. However, his book, written in the form of a fast-paced narrative, is largely and obviously based in a formal sense on the short-chapters model set out by *Event, Metaphor, Memory*, a book by the Subaltern Studies historian Shahid Amin. What implications does this have for the later writer? Does Chaturvedi's book belong to the Cambridge School or to Subaltern Studies? To speak the truth and say either 'I don't know' or 'a bit of both' would not do—certainly not in the USA, and certainly not by a candidate in quest of tenure.

Decades ago, the Indo-Belgian development economist Jean Drèze recounted an anecdote to me regarding a village in northern India called 'Palanpur' (a pseudonym) where at least two generations of researchers had done their fieldwork. The apocryphal anecdote had a budding researcher asking a farmer for details about the type of fertilizer he used, how much, how often, and so on. The peasant responded: 'That depends.' 'On what?' asked the student. 'On whether you're doing your MA or your PhD' was the response.

As to whether I and my cohort belong to Subaltern Studies or the Cambridge School, I suppose many of us are now old and uncaring enough to say 'neither'. For the young unaffiliated scholar—and my point is that there are statistically more of these really than of any other type—the answer must depend, I would suppose, on the concrete nature of supply and demand. It depends in short on whether the question is being asked in Cambridge, Yale, or Chicago. In Paris, Naples, or Tübingen, they still might not care.

But times do change, and have done since 2008, when the present essay was first published. In the last year or two there have been some strange rumours and sightings which suggest a partial reconciliation between Cambridge and the Subalterns. Interviewed in Paris in April 2010 by French historians, Chris Bayly made highly conciliatory noises towards at least some of the Subaltern historians. This notwithstanding, the academic world market may turn out to have its own inexorable logic. What specific actors say or think may not be all that relevant any more. The new market circumstances seem to suggest, in short, that let alone subalterns, sometimes even historians can't speak.

14

India's Discovery of Vasco da Gama

Some historical myths are particularly hard to get rid off. It is now generally accepted that in the tenth and eleventh centuries, Norsemen (or if one prefers, Vikings) had arrived in and settled in some coastal parts of North America. The important site of L'Anse aux Meadows in Newfoundland, which was excavated by Norwegian scholars after 1960, provides concrete proof of such settlement. Still, enough emotional and nationalist investment exists in the idea that European contact with America began in 'fourteen hundred and ninety-two, when Columbus sailed the ocean blue', for this awkward fact to be customarily set aside, at least at the level of popular representations of history. Where Asia is concerned, European contact was far older and far more regular, from the time of the ancient Greeks and the Romans. Every year brings us fresh hoards of Roman coins in southern India which are proof of that contact, while the settlements of Greeks in Afghanistan and even the Punjab are testified to in numerous sources, including sculpture and coinage.

Throughout the Middle Ages, Europeans kept trickling into the Indian Ocean, so that the case of Marco Polo in the late thirteenth century was by no means an isolated one. The problem is that most of them, unlike Marco Polo, did not leave extensive narrative accounts or records. We are thus left with only fragmentary mentions in many cases, or short and tantalizing narratives. Let us take a particularly curious example. At some point in the late 1470s, a Venetian trader called Bonajuto d'Albano already in middle age (likely at least 40 years old) from the Campo di San Bartolomeo made his way to India, in all probability taking the route via Iran and the Persian Gulf. He left behind a family in Venice, including a brother who worked in a commercial establishment there. His itinerary seems to have taken him through Hurmuz and Cambay (Khambayat) to the Samudri Raja's port of Calicut (Kozhikode), and he would also appear to have visited the great South East Asian emporium of Melaka in the course of the 1480s and 1490s. D'Albano came over time to acquire a reasonable fortune, but eventually lost some twenty or twenty-five thousand *ducati* in a ship of his that was apparently wrecked. Reduced to penury, he found himself by about 1500 in central Kerala, now frequenting the ports of Calicut and Cochin as a pauper, with an Asian wife and two children, whom he had not bothered to baptize and who apparently dressed in the 'native' manner.

He was scarcely the only Italian to frequent the Indian Ocean in these years. We know of at least two Genoese, Girolamo Adorno and Girolamo da Santo Stefano in the mid to late 1490s, who traded across the western Indian Ocean and even in the Bay of Bengal; in central Kerala, there were in the late 1490s also a native of Bergamo and a Valencian, both of whom had long experience of the Indian Ocean trade. Still, these men were rather few in number and could not constitute themselves as a community inhabiting a particular quarter of a port-city, even had they so desired. In northern Sumatra, at the port of Pasai, Santo Stefano found a *qazi* 'who had some knowledge of the Italian language' and was helpful to him. But we must imagine that for the most part they communicated using a smattering of Arabic, Persian, or Turkish, as we see from the slightly earlier account of the merchant from Tver, Afanasii Nikitin, who visited India in about 1470.

What were the rules of the game so far as these merchants—who were often called Franks (*afranj* or *firangi*) from the memory of the Crusades—were concerned? From what we can gather, these traders were rarely if ever armed and depended on local and regional states to protect them from the attacks of maritime and overland predators, whether pirates and corsairs or bandits. In the face of demands from tax-gathering states, they usually had little option but to negotiate as best they could. The brief account of Santo Stefano, written as a letter from Tripoli (a port to the north of Beirut, not the one in Libya) to Giovan Jacopo Mainer in September 1499, is rather helpful in evoking the trading ambience of the mid-1490s. He and his companion Adorno had decided while in Cairo to make for India, and purchased a stock of coral and other goods for this purpose. They then found their way overland via Qina to Qusair, where they embarked on a ship to Massawa. After a stop here, they eventually pushed on to Aden whose Tahirid ruler al-Malik al-Zafir 'Amir (r. 1489–1517) they found to be 'just and good'. From Aden the Italians once more boarded a sewn-plank ship—quite a novelty for them—and made their way to Calicut, the great centre for the pepper and ginger trade. Deciding to explore the further commerce of the Indian Ocean, they then resolved to move on to Sri Lanka (for the cinnamon and gem trade), then to south-eastern India, and eventually to lower Burma (or Pegu).

From here on, things did not turn out well. In Pegu, the high roads were closed on account of the wars of the late fifteenth century, following the death of Mon king Dhammacedi in 1492 and the succession of his son Binnya Ram. The Genoese were therefore more or less obliged to sell their goods to this prince, who also proved very slow indeed to pay them. Adorno died during the extended stay, and Santo Stefano then made his way alone to northern Sumatra, where he had to negotiate his way out of escheat demands from the ruler of Pasai, Muhammad

Shah (1495–1507), in regard to the deceased Adorno's goods. He eventually took a ship via the Maldives to Gujarat, suffered shipwreck en route, but at last made it to Cambay.

Here, his luck turned somewhat in a way that is significant. Encountering 'some Moorish [Muslim] merchants of Alexandria and Damascus', they first offered Santo Stefano money for his expenses and then agreed to employ him as an agent on a commercial voyage to Hurmuz. After discharging his tasks in the Persian Gulf, our Genoese merchant then fell into the company of Armenian and Persian traders; it was in their caravan that he travelled to Shiraz, Isfahan, Tabriz, and eventually to Aleppo. On the last leg of the voyage, Santo Stefano once more lost his goods to robbers, and as before it was the Muslim merchants on the caravan who came to his financial aid. This eventually brought him to Tripoli, where he was able (in a rather morose mood) to write his account of what he terms his 'disastrous journey'.

These travails should—like those of the Russian Nikitin a quarter-century earlier—keep us from overly idealizing the trading conditions that were to be found in the Indian Ocean in the second half of the fifteenth century. But whereas Nikitin felt the need to conceal his Christian identity, and tried to pass himself off (unsuccessfully in the event) as a certain Khwaja Yusuf Khorasani, this is not at all the impression that Santo Stefano leaves. The Russian trader also suggests that Bahmani regional governors in the Deccan, in particular, preyed on him, and our Genoese merchant too has his share of complaints on similar scores. But what is interesting in his case is the fact that he finds substantial common ground with Muslim traders from the eastern Mediterranean, and also with their Persian counterparts. Clearly, the mere fact of being Christian did not evoke automatic hostility; and many merchant communities from the eastern churches seem to have flourished in the Indian Ocean at that time, whether the so-called Syrian Christians of Kerala or the Armenians.

The arrival of a small fleet of three Portuguese vessels, *São Gabriel*, *São Rafael*, and *Bérrio*, of somewhat unusual appearance off the coast of Kerala in May 1498 thus need not have caused great consternation there. Even if they were armed with cannon and bombards—which ships in that part of the world usually were not—the fleet was tiny. The inhabitants of Pantalayini, where the ships eventually anchored, included a community of Muslims who had resided there over several centuries. They were habituated to trading with Hindu Chettis from the Tamil country and with visiting Gujarati Banias from further north up the coast; in order to gain access to the pepper grown in the hilly country inland, they often went through Syrian Christian traders. South of this port lay Calicut, where the Samudri Raja ruled from a somewhat modest palace, hardly on the same dimensions as the residence of the Vijayanagara ruler some hundreds of kilometres inland. Still, Calicut was a great market town, which was generally thought however to be less than safe as a harbour, particularly in the months of late May, June, and July, when the full force of the monsoon rains came down with the winds that blew in from the south-west. In June, the monthly rainfall here averages 80 cm, and this was the season when the Portuguese fleet had just arrived. Conditions in short were not quite what the Portuguese were used to, and, in the three months that they remained in Kerala, they never managed to escape from their imprisoning sentiments of cultural and physical alienation bordering on paranoia.

But what did the inhabitants of Kerala, and of western India more generally, make of this first expedition commanded by Vasco da Gama? We do not possess any direct evidence, since no eyewitness from the other side has left us an account to counterbalance the well-known anonymous Portuguese text (the so-called Álvaro Velho account), which is the chief narrative source for the encounter. We must therefore use one of two strategies: read later accounts back into this period; or attempt to draw on Carlo Ginzburg's fruitful idea that 'texts have leaks' and try to read the Portuguese texts for the voices of their interlocutors. Let us attempt the latter strategy first.

Now, according to the anonymous Portuguese text (which is closely followed by most later Portuguese chronicles and accounts), the first Portuguese sent ashore in Kerala was an exiled convict (or *degredado*). It is possible that he was chosen for this task on account of some knowledge of Arabic, since the Portuguese at this point had no notion of the other languages spoken in southern India. It was he who had the iconic encounter then with two Muslim merchants from Tunis, to whom he appears to have been presented especially because they could speak Castilian and Genoese. Their reactions to him are interesting. Overcoming their initial astonishment when they recognized him as Portuguese (and not Castilian or Venetian), the Tunisian merchants fed him and treated him well. Then, one of them returned with him to the Portuguese vessels to assure Gama that 'you should give many thanks to God for having brought you to a land where there are such riches.' They thus viewed the Portuguese simply as another group that had come to partake of a rich trade, in which there was certainly place for more participants. In other words, it seems that, initially, they did not treat Gama very differently from the manner in which the Damascene and Alexandrine merchants of Cambay treated Girolamo da Santo Stefano at much the same time.

But Gama himself was caught in a bind. Since we do not possess his instructions from the king of Portugal, we cannot be certain that he had been told to go to Calicut. This may well have been a destination that he improvised while on the east coast of Africa, based on information gathered at Malindi. On the one hand he seems to have felt he had to impress his interlocutors in Calicut that he was no mere merchant but the representative of a great monarchy. On the other hand he did not have the means to do this, being poorly supplied with both trade goods and gifts. Furthermore, if the Tunisians or other Maghrebi traders present in Calicut were at all well informed, they would have known that Portugal was not in quite the same political league as Castile or Aragon, even if the Portuguese had some footholds and fortresses in North Africa.

We may thus imagine that Gama's behaviour would have puzzled them somewhat. Not knowing at the time that Africa could be circumnavigated, the appearance of his fleet must already have caused them some doubt, for the only other solution would have been if the Portuguese had managed somehow to assemble a fleet in Suez (as the Egyptian Mamluks were to do a few years later). But how could his persistently aggressive stance be explained? Gama's speech to the Samudri Raja on the occasion of their first meeting, as it is reported by the anonymous text, is a rather odd affair and contains a number of implausible claims and half-truths. These include the following:

- That the king of Portugal 'was much richer in all things than any other king of those parts', meaning the rest of Europe.
- That the Portuguese were impelled to set out each year because they wanted to find Christians 'and not because they needed gold and silver, for they had those in such abundance that they did not need them from this land', that is, from India.
- That if Gama returned to Portugal without finding a Christian king in India, 'he would have his head cut off' by Dom Manuel.

Indeed, Gama was not able to keep up these pretences in the next meeting, and when asked to describe the chief products of Portugal spoke of wheat, textiles, iron, and brass, not gold or silver, as he had claimed earlier. By this time, moreover, the poor quality of the Portuguese gifts had already led them to lose face and be rather deflated. This may have lain behind a series of sneering counter-questions that are put by the anonymous Portuguese writer in the Samudri Raja's mouth. If indeed he came from such a rich kingdom, the Calicut ruler asked, why had Gama brought nothing? Why did he not even have a proper letter for the Samudri? And finally, what had he come to discover: stones or men? Now, Gama did indeed carry two letters, but one of these, being in Portuguese, was unusable, while the second—the contents of which are unknown—being in Arabic, was only a little less so. We cannot therefore divine the impression that this second letter, which he handed over with great reluctance, might have made. Was it full of high-flown Christian universalist rhetoric, as has sometimes been suspected? Clearly, it must have been generic in nature, because the Portuguese did not have a proper name for the kingdom where they had landed, let alone of its ruler. An awkward gap would appear to have opened up between Gama's high ambitions and his poor capacity to act on them.

The following two and a half months after these meetings could not have eased tensions or improved impressions. To be sure, Gama contemplated the idea of leaving a factor called Diogo Dias and six other men behind as a longer-term establishment, but he also demanded local hostages in return. Later, on the eve of his departure in mid-August, he actually seized eighteen men (including six Calicut notables), and only released the bulk of them rather reluctantly. Some he did carry back to Portugal, and while leaving Calicut left a rather surly message to the effect that 'he hoped that he would return soon to Calecute, and that then they would know if indeed we were robbers as the Moors had told them.'

The last is a reference to the growing hostility on shore between the Portuguese and Muslim traders, whom the anonymous text accuses of spitting offensively and saying 'Portugal, Portugal' in an insulting fashion. There was also the view that these same Muslim merchants, especially those from the Middle East, had poisoned the mind of the Samudri Raja. In other words, we are here given the first impression that the hostility between the two sides was a product of prior aggressive behaviour by the Muslims, whereas a careful reading of the anonymous Portuguese text suggests that Gama's behaviour could only have seemed rather inconsistent and suspect from the very start.

On the other hand, a reading of later texts produced in Kerala radically simplifies matters and produces a near-teleological vision of the conflict. Some of these texts have been analysed at length by historians, notably the *Tuhfat al-Mujahidin* (Gift to the Holy Warriors), a prose chronicle in Arabic written by Shaikh Zain al-Din Ma'bari in the 1570s. Less well known is a didactic poem (or *urjuza*) in Arabic entitled *Fath al-Mubin li al-Samiri allazi yuhibbu al-Muslimin* (Manifest Victory for the Samiri, who loves Muslims), authored by a certain Qazi Muhammad ibn 'Abdul 'Aziz, perhaps the cousin of Zain al-Din. The events covered in this text are from the period 903–79 AH / 1497–1571, so that it too was probably written in the 1570s. It commences with extensive praise for the ruler of Calicut, and the hope that the tale of his brave resistance to the Portuguese might 'travel over the world, and reach Syria and Iraq in particular'. It is understood that the monarch is himself no Muslim, but he is after all 'fighting against [the Franks] in spite of his own unbelief, while Muslim kings do not do so.' A description then follows of the Portuguese:

> They are the worst of all creatures,
> followers of the most unclean ways,
> The bitterest foes of Allah and His Prophet,
> his faith and his Prophet's community.
> The Frank worships the cross
> and prostrates before images and idols,
> Ugly in appearance and form,
> Blue-eyed like a ghoul.
> He urinates [standing] like a dog,

and those who wash are rebuked and expelled.
Cunning, disobedient, and deceitful,
the filthiest of God's creatures, that is the Frank!

It is the deceitful aspect which is then emphasized in the verses
that follow, which note how the Portuguese eventually set about
demolishing mosques, burning cities, and enslaving people in
the Red Sea, Sri Lanka, and the east coast of Africa. A brief set
of verses is devoted in particular to Vasco da Gama's first visit.

The Frank came to Malabar in guise of a merchant,
but intending cheating and trickery.
To gather all the pepper and ginger for himself,
and leave just coconuts for the others.
In the year 903 from the year of the migration
of the Prophet, chosen of humankind,
the Frank brought some presents for the Samiri
and asked to be one of his subjects.
Saying he would help the country flourish
and defend him against enemies and rebels.
The Samiri preferred him to all others,
and rejected the warnings of his subjects,
Who said: the Frank will destroy our lands.
Now our words have been proven true,
for he lay low like a slave until,
growing in strength, he rose up,
and subdued the lands of Hind and Sind,
and even China: that is no lie.

This would be a lasting image, eventually inscribed in text after
text, from Gujarat to South East Asia. In some versions the
deceit of the Franks would be assimilated to the story of the
founding of Carthage in the *Aeneid* (ll. 365–8), where Dido and
her companions, granted land equal to an ox's hide, stretched
it by subterfuge. The relevant passage is: 'They came to this
place, and bought land, where you now see/ the vast walls, and
resurgent stronghold, of new Carthage,/ as much as they could

enclose with the strips of hide/ from a single bull, and from that they called it Byrsa'. This may appear a great distance from the image of Vasco da Gama in the great Portuguese epic poem from the 1570s, the *Lusíadas* of Camões, but the latter too retains something of Gama's resourcefulness, his capacities as a manipulator and trickster. At the end of the day, all merchants may be seen to be devious, but the lesson that was learned in the Indian Ocean between May and August 1498, and even more so in 1500 and 1502, was that the Portuguese were not just tricky; they were more than mere merchants.

15

Philanthropy, Warren Buffett, and the Bhagavad Gita

E uropean visitors to India in the sixteenth and seventeenth centuries usually found precious little to admire there. The climate they deemed too warm and languorous; they rarely liked the food and drink; the gods struck them as frightful and monstrous. Once in a while, however, something did take their fancy. Amongst these was the Indian habit of giving often and generously, such as when a merchant at the end of his worldly career decided publicly to part with all his material goods. Even the Jesuits, behind their general attitude of superiority and condescension, occasionally praised the mass feeding of the poor that was practised both in temples and by princes and magnates. Usually they saw all this as a form of ritual or religious practice rather than an affirmation of social bonds. The Dutch and the English merchants in their outposts, in places such as Surat and Bharuch, were less certain of what these acts of giving meant, and noted in puzzlement that they extended beyond human generosity to setting up infirmaries for animals and even birds.

Something happened to this tradition over two centuries of colonial rule. It did not disappear but it was transformed in a variety of ways, some subtle and others less so. To be sure, when the great famines of the late nineteenth century ravaged western and southern India, some acts of generous giving were noted. The celebrated bird and animal hospitals of Jains in western India did not disappear. But philanthropy was initially not taken very seriously by those who made great fortunes on the back of the colonial trades, whether opium export to China or jute-making in Kolkata. Trading communities looked after their own, up to a point, with the richer traders bankrolling their poorer cousins. By the time of the Five-Year Plans of the 1950s, it was the state that was looked up to more and more as the ultimate *maai baap*, giver and arbiter of redistribution. Not for nothing has it been argued by Paul Greenough and others that mortality in the great Bengal famine of the 1940s would have been far lower if only social bonds of mutual support had not given way by that time.

This dependence on the state to nourish the people, to create human capital, to ensure social change and development, was a very convenient alibi for some. The Tatas and the Birlas built the odd educational institution for engineers, physicists, and the like, such as the Birla Institute at Pilani (BITS) or the Tata Institute (TIFR) in Mumbai, but few others followed suit. Socialism may have been a nice buzzword in the 1950s and 1960s, but beneath its surface it was really a dog-eat-dog world. If one had not inherited wealth, it was all a question really of who could get access to the state and its mechanisms for redistribution, rent-seeking, and social climbing. So, some social change did happen, and some new groups emerged to the fore. A handful of robber barons also made great fortunes by dint of their strategic dealings with this or that party and leader. It was a far-from-ideal world, but one where the state was meant to keep a lid on things when social tensions came to the boil by a mix of populism, coercion, and handouts.

Many Indians today, especially among the middle class and elite, want to repudiate that past and its licence-permit-quota raj. One can see why. But it may also be useful to see what the alternative, which has been touted for a decade and a half as something called 'liberalization', really means. Fundamentally, what liberalization as a process entails is the reduction of the role of the government in economic and social terms. In the specific case of India, it also seems to imply a gradual process of decentralization, as decision-making moves from the centre to the states on a certain number of key issues. So, let us say one wanted to grow orchids for export in 1965. I imagine one would have had to deal with at least three different central ministries, the customs, Air India and its bureaucracy, and a host of other obstacles. Today, it may be far easier to pull off such deals, though one still hears periodic horror stories from entrepreneurs. That is all very well for businesses, but what of other tasks the state undertook, and which do not bring with them ready short-term profits as rewards for risk-taking? These include the provision of a whole host of public goods, and I want to single out one: education.

Now, some parts of education are well-paying, as anyone who has visited the great public school chains in the metropolitan cities knows. The proprietors of Modern School and Vasant Valley are not exactly starving. Even teaching shops and cramped spaces where students cram desperately for the Joint Entrance Exam (or IIT-JEE) have been doing a roaring business for some decades now. But that is not true for a huge swathe of education across the board, from the primary to the highest level. The market, left to its own, will not educate many of those who do not have the ability to pay and pay amply. This is where only two alternatives exist: the state or philanthropy. This is undoubtedly true for the primary education of a poor farmer's five-year-old child in Belgaum, but the logic of this runs all the way up and down the system. One can see how engineering schools, medical schools, and management institutes can work in a free market. The same is true for the production of software programmers and others who service global industries of various sorts. But what about the social sciences, the arts, the humanities? What would the market want with a social anthropologist or a poet? Should we then imagine an India with crores of software writers and not a single great sarod-player or political theorist?

It is usually imagined that for the reproduction of artists, musicians, and the like, we can somehow depend on traditional family-based institutions to do the job. This may be true to an extent with music, but is it true of the visual arts? Is it true of literature? Will our chief research institutions in sociology, politics, and cinema studies survive eternally on handouts from the Ford and Rockefeller foundations? The Indian landscape is littered with wrecked higher education institutions in Allahabad, Chennai, Mumbai, and Pune that were once great and which now moulder in the dust. It seems to me that the only answer here in view of the gradual (and perhaps even justifiable) withdrawal of the state is the growth of Indian philanthropy and private patronage of the arts and education.

But how is this to happen? There is obviously no simple solution. But one can help to create the conditions for it. First, it should be understood that philanthropy is not altruism or some sort of Gandhian *nishkama karma*. It is enlightened self-interest and also carries some bragging rights; no one should think that Warren Buffett got his ideas from the Bhagavad Gita. There are plenty of people today in India who have more money than they know what to do with. So it is a question of making philanthropy something that is valued, a sort of 'prestige good' if you will. Second, the matter obviously requires some fiscal forethought. Almost all those who give large sums in the US—which is perhaps the single-most successful philanthropic economy in the world—do so in careful consultation with their tax-planners. Even in their generosity, they are careful and calculating. So the state has to motivate such activity through its tax policy, and even perhaps provide some delicately constructed loopholes for those seeking to transform their wealth from a darker to a lighter shade.

But above all there is the question of seeing all this as enlightened self-interest. We can all agree that, two hundred years after 1789, the age of revolutions is over and the age of dreaming about revolution too is mostly over, the case of Nepal notwithstanding. What remains then is a world where societies may not explode, but may still be characterized by a constantly simmering social violence, built on the back of gated communities, private security, and a deep paranoia among the haves that goes along with the resentment of the have-nots. In a society like India, where an extremely affluent class has emerged in the past two decades riding the crest of liberalization, it is a question of whether a new social contract is now not a pressing necessity.

This would not be a contract based on the conjuring tricks of the state, but rather on some notion that went beyond mere taxation and redistribution. American conservatives such as Richard Posner have argued that growing income inequality is necessary and even desirable as a condition for a meritocracy. That they can even dare to make such an argument is because they are confident in the existence of other institutions that will counterbalance such inequality and curb its nefarious social effects. Chief among such institutions is philanthropy. The protagonists of liberalization in India today need to remember that the market cannot exist in a social vacuum, something that would have come as no surprise to Adam Smith over two centuries ago. Giving wisely may be the most sensible way of keeping what's left.

16

9/11, Islam, and the USA

There is little doubt that the period since 11th September 2001 has seen a significant decline in both the reality and the image of American power. To this extent, we may say that the architects of the attacks on New York on that day have to a great extent succeeded in their intent, though not in ways they may have foreseen. By embroiling the US in two costly wars that came out of the events—however avoidable they really were—and thus causing a downward fiscal spiral with larger financial implication, the aftermath of 9/11 has been somewhat astonishing to witness, and we have not yet seen the last of its consequences. The greatest surprise is that the challenge to the US did not come from the two rival politico-economic systems that seemed to be emerging in the 1990s. China has certainly profited from American decline in the past decade to open the sphere of its influence, above all in Asia, but even in other continents. However, this has been largely opportunistic. On the other hand, the European Union has—ever since the adoption of the euro as its currency in the early 2000s—lurched from one crisis to another and seems hardly better placed than the US to face the 2020s.

The collapse of the Soviet Union in the late 1980s and early 1990s is frequently attributed to a version of Paul Kennedy's thesis on 'overstretch'. In this view, the Soviet leadership managed to conceal the deep fragility of their economic base until it was put under severe pressure by the need to compete in an ever more costly arms race. The Soviets here would be compared to other older imperial powers, such as the Spanish Habsburgs in the early seventeenth century, who failed to keep up with competitors because they were attempting too much, over too large a space. There are elements of overstretch in what has happened to the US as well, but the central problems seem to lie elsewhere. After all, neither Iraq nor Afghanistan can be seen as a major sphere of military operations by comparison with past imperial wars of the nineteenth and twentieth centuries. Yet, they have proven too costly for the US to stand up to their burden, perhaps because the US style of war-making now is far too capital-intensive.

Some ten days after the attack on New York, George W. Bush addressed the US Congress and explained that the cause of the attacks was that 'they hate our freedoms—our freedom of religion, our freedom of speech, our freedom to vote and assemble and disagree with each other.' This was comforting as an attempt to seize the moral high ground, but not quite true. The attempt here was to make the US appear to be the paragon of secularism and modernity, as if the real enemy targeted on 9/11 was an Enlightenment vision of democracy. The reality seems to have been rather that the leadership of Al-Qaeda saw the US as a Christian power, often acting in concert with Israel and with a powerful Jewish community inside the country.

Ironically, the aftermath of 9/11 has made this somewhat self-fulfilling. In the later nineteenth and twentieth centuries, while Western Europeans pondered the prospect of the increasing secularization of their societies, the US continued to be strongly rooted in Christianity. This remains even more true today. Slightly under half of the population belongs to various Protestant denominations, and over a quarter is Catholic. Besides, a surprisingly large proportion of adults in the US are

Christian 'converts', in the sense of belonging to a different Christian denomination than the one into which they were born. As a consequence, Christianity weighs very heavily on the politics of the country and no politician today who stands for the Presidency—whether Catholic, Protestant, or even Mormon—can step away from the religious question as a central aspect of their politics. This was already evident during Barack Obama's last campaign. Again, Christianity underpins the so-called 'Tea Party' movement, which though quite small is disproportionately powerful as an ideological force, and is in many ways an outcome of 9/11.

The obsession with Christianity means that US politics is often fought by giving enormous importance to issues such as abortion rights or same-sex marriage. The Supreme Court has over time taken to interpreting the American Constitution as if it were doing Biblical exegesis, with the Founding Fathers cast in the role of messianic oracles. Today's Republican Party is thus a far cry from what the party has at times been in the past. Indeed, Nixon, Goldwater, and even Reagan appear to be paragons of secular reason in comparison to the current crop of candidates.

Communitarian Christianity has also gone hand in hand with suspicion of the state, and with the concomitant rejection of even the most obvious welfare programmes: from childcare, to family planning, to socialized medicine more generally, to interest in a strong system of public education. The results are clear. While still boasting some of the most prestigious universities in the world, the standard of middle- and high-school education has noticeably deteriorated since the 1960s. Though life expectancy still rises slowly, so do rates of morbidity, chronic workplace illness, obesity, and related problems. The US political system today is incapable of addressing these purposefully, as shown by the regular deadlocks over the fiscal deficit.

Therefore, the roots of the crisis the US finds itself in today are not solely, or even largely, to be found in 'imperial overstretch', which has merely magnified the problems that are internal to the society and political system. Inevitably, the response of some on the right, namely isolationism, is based on mistaking a few of the symptoms for the malady. For the US economy is sufficiently entangled with the world economy—at the level of capital, labour, and commodities—to make any dreams of autarchy absurd. In many parts of the US, illegal and semi-legal work done by Latin American immigrants lies at the heart of key sectors of the economy. It is not merely a joke or exaggeration to suggest that, in the absence of such workers, the city of Los Angeles would come to a grinding halt.

It might be said therefore that the central consequence of 9/11 was to disorient the US. The Muslim population in the country had historically been small and not very prominent, and Islamophobia had been a far smaller issue than in Western Europe—with its greater proximity to the Arab world. The most significant wars the US had fought outside its borders in the nineteenth and twentieth centuries had been in Latin America, Europe, the Pacific, and then Korea and Vietnam. Muslims from any country, even the Philippine Moros, had not loomed large on the American mind as potential rivals. However, by 2004–5, surveys found that something like a quarter of Americans held strong anti-Islamic views. It is possible that some of this had been developing in the aftermath of the Iranian Revolution of the 1970s and the first Gulf War, and may even have some relationship to Black Muslim movements of the 1960s. There is, however, no doubt that this view has become deeply entrenched today, and is an essential determinant of the American view of the world.

The state of disorientation means that the US has not coped well in recent times with the two most significant challenges it faces outside its borders, namely its relations with Latin America and China. Religion, so to speak, has overwhelmed considerations of political economy. This is not the only instance in which the US has abandoned principles of realpolitik to pursue self-defeating policies: near-unconditional US political, diplomatic, military, and financial support for Israel—irrespective of that country's occupation of territories—is another instance. There too the principal arguments have a religious flavour to them, namely the support of a Judaeo–Christian alliance. In sum, contrary to what was asserted in the aftermath of 9/11, the principal clash that was seen then was not between tradition and modernity, or religion and secularism. Rather, the US was indeed attacked as a Christian power, and regrettably it has espoused that role with greater and greater alacrity.

The retreat of the secular in the US, from a situation where it was already fragile by the late twentieth century, has thus made of Samuel Huntington's clash of civilizations something of a self-fulfilling prophecy. To be sure, we cannot write the US off today. Nor is it likely that its decline will be as precipitous as was that of the USSR. There will be no territorial breakup. But if, as was stated by Henry Luce, the last century was the 'American century', we can be pretty certain that this will not be the case with this one. So when we look back on it after a few more decades, there is little doubt that 9/11 will still have symbolized the beginning of something significant.

17

'D. School' Days

In the early 1990s, as she was approaching the age of retirement, my former teacher Dharma Kumar decided to organize a volume of essays in which a variety of authors would reflect on their connection with the Delhi School of Economics. Contributors ranged from current and long-lost colleagues to students from the near and far distant past, and ran the gamut equally from bureaucrats and journalists to Nobel Prize-winners. I was asked to contribute an essay and did so somewhat reluctantly since, at the time, I was still teaching at 'D. School' and felt quite constrained by this fact. Some two decades later, having long since left the institution and taught in a variety of others, I feel happier coming back to the subject. Further, I do so in the knowledge that this great educational institution—one of the most significant in the social sciences in post-Independence India—could certainly do with a fuller acknowledgement of its role and place. So, even if this is a slightly irreverent essay in tone, my intentions are not at bottom entirely irreverent.

I came to the Delhi School of Economics and its Department of Economics in 1980, after three more-or-less frustrating and unhappy years doing a BA in Economics at St Stephen's College, diagonally across the road. The college had a significant but in my opinion largely undeserved reputation. To be sure, it had produced a vast number of civil servants, some journalists, and even some intellectuals, including historians and economists, but the atmosphere there was dominated by all-round philistinism and a deep current of anti-intellectual sentiment. Not long before I joined it women had begun to be admitted, but their presence had not dampened the college's most potent 'cultural' force, comprising macho jocks from the posh public schools of Delhi—St Columba's, Modern, Delhi Public School, and St Xavier's—and from the hills to the north. Some of these swaggering hearties were in fact intelligent people, but it was a point of honour for them to pretend not to be so. Few would be caught with a novel in their hands, unless it was pulp fiction, and they spent much time talking up the activities of the hiking club. They generally dressed in a kind of uniform consisting of imported Levi's and Wrangler jeans and carefully laundered full-sleeved designer shirts. Some of the women adopted the same apparel and claimed the same broad ambition, which, by 1980, was also uniform—to devote one's entire student life in an effort at joining one of the prestigious MBA programmes in the Indian institutes of management so as to land a cushy corporate job thereafter. The cachet of the civil services, once the chief ambition of graduates of the college, was now more or less on its way out because changes in the economy had opened up the corporate sector and made it seem more enticing than the bureaucracy. The quality of the teaching, with one or two honourable exceptions, was also remarkably poor, the teachers dictating notes they had been rattling out the previous ten years, complete with such instructions as 'take down, take down' and 'underline'. In these years I turned increasingly to music and literature as alternative pursuits, spent more time in a nearby men's hostel, Gwyer Hall, with musician friends, and eventually managed to obtain a decent set of marks in return for a rather half-hearted effort.

The Delhi School of Economics was thus an enormous relief.

Though by 1980 the institution had the reputation of being somewhat in decline in relation to its halcyon days over the 1960s and early 1970s, many of us soon discovered that the place still had a faculty which included active researchers who had sometimes made prominent contributions to the areas in which they taught. Some of these were fresh-faced youngsters with recent PhDs, barely eight or ten years older than us; others were veterans, or at least seemed so from the perspective of nineteen- and twenty-year-old eyes. The competition was from the other important economics department across town, in Jawaharlal Nehru University. In the narrative presented to us even by some of our undergraduate teachers, the opposition was on the one hand between a progressive, Marxist-oriented, and 'relevant' economics practised at JNU by such charismatic figures as Amit Bhaduri and Prabhat Patnaik, and on the other the mix of liberal, neo-classical, and generally ivory-tower views that D. School allegedly represented. This was of course far from being an accurate representation, but little matter. As a consequence, many of us hesitated long and hard between the two, and even attempted the entrance examination to JNU. Still, in the final analysis, given the choice between a more familiar space and a less familiar one, most of my undergraduate friends who did not depart town for the joys of an MBA joined D. School. In my case, there was a further complicating factor as my maternal uncle, J. Krishnamurty, a labour economist and economic historian, taught at D. School. As a result, I actually knew some of the junior faculty, having met them on social occasions in his home. Still, I do not think I was overly influenced in my choice by his presence there.

It became clear to me from the very first days of the MA programme in D. School that this was quite a different order of education than the farcical years at St Stephen's. A couple of courses, like statistics, were taught by professors who had a weighty international reputation, and others were put across with a degree of enthusiasm that was infectious. Naturally, this was not true across the board, and there were also some dreadful teachers and tutors to be found, some of whom could barely communicate intelligibly in any language. Whether it was their fault or mine, my grasp of macro-economics, rather poor from undergraduate days, did not improve a great deal, and the approach to the Indian economy remained curiously arcane and disembodied as well. Perhaps overly conscious of the alleged contrast with JNU, the professors in the area of development and current Indian problems tried to peddle their own party line to us, so that the readings seemed often to consist of confidential 'cyclostyled' notes rather than published work. But my interest was much caught by courses in two distinct areas: micro-economics, as taught by a young and charismatic London School of Economics graduate called Kaushik Basu; and economic history, taught by Om Prakash and Dharma Kumar. Basu's classroom delivery and organization were crystal clear and he also ran very entertaining tutorials where he set puzzle-style problems to be solved. He was particularly strong in areas that were close to his own research interests. The male students sometimes thought that his female fan-base was excessive and rather too enthusiastic, but there was nevertheless general agreement that he was an effective teacher. Unfortunately, he went on leave part of the way through the year and his substitute—a World Bank employee on leave, with an accent that teetered between Gurdaspur and Georgetown—left us feeling less than enthusiastic. Basu was also part of a group of younger faculty, which included Ashok Lahiri and the glamorous Prannoy Roy, later to become a media star, who were known as the Young Turks. They would frequently gather together outside the coffee-house, a shabby but welcoming restaurant of sorts run by the Indian Coffee Board which served bad coffee and worse food, and students would at times timidly join them in discussion.

But it was my interest in economic history which led me in the direction of a veritable treasure-house, the Ratan Tata Library at D. School. For it soon became clear that, rather than provide intelligent summaries of our class lectures, as we had done when undergraduates, in this institution one actually had to read in order to distinguish oneself. The readings included the odd textbook, but mostly a number of chapters from monographs as well as journal articles. These would be carried by us to the very primitive xerox facilities that were to be found behind the coffee-house, and we would then pore over them at leisure.

The contrast in style between the two economic historians was marked. Om Prakash was well-organized if somewhat rigid in his style, and also known for being a stern disciplinarian with a sarcastic laugh which he deployed to great effect in tutorials. Dharma, on the other hand, was as enthusiastic as she was chaotic, and would hand out enormous reading lists which were meant to give us a sense of the whole field rather than what was really to be read. She was also capable of recommending something she had caught sight of in the latest issue of a journal, without having read it carefully herself; this was apt to create confusion in our impressionable minds.

A year into the two-year Master's degree, I had become far more serious about academic life than I had ever been before. Lingering thoughts of a degree in comparative literature, which had been on my mind over the previous couple of years, vanished. Unlike my siblings, who had taken the regular family route into the civil service, I had begun to experience academics as something like a calling. The question was which part of economics would prove the most welcoming. As it happened, Kaushik Basu continued on leave and I was unable to take advanced courses with him. Most of the other options available at the time seemed unattractive, and so the decision to specialize in economic history and the history of economic thought came as the default.

The first of these brought me back in contact with familiar faces, and the latter to dealings with a rather curious figure, Khaliq Ahmad Naqvi. Naqvi belonged to a family of intellectuals from Uttar Pradesh and himself had some pretensions in that direction. (I later discovered that he was a relative by marriage of my friend Muzaffar Alam, now a professor of history at the University of Chicago, who knew him then as Husaini Uncle.) But his reading in the area of 'classical political economy' was by that time rather out-of-date, and he came across as less a scholar than a *bon viveur* with a fondness for Scotch and kababs. But I no longer needed encouragement to find my way to the library and was able to construct my own reading list on the basis of the rather rudimentary one he provided. Further, it was always possible to drop in more-or-less unannounced in the morning at the campus house of Sukhamoy Chakravarty, a near-mythical figure who was on the D. School faculty but who in fact taught very little. Chakravarty was known for his encyclopaedic grasp of the social sciences, and, so long as he took to you, could be immensely helpful. Both as a Master's student and thereafter my episodic contact with this rather enigmatic figure proved important to me in reshaping ideas, and also in opening the horizons of my reading. In later years, there is only one scholar whom I have met who has given me a similar impression of exceptional intellectual weight, Carlo Ginzburg.

But it was in the advanced economic history classes that my interest really bloomed. Freed of the constraints of textbooks, Om Prakash waxed enthusiastic about the history of Indian Ocean trade in the seventeenth and eighteenth centuries and the place in it of the Dutch East India Company, and within a few months I had decided this would be my field of research as well. This was a doubly unfashionable choice in comparison with those made by my classmates, such as Prajit Dutta and Ajit Mishra, who were inclined towards economic theory or econometrics. Then again, they were mostly bound for economics departments in the United States or the United Kingdom, and I was not sure of my destination.

In this phase of indecision, Dharma Kumar was a decisive influence. She was quite an Anglophile, having done both her undergraduate degree and her doctoral research in Cambridge. Something of a *grande dame*, she was often driven in to D. School in a Mercedes-Benz, and her posh lifestyle set her apart from the rest of the professors. Yet she turned out to harbour an unexpected nationalistic streak and was quite insistent about there being no need for me to seek out a doctoral programme abroad when a 'perfectly good one' (her phrase) existed in D. School itself. A decision was thus taken: if everything went well, I would be admitted directly into the doctoral programme and jointly supervised by Dharma Kumar and Om Prakash. For the rest, Dharma assured me, I could count on her. She would arrange for research funds and all else that I might need by way of facilities. By early 1983 I was duly appointed into a five-year contractual position as Research Associate in D. School, which allowed me to do some teaching and yet permitted me enough flexibility to pursue my own research.

But truth be told, the institutional situation in these years was far from idyllic. There was no 'programme' as such, only a couple of research students, each pursuing his or her own individual agenda. When the time came for me to begin to apply for funds to do research in the Netherlands, England, and Portugal, matters turned out to be far from simple. I applied to an organization called the Inlaks Foundation for a year's funding and was dismissed with a sneer by an ill-mannered Italian with an aristocratic name who made its decisions. More complicated still, I found myself caught in a murky power game between D. School and the university bureaucracy.

At this time a rather corrupt professor of library science—he was, for some reason, important on a variety of university committees—was attempting to get his dim-witted daughter admitted to D. School. He decided to use my case as leverage and threatened to prevent me getting a 'final' (rather than a 'provisional') registration in the PhD programme unless his daughter was accommodated. The situation was as ludicrous as it was shameful. On one occasion a couple of professors from my department, including Kaushik Basu, went off to visit the library scientist to make him see reason; he cast a lofty glance at my file and said to them that he thought economic history a useless subject anyway, the implication being that he would only be saving me from wasting my time. The tug-of-war went on for months together. By early 1984 I was very nearly at the end of my tether and beginning to give up hope of ever getting my research done. But then, all of a sudden, everything came together. I received two reasonable grants for archival research and also managed to get access to the office of the vice-chancellor of the university to plead my case. The library science professor's daughter got admission into a second-rate MBA programme and he decided to cease harassing D. School.

Behind all this was a profoundly uncomfortable lesson: it was clear to me at the end of this experience that the doctoral programme in D. School was of no real consequence to anyone. Most members of the faculty had done their own dissertations from Europe and the United States. There was also the question of the extent to which D. School counted within the university, and for the university's bureaucracy—which had done all it could to slow the progress of my research. After all this, when I submitted my thesis in 1986, it took them a further year to process it and have it examined, so that my degree as awarded dates to 1987. Little wonder, then, that at D. School the Master's programme has been seen by most as a terminal degree, after which further work is best pursued at other, distant institutions.

And yet my thesis years were not exactly times of misery. I became close to a number of my former teachers, including

Kaushik Basu and Ashok Lahiri, whom I could now think of as friends. A jovial and excitable econometrician, Ranjan Ray, joined from Manchester, and he, Kaushik, and I would sometimes hold small wine-tastings after-hours. In the absence of a proper community of research students I would often run ideas and projects by them, and even if they found them very exotic, they would give them a patient hearing. A young economic historian called Omkar Goswami, fresh from a doctorate in Oxford, also joined the faculty for a time, and he too was a ready interlocutor. Goswami had a theatrical personality with a booming voice, and a great desire to make an impression on students. But he was also a patient listener, and an ideal reader of draft thesis chapters. Not least, these were years when I came to have a keener appreciation of my anthropologist colleagues in what is known in D. School as the Department of Sociology. If as an MA student their work had sometimes seemed to me terribly exotic, the passage of the years and the effect of their conversations in the coffee-house was eventually to make me take in their approach to both social and cultural questions.

Still, when I look back to the 1980s or the early 1990s, when I taught economic history and economic development at D. School, there is something of a sense of wasted opportunity. This was epitomized in a way by Sukhamoy Chakravarty, who died in 1990 at the age of 56, without having realized even a small part of his intellectual potential. I wonder if, had he not wasted precious years within the Indian government (heading the Planning Commission), and instead devoted the time to productive conversations with his colleagues, D. School would have been a different place. Of course, the institution was strapped not just for elevated human resources but resources of every other kind as well. I recall colleagues having to find all sorts of complex ways and means merely to submit papers to journals abroad. In general, communications were a real problem, and each time you managed a simple telephone call the feelings of relief and exhilaration that ensued were of the variety experienced by climbers at high altitudes. There was barely a functioning toilet in the place, and the building had the air of being eternally in a state of imminent collapse. But the problem had ultimately less to do with resources than with institutional self-confidence and a proper institutional identity. Was D. School merely a finishing school for students heading for a graduate education abroad, or had it something else to offer? This remained the great unanswered question.

In retrospect, I cannot subscribe to the view that D. School had undergone a vast decline between the 1960s and the 1980s, a perspective based I feel on the excessive romanticization of a handful of teachers there. Nor do I think it was necessary for the institution to align itself to some form of Marxist orthodoxy in order to show its relevance to the Indian reality of the day. But the real conversations that existed there—however contentious they may often have been—between economic theorists, economic historians, and social anthropologists have often been difficult for those very participants to find again in other contexts. Only the odd concrete project properly reflects this atmosphere, such as a book that Kaushik Basu and I edited just after we had both left D. School, entitled *Unravelling the Nation* (1996). It seems at any rate that, like King Dushyanta in Kalidasa's *Sakuntala*, we were probably incapable of seeing the elephant when it stood there, right in front of us, and have only much later recognized traces of it in the footprints of time, long after it disappeared.

18

An Ambiguous Parisian

In the mid-1990s, when I was on the brink of first accepting a job teaching history in Paris, my friend and sometime mentor Jean Aubin wrote to me: 'We all look forward to the day when you will become Parisian.' I noticed he did not say 'French' but rather 'Parisian', and thought he did so deliberately, for neither he nor anyone else at the time expected me to change my citizenship or national loyalties.

Aubin knew something about living across and between cultures. In the 1950s, as a young researcher, he had spent a great deal of time in Iran and knew both West Asia and Central Asia well, whether through texts or lived experiences. And yet he remained very French—even a bit *vieille France*, some would say—in terms of his speech, comportment, and above all writing style. By the time I first met him, in the late 1980s, he was around 60 and had taken to living a deliberately archaic lifestyle in a country house not far from Angers in the west of France. He visited Paris only when he had to teach, and often made a day trip there on a train through the Gare de Montparnasse. He confessed to me that he usually found Paris tiring even on the few occasions that he spent the night there in a hotel. At the same time he acknowledged that a younger man like me was not about to come to France to live in the countryside, but because of the attraction of the big city. It is my attraction—a very ambiguous attraction—for Paris which I now recall. The somewhat peculiar way in which I experienced the city seems worth recording.

I first visited Paris for a month in May 1988. It was at Aubin's invitation, and I came there after having spent time doing research in both Portugal and the Netherlands, which had served as my introduction to Europe. My first impression of Paris was for this reason a strange one—I saw the place as a larger and distorted version of Lisbon. I was driven by an obliging graduate student called Laurent from the airport to the Cité Universitaire, where I was given rooms in the Maison Franco-Britannique. Located in a relatively deserted part of the 14th *arrondissement* near the Parc Montsouris, this was a quite unpromising beginning to the city. Even if the area was calm, the Maison itself was not. Being the month of May, it was full of visiting undergraduates from abroad who came back drunk at all odd hours of the night and made an infernal noise. After three sleepless nights of this I decided to move out. But my budget was quite limited, as were my options. I eventually settled for a small hotel run by Algerians near the Oberkampf metro station, not far from the Place de la République. It was a rather curious place, with only a flimsy curtain separating the main room from the bathroom—a condition of domestic architecture not uncommon in France, and which seems not to strike the locals as abnormal, but the cause of deep unease in an Indian accustomed to believing in this part of his house as, quite literally, his privy. That apart, overall the effect was just the opposite of where I had been: the hotel was quiet, but the area around was really very lively.

From my base at Oberkampf I set out to explore the city day after day. During the week, besides giving lectures and seminars, I plumbed the Bibliothèque Nationale and other libraries. In the evenings and on weekends I took the metro everywhere, discovering amongst other things that Paris had a secret life to it if one spoke Portuguese. This was of particular use to me because my French was quite elementary at this point, the result of a hasty course I had taken in Philadelphia while visiting there to teach. The Portuguese in the city were often to be found running restaurants and cafés, besides a number—of less use to me at the time—who worked as building concierges and in the construction business. I cannot overstate the number of times the Portuguese connection served me well in Paris. Once, while taking a taxi in the early hours of the morning to the airport, I dropped my wallet on the back seat while stepping out. The wallet contained not only money and credit cards, but also my precious *carte de résident*, the French equivalent of the American green card. When, at the point of clearing security at the airport, I found the wallet was lost, I panicked and rushed home. But a few hours later, the taxi driver called. She had found the wallet with a phone number in it and remembered me because we had talked Portuguese on the way, which in turn had happened because she was listening to a Portuguese radio station at the end of her night-long stint. The next morning I recovered the wallet from her and, despite the shortness of our camaraderie, she absolutely refused every offer of a reward.

Paris today is very much an immigrant's city, but the Portuguese are no longer at the cutting edge of immigration, as they were in the 1960s. That role has passed on to West Africans, Maghrebins, Serbs, and increasingly South Asians. It has been an immigrant's city of course for a long time, even though the immigrants in question were once Russian Jews or Italians. This is a fact that is apparently difficult for many foreign visitors to accept, and cinéastes like Woody Allen persist, in movies like *Midnight in Paris*, in producing a painfully clichéd vision of the city within which none of these populations exist: there are only the 'real French' (or *français de souche*). Such visitors are looking for something mysterious and exotic called 'Frenchness', the quest being a pastime that has long preoccupied both the

British and the Americans. I have lost count of the number of Americans, from Hemingway to Jacqueline Kennedy Onassis, who have written memoirs of Paris, not to speak of those who have written books about those memoirs. They mostly ring a bit false, as do the columns regularly written by Americans for the *International Herald Tribune* with ludicrously improbable recipes for *bouillabaisse*, or advice on the most 'hot' and fashionable *boulangeries* in the Marais district, or whatever it is that has temporarily taken their fancy.

Celebrating Paris in these ways, or offering yet another paean to the gastronomic wonders of the City of Lights, seems less interesting than reflecting on what struck me as its quirks and oddities, things that made life there harder rather than easier. Having lived in the Parisian suburbs (the 91 area, that is, the Essonne), then in the 13th *arrondissement*, and finally for an extended stretch in the 5th—which is ostensibly a more chic address but not without its own complications—a certain amount of hard-won experience lies behind what I say. This experience is what makes of me, as Aubin predicted a couple of decades ago, a Parisian as much as a native of Delhi—but an ambiguous Parisian all the same.

Paris in 1988 was, as it is now, very much a city both of and for North Africans or Maghrebins. A survey some years ago claimed that the dish Parisians ate when they went out more than any other was *cous-cous*, and this rings very true. The area where I lived in 1988 near Oberkampf and République had its fair share of this North African population. They mainly ran restaurants and cafés, and a large number of them frequented an extensive and busy store—devoted mostly to discounted clothes (what people rudely called *la fringue pas chère*)—with the name of Tati. Created in 1948 by an entrepreneur called Jules Ouaki who had migrated from Tunisia to France, the store had initially been based further north, near Barbès, but then opened its République branch in 1978 (it eventually closed in

2002). The store was also favoured, as it happened, by Indian academic visitors who were in Paris for a month in the 1980s and 1990s and needed to buy cheap 'made-in-Paris' clothes as gifts to take back home.

Soon after arriving in Paris I was told a version of a common urban legend by my graduate student interlocutor Laurent who himself lived on boulevard Voltaire, not far from Oberkampf. Emerging from the metro near home one day, his wallet was deftly stolen from his back pocket. As it happened, Laurent, who was married to a rather striking Franco-Algerian woman, had his father-in-law visiting him for the day. When he reported the incident, the father-in-law strolled out, walked up to Tati, and after an hour or two of conversation was not only able to locate the pickpocket but have him return the wallet. I was perplexed by the layers in this story when I first heard it. On the one hand it displayed a certain sort of anti-Maghrebin prejudice, but on the other it suggested the existence of a sort of moral economy which people seemed to regard as quite admirable in its own way. It also became a part of a running theme for me in Paris—the very odd attitudes that many people there had towards criminals and criminality.

An episode still much in the news in the late 1980s encapsulated a part of this quite effectively. This was the rather strange case of a certain Michel Vaujour, who had served a series of prison terms for crimes ranging from car theft to armed robbery, and who also had an extended track record for escapes. Vaujour—a man with a certain charm and gift of the gab—had married the sister of one of his friends, had a child with her, and, after he was once again arrested and sentenced for one of his numerous acts, had convinced her that it was psychologically impossible for him to serve out a term in the highly-guarded Santé prison in the 14th *arrondissement*. So persuaded was she that Nadine Vaujour eventually carried out a rather spectacular operation: she learnt to pilot helicopters, rented one in Yvelines on 26th May

1986, flew down to the 14th, and managed a difficult stationary manoeuvre over the prison roof which allowed her husband, brandishing a fake revolver, to clamber up a rope ladder to join her. She then landed the aircraft in the nearby Cité Universitaire and they both made off successfully, leaving the city's public stupefied with admiration.

A friend of mine who was teaching in the nearby Ecole de Télécom remembers the day quite clearly, and how people in the area came out to look, startled by the sound of the helicopter so close overhead. After his escape Vaujour went back to his criminal ways, was shot in the head by the police, stayed semi-paralysed for a time, and split up with his wife. Back in prison he attempted to persuade his next female companion—Jamila by name and a budding lawyer by profession—to repeat the helicopter stunt. Unluckily for him, by this time the authorities had taken the precaution of covering most prison yards with wire netting.

Nadine Vaujour eventually wrote a book that was made into a film, *La fille de l'air* (1992), starring Béatrice Dalle. In recent times her husband, released after some twenty-seven years behind bars, has become quite the media star, referred to in one newspaper account as 'a cross between Houdini and a yogi philosopher'. The assiduous trawler of websites can even find some interviews in which he answers questions from admiring interlocutors regarding the true nature of happiness, the meaning of life, and suchlike, based on a combination of his practice of yoga and his childhood affinity—if he may be believed—for Catholic mysticism.

We can track an episode such as this and its significance both backward and forward in terms of its resonances in Parisian culture. For the Vaujour affair took place less than a decade after the flamboyant end to the career of post-war France's best-known criminal, Jacques Mesrine, mowed down in the midst of traffic at the Porte de Clignancourt in his BMW 528i by a fusillade of some twenty-odd police bullets on the afternoon of 2nd November 1979. Mesrine's criminal career had some odd parallels with that of Vaujour, including his penchant for spectacular escapes, such as one from the very same prison, Santé. But Mesrine's activities ranged farther afield, even as far as Quebec, and were far more violent, running from casino holdups to kidnapping to torturing a journalist to outright and cold-blooded killings. He tended to exaggerate their number and nature, saying he had mainly done in rather a lot of elevated 'pimps'. There was also a more complex political subtext to it all, perhaps relating to an earlier period when Mesrine was active (as compared to Vaujour). He had served as a paratrooper in Algeria and been decorated there, but also alleged that he had been obliged to perform a number of dirty tasks by the state, such as summarily shooting Algerian prisoners. After briefly joining a right-wing fringe outfit called the OAS (Organisation de l'armée secrète), Mesrine had then turned by the 1960s to various forms of violent crime. Aided by a considerable talent for self-promotion and a certain complicity on the part of the media, he managed to transform himself into a spectacular figure, an official 'Public Enemy Number One' who even directly threatened prominent politicians and judges.

By the later years of his career Mesrine had also begun to exploit the political potential of his image, claiming to be a sort of primitive rebel standing up against the system. His acquaintance with a number of far-left figures in prison seems to have helped him refine his rhetoric, as we see from a cult book that he produced while incarcerated, *L'instinct de mort* (1977). In his last years he transformed himself into a sort of Foucauldian activist against the conditions experienced within French prisons of the time, notably in the Quartiers d'haute sécurité (or QHS), where radical solitary confinement and other extreme practices prevailed. For here, in those very years, as one of his fellow prisoners was to recall in a television documentary, bandits and kidnappers found themselves cheek by jowl with sophisticated theorists of the revolution and were informed by the latter that they were all conjointly part of *le même combat*.

Mesrine's claims went very far by this time, even to the point—ironical in his case—of boasting about dealings in the mid-1970s with 'revolutionary movements in Algeria'. Journalists for the newspaper *Libération* wistfully compared his actions with those of the Red Brigades in Italy; several of his neighbours declared that, even had they known who he was, they would never have denounced him to the police; and by the end of 1978 some French magazines were even considering him 'Person of the Year'. The number of women he attracted, including his own female lawyers, was not inconsiderable either, suggesting that the Mesrine phenomenon had unsuspected social dimensions. The fact that the leading actors and publicists of the two-part film *Mesrine* (2008), by Jean-François Richet, went strenuously out of their way to assert that he was by no means a hero to them was also rather telling in its own way.

We can also follow this story forward into the mid-1990s, which was when I moved to Paris to settle there for some considerable time. The year I was offered a position there, 1994, was when another incident took place that recalled Vaujour and, especially, Mesrine. This concerned two students living in a squat in Nanterre, Audry Maupin and Florence Rey, the former in his early twenties and the latter in her late teens. After desultory readings in anarchist philosophy, the two embarked on a strange enterprise on the evening of 4th October 1994. They began by attacking a police car impound with teargas canisters and seizing arms carried by a couple of policemen on duty. Then, in a state of panic, they hijacked a taxi at the Porte de Pantin, compelling the Guinean driver to enter Paris. At the crowded Place de la Nation the taxi-driver attempted to escape them by colliding with a police car. In the ensuing confusion—even at 9.30 p.m. Nation is a busy intersection—shots were exchanged and several policemen as well as the taxi-driver were shot dead. The couple then hijacked another car and drove off towards Vincennes, where they shot yet another policeman—he had been following them on a motorcycle. Finally, they were trapped and, despite Maupin's apparent wish to surrender, he was shot and succumbed to his wounds. Florence Rey stood trial. In 1998 she was condemned to twenty years in prison instead of the thirty years the prosecution had demanded. In May 2009 she was released on grounds of good behaviour and reformed conduct.

A part of the French press had taken to calling this duo the new Bonnie & Clyde, a term that had already been used for Mesrine and his girlfriend when he was in Quebec. The reference was not so much to the real Bonnie Parker and Clyde Barrow, the notorious Depression-era Texans in their mid-twenties who had carried out a series of petty robberies at gas stations, banks, and stores before being brought down by a hail of police bullets in Louisiana in 1934. Had the parallel been properly established, it might have been noted that, for a certain time, Florence Rey, like Bonnie Parker, had been thought of as an exemplary student who possessed some literary talent and wrote poetry. But in fact the allusion was to the cynical chic of the 1967 film *Bonnie and Clyde*, with Warren Beatty and Faye Dunaway, and—even more important than that from the French viewpoint—the song that Serge Gainsbourg wrote and recorded later that same year with Brigitte Bardot (where it is unclear which of the two is the less capable of carrying a tune). Besides, Bonnie and Clyde had been known as 'cop-killers', an epithet also used in this instance, though Florence Rey's defence team insisted that all the killing had been done by Maupin and none by her. This became one of the central points at the trial, in which the driver of the second hijacked car testified that she had fired the guns herself, and also explicitly encouraged Maupin, for example, to kill the motorcyle policeman. The public image of Rey emerged, consequently, in an oddly fragmented manner. If one part of the press saw her as little more than a misguided schoolgirl who had fallen under the influence of a dominant male personality, but who even in prison read William Blake and participated in a theatrical production of Shakespeare's *Richard III* (an odd choice, one might have thought), another linked her and Maupin variously to 'autonomist' movements that drew on anarchist thought, to the heritage of 'political bandits' such as Mesrine, and to the consumption of recent films of a highly violent variety such as Luc Besson's *Nikita* or Oliver Stone's *Natural-Born Killers*.

Living in Paris in the latter half of the 1990s, this story, and its aftermath in the form of the trial, was impossible to escape. What struck me most was the degree of sympathy for the couple, who were celebrated by a number of radical singers and stage performers, and even by a prize-winning writer well known for his provocative postures. In a television documentary it was amazing to hear one of those who had been caught in the crossfire on the Place de la Nation declare that his main thought at the time was: 'Why don't I have a girlfriend like this?' Not much was ever said about Amadou Diallo, the Guinean migrant who, having moved to France in the 1970s, found himself driving a taxi on the wrong day in the wrong place. Including him in the list of victims made matters too complex morally; it was far simpler to narrate this as a straightforward cops-*vs*-bandits affair, or a case of anarchists resisting the oppressive forces of the state. Indeed, from a certain left-wing standpoint, the moral position of Maupin and Rey was largely impeccable: not only had they read Bakunin, they were also activists against the right-wing Front National.

A part of this sympathy was undoubtedly the unfinished business of May 1968. By the late 1990s, even though those events were some three decades old, the spectre of failed revolution—or whatever May 1968 can be classified as being—was still on many Parisians' mind. Though for some categories of people it did not seem to matter very much—notably those either too young to remember it or too old to have been affected by it, and also many migrants who did not see it as having much meaning in their lives—in the academic milieu that I frequented the subject was all too present in one fashion or another. This was because there were in that mix quite a few Maoists, whether disillusioned or those who still clung to some form of the ideology, as well as many who saw themselves as fellow-travellers of the 1968 movement. In similar vein there was a substantial presence of former 1968-ers (or *soixante-huitards*) in the ranks of journalists, notably in newspapers like *Libération*, but also in *Le Monde* which reported on the matter.

Years later, while attending a literary festival at Saint-Malo in the context of the publication of one of my books in French, I was struck by how much the solidarities forged in the context of groups like Gauche prolétarienne continued to function even forty years later. Certain politicians, high officials, influential journalists, and literary figures would all refer back to those times with nostalgia, even though their party affiliations had long since shifted. There was a real desire amongst such people to see these kinds of violent acts as a form of social banditry, and I suspect that there was even a sense of regret that France had not had its proper equivalent of Italy's Red Brigades, or Germany's Red Army Faction, or some of the more extreme Japanese groupuscules. This is not to say that there was no soul-searching at all, especially since many of those of whom I am speaking had in the intervening decades made the transition into successful, and even at times highly prosperous, careers.

I recall one particular case of a Maoist who had become one, in part as a rebellion against his parents who were hard-core members of the French Communist Party. Ebullient and garrulous, Luc (let us call him that) was a great connoisseur of French popular music, of which he had a considerable repertoire. When in his cups he would sing songs like Boris Vian's *Le Déserteur* and reminisce about the time he had spent in jail,

at which time as an *établi*—a Maoist agitator sent to work
after 1968 in the factories—he had been framed on trumped-
up charges. What was remarkable about him, whether in his
public pronouncements or his rather tumultuous personal life,
was his great sense of moral certitude. There was one moment,
though, when I saw his confidence somewhat shaken. This was
after a meeting late in the 1990s with the celebrated Benny
Lévy, a figure whom he, like so many others, had looked up
to in the context of 1968 and had known very well indeed.
Lévy, who died not long after this meeting in 2003, had
been a brilliant student at the Ecole Normale Supérieure,
and was known in Maoist circles and beyond as a charismatic
speaker and theoretician. After taking various initiatives in the
1970s, including helping to found the newspaper *Libération*,
he eventually became secretary to Jean-Paul Sartre in the
philosopher's declining years. In this role he became increasingly
controversial and fell afoul of several of Sartre's close associates,
including Simone de Beauvoir. She accused him of manipulating
the writings and pronouncements of her companion who, by
then, was physically quite incapacitated. The manipulation, she
said, included taking Sartre towards more and more pro-Israeli
positions, a fact commented on rather sarcastically by Edward
Said, who had occasion to meet them both in the 1970s. By the
1980s Lévy openly claimed that he had moved from 'Mao to
Moses' and embraced Orthodox Judaism, becoming part of an
increasingly conservative milieu. It was roughly at the moment
when he eventually emigrated to Israel that Luc met him. He was
shocked not only by what had become of the political opinions
of his comrade, but also by the fact that Lévy's young daughter
would not even speak to him until she had ascertained if he
was indeed Jewish—which Luc was, as a matter of fact. All of a
sudden it seemed as if the old solidarities meant nothing at all
in view of the new ones.

Lévy's death a few years later was the occasion for a widely-attended public meeting at the Mutualité, not far from where I lived. It was one of those occasions which could produce the illusion that what Paris was all about was a lively collective existence, something like the great winter transport strike of 1995 against the Alain Juppé government, when I, like thousands of others, had tramped the snow-clad pavements of the city to work and back. To be sure, the meeting at the Mutualité did not quite attain the dimensions of Sartre's funeral in 1980, which tens of thousands attended. But this fondness for public *manifestations*, a recurrent Parisian feature that regularly disrupts traffic, is in my view a mask for a real paradox—the disastrous lack of civic spirit and real solidarity in the city. There is a disquieting sense in which those who applaud the glamorous bandits and jail-breakers represent the spirit of a city in which everyone seems to live for himself or herself, justifying this by the common French claim: 'Well, I pay my taxes' (*Moi, je paye mes impôts*).

A striking example of this came during the disastrously hot summer peak (or *canicule*) of August 2003, when, as is usual at that time of year, younger and able-bodied Parisians had left the city for their vacations, leaving the place abandoned to tourists and the elderly. By the time they returned, the heat had claimed over a thousand lives by way of excess mortality, mostly of the elderly, especially those living alone. The peculiar conditions of the *canicule* also revealed the disquieting fact—this I heard on the radio France Info—that several Parisians kept illegal and exotic pets such as pythons in their apartments, at least one of which smashed open a window and went to forage for food in a neighbouring flat. Its owner had paid his taxes too.

While my next couple of examples with regard to the tension between the discourse of collective solidarity and the reality of runaway individualism will strike a lighter note, the bitter truth of experience underlies them nonetheless. The Parisian neighbour is an excellent example of the rampant individualism that characterizes the city. Typically, he is utterly unconcerned by how much noise emanates from his apartment, and oblivious of the effect of his lack of consideration on his neighbours. Parisians who are chain-smokers will blithely lean out of the window in the summer months so that their smoke wafts systematically up into your apartment. I once lived not far from Censier and Jussieu, two of the universities in central Paris, and the flat above mine had a steady turnover of rich kids. They would play techno music until the early hours of the morning, causing the whole building to shake with bass vibrations. It was only when I pointed out to them that the police might be interested in what they were smoking that I obtained a temporary ceasefire. The Parisian neighbour seemed to me to have taken a leaf out of Rousseau's book: since he loved humanity—in the form of social bandits, for example—he felt justified in his contempt for the fellow human being who lived below or above his flat. Another particularly noisy upstairs neighbour, who was eventually given the nickname Heffalump, once responded to complaints by saying that she had 'her life to live', and that my objections to her noise were nothing but a form of 'harassment', an infringement of her freedoms.

But it is in their relations with dogs that Parisians most come out in their true colours. Since most of the city's inhabitants live in flats and not houses, and since these flats are often rather small, it has always been a matter of considerable astonishment to me that so many of them have dogs. These dogs are, naturally, adored by their owners, and the devotion seems to flow horizontally across the boulevards, so that it is not uncommon to see them being caressed and petted by perfect strangers in passing. The tolerance for them in restaurants can be startling, and I have heard more than one story of a dog snatching food from a plate at a neighbouring table while its owner shrugged his or her shoulders. It must be more than a Brahminical residue in me that causes me to find this quite appalling. It turns out that of about eight million dogs in France, roughly a third are to be found in the greater Paris region, and 150,000 to 200,000 within the city proper. In other words, one household in six owns a dog, and the greatest intensity of ownership may be found in the 4th, 8th, and 16th *arrondissements*. While even two decades ago the ownership was largely a bourgeois phenomenon in the city, it has now been 'democratized', making it not uncommon to see young men from a more humble background owning and aggressively presenting their dogs in a show of competitive machismo. (Interestingly, whatever its significance, the popular French slang word for dog is *clebs* or *clébard*, from the Arabic *kalb*.) The central problem that all this presents—not in itself, but on account of Parisian attitudes—is of pavements and streets that are almost everywhere filthy with dog faeces, a side of Paris that Woody Allen's cameras do not choose to capture. Despite the considerable fines that exist in theory, rare is the Parisian dog-owner troubled by the law. The fact that the same pavements are toddled on by toddlers seems not to interest Parisians either. A superb form of 'I'm-all-right-Jack' individualism decrees that this is a collective problem and not an individual one, so that the city of Paris spends 7.5 million euros a year to address it—with rather limited success. When Jacques Chirac was mayor of Paris he went so far as to introduce a system by which a legion of city employees went about on mopeds with portable vacuum cleaners to deal with canine contributions to the streets. These machines, derisively termed *chiraclettes*—a portmanteau word combining Chirac and *raclettes* (a dish made from scraping cheese)—have long disappeared, but the problem remains. And Parisians, for their part, continue to visit Berlin, Lisbon, Madrid, and London without wondering how these other capitals miraculously keep their pavements clean.

Every summer, along with millions of other visitors, thousands of students from universities like mine in Los Angeles descend on Paris. Those that are somewhat literate may find their way to the Closerie des Lilas in search of the ghosts of Hemingway or Fitzgerald; or to the Père Lachaise cemetery in search of a celebrity tomb. Increasingly, they are joined by a new phenomenon: the well-heeled Indian tourist who has little or nothing to do with the Indian, Pakistani, Sri Lankan, and Bangladeshi working-class migrants settled already in Paris by the 1990s. These young migrants can be found working in the kitchens of a variety of restaurants, or selling trinkets in markets, or running convenience stores. Not long after Princess Diana was killed in a car crash near the Pont de l'Alma in 1997, it was they who kept alive a sort of small cult near the spot, with flowers and posters of her visiting Pakistan with Imran Khan. They are nowhere near as integrated as the Maghrebins, or even the Portuguese—amongst whom some have even become supporters of the xenophobic Front National, militants against African immigration to France.

The wheel always turns in a great city like Paris, which is why, in spite of all complaints, it is so easy to become, and then remain, a Parisian: an ambiguous one, of course.

19

A Lisbon Summer

I first came to Lisbon as a penurious doctoral student in the spring of 1985, after a particularly brutal winter spent in the Netherlands working in the archives of the Dutch East India Company. I had stayed in the windy suburb of Scheveningen north of The Hague, and it had been a difficult business forcing myself out every morning, during that freezingly cold and dark winter, to take the tram across snowed-in streets and down to the Centraal Station next to which the archives were located. The time and money I had on my hands were limited, and the archives were copious, so that the only solution was literally a nine-to-five routine of all work and practically no play. After some months of this I had some notion of what it felt like to be a Calvinist. Lisbon promised to be something else, even though I only had the vaguest notions beforehand of the city itself and its topography. Of its history and that of Portugal I was somewhat better informed, thanks above all to an elderly Brazilian called José Leal Ferreira (Jr), who taught Portuguese at the Jawaharlal Nehru University in New Delhi. Ferreira had stumbled into language teaching after a career as a diplomat and then more briefly as a journalist; when the military seized power in Brazil in April 1964 from President João Goulart, he, like many others, had been summarily dismissed from the diplomatic service and decided to make his home in India where he had been a diplomat. I had gone to see Ferreira in the summer of 1982 on the recommendation of a few historians in Delhi who had heard he was the only person who taught the sort of Portuguese relevant for historical research. He lived then in a cramped *barsati* flat in Sarvapriya Vihar, and agreed without any hesitation to begin teaching me on an individual basis and without any fees or other recompense. I eventually enrolled later that year for a course with him in JNU, but our specialized classes continued, sometimes involving another student who was working on a historical subject as well.

Senhor Ferreira's ideas of language instruction were eccentric but effective in their own way. He was old-fashioned, refined, and polite to the point of being precious at times. He was also an avid Francophile who would spend hours every week looking for French films in the various cine-clubs of the city. His historical references and readings largely came from the 1930s and 1940s, when he had been at high school and the university. From the very beginning his idea was to drill me (and his other students) in formal grammatical structures and then in composition and translation. He would type out long passages, first from modern authors, and then from the sixteenth- and seventeenth-century chroniclers, on his typewriter, and we would pore over them; but as for spoken Portuguese, we barely exchanged a few phrases at the beginning and end of each lesson. Still, thanks to this mode of functioning I had begun reading printed Portuguese documents on my own at the Jesuit Vidya Jyoti library in Old Delhi, and then by the early months of 1984 was able to make a profitable trip to the archives in Goa. And yet I had neither the desire nor the confidence to put together two sentences of conversational Portuguese.

This made me somewhat nervous about dealing with Lisbon, where I knew few people other than a handful of Portuguese historians I had met while in Goa. So it was a godsend when, one day in the archives in The Hague, I ran into a young Dutch scholar who said he was doing research in Lisbon too and could find me cheap and comfortable accommodation where he was staying. I accepted his offer with alacrity; it was agreed that Jan Jakob would arrange a room for me in Avenida Elias Garcia for the three months I intended to stay in Lisbon.

So, some months later, I arrived on a bright March afternoon in Lisbon from London, and on taking a taxi in from the airport found myself faced with the task of carrying my suitcase up five flights of stairs to the room I was to stay in. Everything about Lisbon seemed a little rundown and grimy, but quite charming in its own way. The prices were strikingly low after northern Europe, as I had noticed already from the taxi fare. And the room rent was simply astonishing, just a small fraction of even the far-from-generous stipend I had been given by the Indian Council for Social Science Research.

Living arrangements in the Elias Garcia flat were complicated. It was enormous, with six bedrooms, three or four bathrooms (I was never exactly clear on how many), a salon, a large dining room, and a kitchen. Our live-in landlords were Raul and Alexandrina, he a bandy-legged, sickly, seventy-something man of few words, and she a voluble and hard-working forty-something woman, who was really in charge of the whole affair. After a few weeks their story became clear: she had been a nurse of sorts who had taken care of his dying wife and then married him; the flat was in fact rented by them from someone at a ridiculously low price determined by an archaic law, and they then made money by subletting. The sublets were three rooms in a row along a corridor, and then two others at the back of the house. The last two were occupied by two widowed old ladies with whom I exchanged just a few sentences over the months I was there (usually while they were groaning their way up the five flights), and who still wore the traditional black of their tribe. As for the first three rooms—the better ones I suppose—they were taken by Jan Jakob, myself, and a suave Portuguese MBA student called João Pedro whose parents lived in Oporto, where he usually left for the weekends. We shared a bathroom and toilet between these three rooms, but the arrangement was just for room and not board.

There was however an unusual feature: Alexandrina agreed to do our laundry, and these items would be placed neatly on our beds every few days, washed and pressed down to the last undershirt and pair of socks. I was impressed, as I had never seen, let alone worn, an ironed pair of socks. Once in a while, when she was in a good mood, she would bring João Pedro and myself coffee and a roll for breakfast. In the evenings she and Raul would also invite us and the taciturn old ladies after dinner to watch the Brazilian soap-opera (or *telenovela*) which was quite the rage in Portugal those days: this was *A Sucessora* (1978), based on a novel by Carolina Nabuco. It had a plot suspiciously similar to that of Daphne du Maurier's book, *Rebecca*, which had appeared later. Nabuco and du Maurier had in fact been involved in a slanging match on the question, a fact of which I was unaware in 1985.

The day after I arrived, we went down early for breakfast to one of the nearby bars which doubled as coffee-shops. This was on the cross-street called 5 de Outubro, the 5th of October, on which I was to spend a lot of time. We were joined by an African historian—from Tanzania, if I recall right—who had been the previous occupant of my room in Elias Garcia, and was now on his way back home after having spent a year doing research in Lisbon on Portuguese Africa. The first linguistic experience in a public place was overwhelming. This language sounded nothing like the few musical phrases I periodically exchanged with Senhor Ferreira with his quaint 1940s Rio de Janeiro accent, full of sounds like *ji* and *chi* which did not seem to exist in Lisbon. It was rapidfire, quite guttural, and the words seemed to be radically truncated. It sounded rather more like Russian than Spanish. I learnt quickly that there were many words for coffee, and that few of them were actually *café*. There was *bica*, meaning a short black espresso-style coffee; or *galão*, which was coffee in a glass with a lot of milk; or even *cimbalino*, a more obscure usage deriving from the brand of the Italian machines. Accompanying them at breakfast was the *coração*, a soggy Portuguese version of the croissant, often with ham and cheese. Bolder eaters could take their pick of various breaded and fried products, or a roll with a piece of fried egg inserted in it. All this was eaten standing at a counter, where one rubbed elbows with shopgirls and suited men on their way to work in one of a vast variety of banks, or with workmen from nearby construction sites in their paint-splashed overalls—who were by then on their first break, and accompanied their *bicas* already with sizeable *bagaços*, the potent white or pale-yellow 'fire-water' (or *aguardente*) that was designed to take the top of your head off. The exchanges flew by fast, far too rapidly for my poor comprehension. I only remember one, when the pretty young waitress asked our African friend whether there was anything else he wanted, and he flirtatiously replied '*Só um sorriso*' (just a smile). It's funny what sticks in your mind.

Elias Garcia was not part of a posh neighbourhood, but it was very well located. A few minutes away was the Calouste Gulbenkian Centre, a strange modernist building surrounded by walls like a fortress, which was the unofficial Ministry of Culture. Gulbenkian was an Armenian from Scutari who had settled in Lisbon in 1942 after a long and chequered career, and who until his death in 1955 had put his substantial resources—deriving from the petroleum industry—to use in Portugal, where his foundation still ran several museums, an orchestra, and paid for research on Portuguese history both by nationals and foreigners. Also close at hand was the Universidade Nova de Lisboa, the new university that had emerged after the 'Carnation Revolution' of 1974 to challenge the hegemony of the other university, which people called the *clássica*. A primitive metro system existed by the time I visited, and my nearest station was Campo Pequeno, named for the bullfighting ring just round the corner. It took you on the one hand towards the old university, and on the other hand towards the *baixa*, or downtown, including the Restauradores area where one could make long-distance international calls from the post office. The other nearby attraction from Elias Garcia was the Parque Eduardo VII, named after Queen Victoria's dissolute son and heir; it had a splendid view over the downtown and onto the Tagus estuary, but was reputed to be dangerous since by late evening it was full of drug dealers and addicts. The downtown itself, and the area around Restauradores especially, was also quite seedy; even though it was favoured by English tourists looking for grilled fish and roast chicken, by dusk prostitutes were to be seen standing in the doorways of many buildings.

I barely had time to take any of this in over the first few days. Rather, I at once began to frequent the archives, initially lulled into illusions by my experiences in the hyper-efficient archives of The Hague. Aided by a hard-won *passe social*, a travel-pass with a photo that required some patience to acquire, Lisbon's buses took the place for me of the trams of The Hague. But I quickly realized that the Dutch archives had no relation with those in Lisbon. The Biblioteca Nacional, near the Universidade Clássica, was the easiest for me, and also the closest in terms of access. But its catalogues were poor, and the materials seemed of limited relevance for me at the time. So I decided to attack the two major archives: the National Archives (or Torre do Tombo), located in a wing of the Parliament building, the Palácio de São Bento; and the Overseas Historical Archive, located even farther out from my point of view in the Junqueira area.

Each of these had its own problems. The Torre do Tombo opened at 10.30 and only had twenty places in its reading room. You had therefore to show up before 10, take a brass token (or *chapa*, a familiar word for an Indian), and twiddle your thumbs or drink coffee until the doors opened. When there was a rush you had to arrive as early as 9.30. The Overseas Archive only opened at 1.30 p.m. and had a single large table around which researchers sat, trying to ignore the noisy and disruptive conversations between quarrelsome staff members until the archive closed around 7 p.m. I had initially hoped that Jan Jakob, with what I imagined was his deep experience in the archives, would help me find my feet, but he proved to be quite reluctant to accompany me. The archivists and staff, faced with my questions in English, responded rarely, and when they did it was with little enthusiasm. Everywhere, it seemed, there was little by way of catalogues. Moreover, the archivists—usually elderly women dressed in what looked like grey uniform lab coats over their street clothes—found it hard to believe that someone who could not speak Portuguese could actually read the language, and that too in its somewhat archaic forms and scripts.

After a week or so of this I was frankly in a state of panic. These archives were totally opaque and my prospects seemed hopeless. I then began thinking of the few contacts and telephone numbers in Portugal I had gathered when in Goa, or heard of in Delhi. Only one stood out: that of a small, bearded, Portuguese historian in his forties, who in Goa had patiently answered some of my questions and even given me a few bibliographical leads which I had followed assiduously. I called him several times and received no useful response because the old lady at the other end of the line, apparently his mother, could not really understand my English. Finally, one evening Senhor Thomaz picked up the telephone and suggested in strongly-accented but excellent English that I visit him at his home in the suburb of Parede. All I had to do was take the train from the waterfront station of Cais do Sodré in the direction of Cascais, get off at the Parede station and walk a few hundred metres to his house. For once, Jan Jakob decided to accompany me, and we made the expedition a day or two later.

Entering the Parede residence of Luís Filipe Thomaz was an odd experience. The house seemed half-museum, with all sorts of objects, knick-knacks, and pieces of furniture from the Indian Ocean world, and especially Goa. Old photographs hung on the walls, some of which I came to understand were of the former Portuguese royal family. Several of the rooms constituted a large private library, with shelves from floor to ceiling with all sorts of books that I had only seen before in public libraries and archives. I reintroduced myself, reminded him of our meeting in Goa, and tried as best I could to explain my research. In a relatively brief conversation it seemed all of a sudden that several leads opened up. Thomaz suggested that I work for a few days in his house, consulting a few of his own published and unpublished writings and taking notes from them. He mentioned an upcoming conference on South East Asian Studies in nearby Sintra, and suggested that I attend it. He also gave me the names of a few other young historians I could contact, some of whom were his students or former students and working in the same archives.

I soon discovered that the world of Portuguese historiography in general, and that on the Indian Ocean more particularly, was a very small one. So, someone like Thomaz knew everyone and they all knew him. This had its advantages but also some notable inconveniences. It was known for example that the historian was the nephew of Admiral Américo Thomaz, who had been the dictator Salazar's handpicked candidate for President, and had then been exiled to Brazil in 1974 when the Caetano regime had fallen. Further, the younger Thomaz had been the student of Virgínia Rau, a formidable and quite conservative economic historian at the Clássica. So did that make Luís Filipe Thomaz a conservative historian, determined to whitewash the Portuguese empire and its past, as some left-wing Portuguese and even Goan historians would claim? I hardly found this to be the case. For one, his declared political opinions were those of a 'monarchical populist', a paradox in terms if ever there was one. Further, unlike most Portuguese historians, whether on the left or right, he had an enormous curiosity regarding Asia, had spent large amounts of time in Timor, and had also been for long periods in Paris, where he had studied not only Malay but also Sanskrit. Almost alone in Portugal at that time, he had a collection of the most important secondary works in French and English on Indian Ocean history.

The other major figure, part of the official leftist pantheon, was Vitorino Magalhães Godinho, by that time in his late sixties. Godinho had briefly been Minister of Education and Culture in 1974 and later Director of the Biblioteca Nacional. Logically, he would have been someone for me to contact as a central figure in economic history, but he was inaccessible and his reputation was that of an irascible and sectarian man who generally surrounded himself with yes-men. I failed, at any rate, to gain access to him, and when he came to know of my published work somewhat later, his reaction was one of violent rejection, couched in quite insulting and more-or-less racist language. So the left–right division in Portugal was no more simple than elsewhere in the world. What made it worse was that in 1985, the revolution, or *vinte e cinco de abril* (25th of April) as everyone called it, and its consequent democracy were barely a decade old. The wounds, even if they were far less deep than in neighbouring Spain, were still fresh. The trial of Otelo Saraiva de Carvalho, a very high-profile and left-wing army officer and sometime presidential candidate, accused of mounting a coup, was on everyone's minds and lips in those times.

In the days that followed my first visit to see Thomaz, a new coherence emerged in at least a part of my work. I spent the days in Parede, returning every evening to Elias Garcia to mull over my findings of the day. There too, a routine crystallized as Jan Jakob, João Pedro, and I went out every evening for dinner together to the same restaurant, located in a shopping mall on the 5th of October Avenue. This was run by a certain

Senhor Carlos, a jovial Chinese from Macau who had settled in Mozambique before moving to Lisbon in the mid-1970s. His restaurant, essentially a set of chairs set at a counter, had nothing Chinese about it; it consisted of an assortment of half a dozen rather greasy *pratos do dia*, which were a mixture of basic fish and meat offerings, running the gamut from pork chops and strips of beef to grilled sardines and eel and back. On the side there were boiled potatoes, some rice, and a leaf or two of salad. To wash this down Jan Jakob and I usually drank copious amounts of wine, which was just as basic as the food and as limited in its variety—a couple of whites and a couple of tough reds, all from the Alentejo. João Pedro, more restrained, often just drank bottled juice, and either practised his English on both of us, or his German on Jan Jakob. Senhor Carlos with his own curious humour began calling them João do Porto (referring to João Pedro), and João Gordo (or Fat John, referring to Jan Jakob, who actually had the size and look of a rugby player).

The behaviour of Jan Jakob, for the rest, continued to be quite mysterious. During the day, he would disappear and I rarely spotted him in the archives. He seemed to have the most interesting connections in Lisbon, where he drove around in a large and expensive car that he had brought from the Netherlands. These connections included some of the booksellers of Lisbon to whom he later introduced me. It appeared Jan Jakob belonged to a well-placed bourgeois family, and he had studied at Leiden University and been a member of the prestigious Club Minerva. Conspicuously placed on his bedside table was a photograph of his Dutch girlfriend, who called the Elias Garcia flat every other day just before dinner time. From time to time, his parents would call too. When he was not there, it was up to João Pedro and me to respond to these calls, as Alexandrina was completely flummoxed by all this. She and Raul could hardly pronounce his name, and preferred to call him 'Eanes', the name of the Portuguese president of the time and a rough approximation of 'Jan'.

In day-to-day life, the real issue for me continued to be spoken Portuguese. At times it seemed to me that the more I heard it the less sense it made to me. Then, quite quickly, the situation was transformed and I began to speak Portuguese. It is difficult for me to understand how this happened but the change was quite sudden. My recollection of it goes back to a lunch with Thomaz in Parede, after I had been reading some documents with him. He told me it was absurd for me to have the reading skills I possessed and, even so, refuse to speak the language. From that point on, he declared, he would only speak to me in Portuguese. In a sense, I thus learnt to speak Portuguese not in the manner of Senhor Ferreira, but by imitating Thomaz's accent (though not his rather particular intonation). This had quite interesting consequences, since his accent is to a large extent the 'open' one of the Portuguese north-east (or Trás-os-Montes) rather than the mumbled version of Lisbon. Years later, I was often told—when my Portuguese was at its best, which is no longer the case today as a result of disuse—that I nearly had a native speaker's Portuguese, except that the region was not quite identifiable. Between Ferreira and Thomaz might have been the answer.

As I began to speak, many doors suddenly opened. The younger lot of Portuguese historians in the archives quickly became my friends, inviting me out for coffee and exchanging notes on their own research. The grumpy staff ladies in the archives thawed a little and documents began to arrive a little more quickly at my desk. Indeed, even the archives themselves began to make more sense as I was given all sorts of tips regarding this or that obscure collection that no one had looked at with any great care. My pile of archival notes grew larger and larger, and I found a routine by which I could spend the morning in one archive and the afternoon in another. The three months that my grant allowed me began to appear too short for what I had in mind. There was also the question of acquiring a collection of old books and sources, many of which were still available for a reasonable price.

Here, Jan Jakob proved invaluable, by introducing me to a cantankerous old German bookseller called Birkemeyer who worked just off the Rua da Misericórdia near the Bairro Alto. Birkemeyer spoke fluent Portuguese with a strong German accent, and with an equally strong predilection for four-letter words. But he was ever ready to make you a deal, and had an astonishing collection of works published in the nineteenth century. It was just a question of sitting in his chaotic warehouse while he chatted with his Portuguese workmen about their love-life in his own version of *calão* (or slang), and the mood presently came over him to offer you the right price.

I had arrived in Lisbon in March. As April turned to May, and the temperature began to rise well into the 30s, things began to move even more rapidly on all fronts. The paradoxical advantages of working in disorganized archives became evident, since every other day I would run into a cache of documents that no-one had exploited or looked at with care. The great advantage of a network in the archives became obvious too; every now and again, someone would tap my shoulder and show me a document in a collection they were working on that was possibly relevant to me. Luís Filipe Thomaz then presented me with a new challenge: why did I not give a small series of lectures in Portuguese to his students in the Universidade Clássica on the materials I had found? I began laboriously writing out these lectures, asking both Thomaz and my neighbour João Pedro for help with corrections. I was also offered a small supplemental job by one of the archivists, who asked me to translate some Portuguese documents into English for a mysterious patron from the Persian Gulf. Thinking this would help me extend my finances and thus my stay by another month, I agreed. So, even the evenings in Elias Garcia came to be occupied after dinner with a continuation of the workday.

As time went on, however, João Pedro and I noticed that Jan Jakob joined us less and less often for dinner. Moreover, he was frequently not there when calls for him came from the Netherlands, requiring us to answer the phone and improvise explanations on his behalf. Occasionally, he would now appear in the archives, but with odd requests. He once showed up with references to a set of documents which he could not read, regarding a shipwreck in South East Asia in the seventeenth century, and said he needed my help with them to facilitate a project of treasure-hunting. Then, on another day, he let us know that he had found religion, and that the real reason for his extended absences was that he was spending swathes of time in an American evangelical church in the Estoril area. At much the same time, Alexandrina—who had discovered to her puzzlement that I was not a Christian—began trying to persuade me to accompany her to church. I was initially curious about what Portuguese Catholicism looked like from the inside. However, when I found that the church in question was one of those Brazilian evangelical affairs that had begun to penetrate Lisbon, I politely declined. When I told her about 'Eanes' and his newfound religious enthusiasm, she sniffed and looked dubious.

Matters came to a head in late May or early June. Jan Jakob had been returning later every night, or sometimes not returning at all. As the temperatures in Lisbon rose still further, his pink complexion was becoming redder and redder and he was growing less communicative by the day. One evening, after dinner, he invited João Pedro and myself into his room. Lounging on his bed in a pair of boxer shorts, and taking large shots from an enormous bottle of whisky he had obtained from somewhere, it became clear that he not only had a terrible case of sunburn but something else on his mind. It took a while for it to come out, and as he spoke he peeled off large chunks of skin that he arranged around his sizeable frame on his sheets like some form of animal sacrifice. He had not quite told us the entire truth, he began by noting. The fact was that he had fallen in love with the daughter of the American pastor at the evangelical church. The further fact that she was somewhat young made the matter delicate, and they had to conceal it from the father—as well as from Jan Jakob's own girlfriend back home and his parents. However, the couple had developed a daily routine now by which she left home on some excuse, he picked her up in his car, and they then spent the whole day on one or the other beach between Estoril and Cascais. This explained his rather odd physical state, though we hesitated to probe him further on their beachfront activities. Still, João Pedro and I pointed out to him that it was becoming difficult for us to make excuses for him on the phone. If, as he swore up and down, he was deeply in love with the American girl, he might want to break things off with the Dutch girlfriend. Jan Jakob, whose mood on the evening seemed to veer between sentimental romanticism (he had found True Love, after all) and a sense of self-pity that was fuelled by whisky and sunburn, eventually came around to our point of view. We did meet the American girlfriend a few days later, and were not impressed either by her clinging manner or her evident lack of intelligence.

And so, in a welter of last-minute archival forays, talks in the universities, and social engagements with my new friends in Parede and elsewhere, I eventually left Lisbon for India in mid July, laden with papers from the archives and two suitcases of Birkemeyer's books as unaccompanied baggage. Getting those books released by customs at Delhi's airport took me a whole further day. For a full month after I returned to Delhi, I think I could talk of nothing but Lisbon. My stay in the Netherlands had been largely forgotten by then. I went back to see Senhor Ferreira in his *barsati* in order to show off my newfound spoken Portuguese to him. Such was my enthusiasm that even my research adviser, Dharma Kumar, was somewhat affected by it. Early the next year, she was invited by the World Bank for a conference in Lisbon and took various tips from me about the city. But her experience was quite different from mine. She stayed at the Sheraton, not far from my old haunt of the Avenida Cinco de Outubro. But she detested the food, and found Lisbon a provincial version of great cities like Rome and Paris that she already knew. One evening, while she was walking with a few of her colleagues, two young men in an open sports car that they had just stolen tried to snatch her bag. Unfortunately for her, the strap did not give immediately and she was dragged behind the car for some yards, resulting in extensive bruises and scrapes. She never forgave Lisbon, '*your* Lisbon' as she thereafter always said to me. I apologized profusely of course. But she never did see my Lisbon in the end.

20

Across Three Continents

An Interview

This interview with Sanjay Subrahmanyam was originally published in Portuguese in the Lisbon-based journal *Cultura: Revista
de História e Teoria de Ideias*, vol. 24 (2007), pp. 253–68. It was
carried out by two Portuguese scholars, Ângela Barreto Xavier and
Catarina Madeira Santos, on behalf of the journal. The version
below has been revised by Sanjay Subrahmanyam.

*Did your interest in the study of history—and of imperial history,
in its various facets—come to you very young? Did you remember
how this happened? Does this have anything to do with our personal
history?*

I come from a family of bureaucrats, initially colonial bureaucrats and functionaries working for the British and then—
with my father's and brothers' generations—bureaucrats
working within a broadly 'nationalist' frame of mind in such
areas as defence and diplomacy. There was always some interest
in history in the house, but it was largely political and military
history, and strategic studies. Those were the sort of books
that one mostly found on the shelves at home, besides plays
and fiction. One of my older brothers, for example, whom
I looked up to a lot, was greatly fascinated by figures such
as Napoleon. Later, though he studied political science and
international relations in university, he also grew interested in

British-style left-leaning social history, Christopher Hill and the like, but eventually became a career diplomat. I was interested in history in middle school (between the ages of 10 and 12), when I had an excellent teacher who taught us a lot of colonial history. But then I lost interest in it for nearly ten years, until I began my Master's at the Delhi School of Economics. In these intermediate years I was interested first in mathematics, then literature, though I studied economics intensively from the age of 16. But from about 1980, two influences played a role. One was that of my maternal uncle, J. Krishnamurty, who was an economic historian who worked on colonial India, demography, and labour in particular. The other was that of my main teachers, Dharma Kumar and Om Prakash. Om Prakash introduced me to trade history and Indian Ocean history. He was himself trained to work on the archives of the Dutch East India Company by Tapan Raychaudhuri (also at the Delhi School of Economics), and his circle of friends included Ashin Das Gupta, Michael Pearson, John Richards, S. Arasaratnam, Anthony Disney, and many others. By the time I began my Master's degree, I was quite suspicious of economics, in which I had been fully trained. I was quite good at it, especially micro-economics (where I had a brilliant teacher in Kaushik Basu), but I eventually opted for classical political economy and economic history as specializations. The person who encouraged me above all to do it, and gave me the courage to switch from economics pure and simple, was Dharma Kumar, best known for her work on the economic history of South India in the colonial period. She also persuaded me to stay in India for my doctoral research, rather than go to the UK or US (like most others amongst my contemporaries). So, I finished in Delhi in 1986 (and got my degree in 1987).

To what extent were you—like some other young Indian in-tellectuals—influenced by Maoist ideas from neighbouring China, or Soviet Marxism, or even the critical discourse coming out of May 1968? Were you ever politically engaged during your career, or have you always steered clear of politics?

I was too young to have directly felt the influence of the Maoist moment in India. That was the generation somewhat before mine, of Partha Chatterjee, or my close friend from Paris, the historian of science Kapil Raj. By the time I was in my mid-teens, the political landscape was different. The leftists were already a bit in disrepute, especially the Communist Party of India (Marxist), because of their rigidly Stalinist bent of mind. The revolutionary violence that the Maoists (what in India we termed Naxalites) espoused was by that time not all that attractive. Chopping off people's hands and heads in response to local feuds was what a lot of it came down to, in the name of class warfare. The people who called themselves Maoists were often devoid of much real (let alone sophisticated) ideological reflection by the late 1970s. Still, I had some friends in that milieu. I suppose the key political moment for people in my cohort was the Emergency, which Indira Gandhi declared for two years in 1975, and which marked all of us because of the suspension of democracy, of human rights, and the brutal programme of forced sterilization that was carried out with respect to the urban poor. Though I was 14 or 15, I remember being part of a group in high school which was outspoken in regard to this, along with my friend Kapil Paranjape, who is now one of India's better-known mathematicians. But my point of view like his was, I suppose, that of a liberal rather than a Marxist.

Since the time I have been a professional historian, I have never been involved in organized politics. But I have often written things which have had political meanings or implications. This is especially in terms of more popular articles in the Indian press (in the *Times of India, India Today* or *Outlook*), or occasionally when appearing on television in India (as I did once, to debate an extreme right-wing politician on the nature of Indian nationalism). Here, the doctrinaire Marxists like to portray me as a right-wing person, the right-wing Hindu nationalists accuse me of being a Marxist, and so on. Of late, I have been the periodic target of attacks by Hindu fundamentalists in particular because they think I am pro-Muslim, and by a certain brand of 'anti-modernists' (the disciples of the guru-like figure of Ashis Nandy), because I have criticized their views on secularism and other related issues. No one can write a history that is totally devoid of political implications. However, I try to draw a distinction between my more popular and my more scholarly writings, saving explicit political arguments for the first. Sometimes, things become blurred though.

What names would you mention amongst your closest intellectual preferences and affections?
     It is a very ecletic list. If I think of those whom I have admired from afar, the list would run to such an odd collection of names as Voltaire (who I was an enormous devotee of in my teens), Gogol, some of Flaubert (*L'Education Sentimentale* in particular), G.K. Chesterton, Akira Kurosawa, Vladimir Nabokov, Jorge Luis Borges, but also the early John Barth. These are mostly literary figures. I should add Joseph Schumpeter to that list, from a rather different angle. Amongst people I have known close at hand, and who left a great intellectual influence on me, I would mention Velcheru Narayana Rao, Muzaffar Alam, and David Shulman. I have in recent years come personally to know, and admire the clarity and uncompromising rigour of Carlo Ginzburg. I have also learnt a lot over the years from Serge Gruzinski in Paris, especially in regard to the analysis of visual culture. When I was younger, I was very influenced in terms of historical and philological method by Luís Filipe Thomaz and Jean Aubin, as well as by my favourite Indian historian, Ashin Das Gupta. Before knowing them well, one of the crucial

meetings I had in my life was with Geoffrey Parker in Goa, in 1983. He gave me the shock of my life, when he explained the diversity of materials and archives he mastered, and set a new standard of excellence and breadth of vision for me. The late Friedhelm Hardy in London, though we were quite opposites in many respects, also taught me a lot about working with textual materials from his perspective as a historian of Indian religion. At the other end of the spectrum, in terms of sheer panache, I must admit a weakness for Charles Boxer, who I got to know in his later years. Another historian who influenced me with his breadth of vision, and also gave me the courage to venture in new directions, was Chris Bayly in the 1980s, as did the late Denys Lombard later on, when he brought me to Paris. So that is quite an eclectic collection, and you can see that quite a few—but not all, and certainly not Das Gupta and Aubin—of them had a pronounced tendency towards macro-historical projects.

In the sixteenth century, Erasmus of Rotterdam liked to be seen as a 'citizen of the world', and in the eighteenth century the Enlightenment philosophers produced an apologia of cosmopolitanism. These two images have greatly influenced the European intellectual imagination. In your world, who would be the equivalent of such European intellectual icons?

Erasmus and the Enlightenment philosophers have the advantage of having been universalized, so that they seemingly belong to the patrimony of the whole world. In India, I suppose, some of the greatest minds from the philosophical tradition are not so accessible to us for reasons of language, or because they are somehow automatically seen as obscure or provincial. But if you look at a whole series of writers from the fifteenth and sixteenth centuries, such as the poet Annamacharya, or the historian Abu'l Fazl, they are still available to us as intellectual resources that do not require us to position ourselves constantly in respect of a single (Western European) intellectual genealogy.

We could add dozens of names to that, from the many regions of South Asia and beyond. People like Narayana Rao have done just that, in their many recent works, on Srinatha, Dhurjati, Gurajada Apparao, Vishvanatha Satyanarayana, and so many others. These last names I mention all derive just from one regional tradition, that in Telugu. Were they 'cosmopolitan'? I cannot answer that easily.

In your academic career, one can discern a move from a more economicist focus and interpretation of historical processes to one that is increasingly political and cultural. Is there a reason behind this dynamic? Is this the result of a desire to see the same process from different angles, or rather the result of your own transformation as a historian?

I do not see this process in the same way as you suggest. My earlier works were not 'economicist' in the sense of Gary Becker or Douglass North. I did not seek to find economic logics and motivations behind all sorts of processes, and in fact have always been opposed to that sort of reasoning, even as a student. Rather, it was a question of the objects of study. I began as a historian of trade and commerce, within a tradition (that of the Delhi School of Economics), but if you even look at my first book, *The Political Economy of Commerce*, I was struggling there already to find a way to enlarge the context of trade history. In fact, Om Prakash and I were constantly in a non-violent struggle when I was writing my thesis. He would urge me to drop certain issues, because that was not what 'we' (meaning economic historians) were supposed to study. But if you look at his work and mine even in that phase, you can see the growing difference in conception. As soon as I finished my thesis, and was liberated from the need to answer his critique and reproach, I began to look for a wider set of problems. The problem was my training at this point, which was quite limited, in terms of both access and knowing what and how to read materials in a different way from the obvious one. But in 1992, just two years after my first book, Narayana Rao, Shulman, and I wrote *Symbols of Substance*, on the political culture of sixteenth- and seventeenth-century South India. You can see that I had learnt some new tricks by then, from both of them, and from others I had met meanwhile. So, the struggle for me all my career has been to widen my horizons and to understand how people from other intellectual trainings and traditions have dealt with their materials. I remember the anthropologist Veena Das once taking me to task for a sort of blind spot in a seminar I gave as early as 1983 in Delhi, where I failed to pay adequate attention to kinship structures in Portuguese Asia. It took me a few months to understand what she was talking about, but I did eventually understand. To take another example, in 1985, I would have been incapable of knowing what to do with the rhetorical structure or content of a Mughal chronicle, and might even have dismissed it. By the late 1990s, I was feeling far more comfortable with such materials, because of years of conversation with Muzaffar Alam. So, this was a painful and uphill task, and one in which I have frequently felt discouraged because the general tendency is to have a sort of 'field of your own' by 30, which you go on cultivating for the rest of your life (you can see the influence of Voltaire!). My view has been to try to open new areas for myself, but not abandon my earlier ones. Of course, the fact that historiography in general has become more culturally oriented (the so-called 'cultural turn') over these years has provided the wider context for this. Still, I dare say that I have moved over more ground, and more diverse materials, than a lot of my contemporaries. The other great difficulty has been one of combining this eclecticism with some degree of intellectual coherence, so that one is not arbitrarily combining methods and perspectives that are actually radically dissonant, and not saying the opposite of what one said last year.

Despite being relatively young, you have written many books that have been influential for an understanding of early modern imperial history. How do you maintain your level of productivity? Is there a political impulse behind it, even as you are trying to put out new historical interpretations?

To return to what I said before, I am not a very explicitly political person at all. I care about politics of course, both the politics of the places in which I live (which includes my workplace), and international politics. But I don't see it as the prime force behind what I do. I think I am motivated by two or three things. One is affinity and friendship. A lot of my work is done in the context of collaboration, and this is the chemistry that motivates me. I talk constantly to my friends and collaborators, and have an enormous telephone bill every month. Collaborative work also provides some kind of real check on quality. A second factor is a sense of dissatisfaction with myself. I don't think I have used my time efficiently in the past, indeed I have wasted a lot of time if I compare myself with, say, David Shulman. I have a fear that one day, soon, time will begin to run out and I will not have done enough (whatever that is). Also, I have made significant mistakes in the past, both of interpretation and of textual reading. That makes me angry with myself sometimes. Whenever a book of mine comes out and I read it, I feel deflated. Still sometimes, you read it again ten years later and say: 'Actually, some of it is not bad.' A third factor is the expectations that people have of me. I find it hard to say no, and so I wind up doing things so as not to disappoint others. It is a bit like a treadmill sometimes, hard to get off. These are all rather psychological as motivations. If politics were the driving force, I would write a lot more popular articles, and use other media rather than books and journals. If money were the object, I would be writing for trade presses like Felipe Fernández-Armesto. Or I would still be an economist.

Can you say something about your work, Explorations in Connected History, *and explain the advantages of the methodology
you espouse there? How does the 'local' fit in a larger space? Are
'Connected Histories' a way of looking at globalization?*

Actually, the idea of 'connected histories' came up because I
was responding to the work of the South East Asianist Victor
Lieberman, who had come up with a vast project of comparative
history, suggesting that Burma, Laos, or Thailand were quite
like France or Spain from a certain political-institutional
perspective. He later published a two-volume work on this called
Strange Parallels. In the context of a conference on his work,
I responded to his proposal not by writing an essay on India
(which is what he really wanted from me), but by suggesting
that the usual comparative history was not necessarily the most
fruitful way of proceeding to understand the early modern
world. As I proceeded, I realized that the late Joseph Fletcher had
proposed something a bit similar, though not quite the same.
So, my proposal then was to look at some of the phenomena
that connect histories across the usual boundaries of thought,
which push us to constitute the objects that are compared in
banal ways. This may have something to do with 'globalization',
but not necessarily. It is just a way of insisting that one may do
something better with the context of the history of Portugal
than, say, comparing Britain and Portugal, and seeing the latter
in the mirror of the former as the case of a failed bourgeois
regime, or of delayed industrialization or capitalist development,
as even Vitorino Magalhães Godinho does.

*Continuing with globalization, how do you see globalization in
relation to colonial and post-colonial experiences? Is it a new form
of imperialism? Or is it something that needs to be thought of
otherwise?*

I am less invested than the French historian Serge Gruzinski in
the idea of 'globalization'. I even agree to an extent with Frederick

Cooper that it may be too flabby and loose a concept to give one much intellectual purchase. And further, it is very clearly ideological, and corresponds to a recent need to give capitalism another, more respectable, name. So, if one looks at it like that, the history of commercial capitalism and of interregional markets is of course an old history. Indeed, everyone knows some empires were either underpinned by or even fundamentally motivated by the desire to find new sources for commodities, or new markets for goods, what in the case of the nineteenth-century British empire has been called the 'imperialism of free trade'. This is also the banal story that Immanuel Wallerstein told in part, and in boring detail, for the period after about 1450. But the history of the market is certainly not contained within the history of colonial or imperial experiences. The history of Indian Ocean trade between, say, 1100 and 1500, is for the most part, not one of the creation of great commercial empires. Most of the empires that existed then, of the Mongols, the Ming, or the Timurids, were land-based. The problem on the one hand is that the apologists of 'globalization' as ideology want to invest it with nothing but positive virtues, or give it an inevitability by inserting it in a teleology. This is the sort of telos that Francis Fukuyama had in mind (and which more economically-minded writers like Jeffrey Williamson still have in the backs of their minds). On the other hand, it has certainly been possible in the past to study colonialism and imperialism without resorting to the vocabulary of globalization. Still, I am curious to see whether Gruzinski's attempt, in *Les quatre parties du monde*, to give the idea of globalization a specific historical temporality and trajectory, finds echoes in the future historiography. The situation with regard to that is unclear at this point.

As an Indian historian, coming from a part of the world that witnessed many imperial projects, how do you see the future of India in the new context of a globalized and post-colonial world?

The Indian situation is both worrying and interesting. Recent growth has been very rapid, but the effects of it on cities in particular has been rather crazy. It is a sort of wild growth, with all sorts of questions regarding its sustainability, not to speak of its ecological consequences. (The same is also true of China, as historians of that region like R. Bin Wong assure me.) I grew up in part in Bangalore, an idyllic city that has become an ecological horror story of sorts in recent times. At the same time, we cannot idealize the sort of low-growth regime, of constant mass poverty, that arose under colonial rule and has continued since. I suspect that eventually, in the medium term, there will have to be significant population transfers from the 'South' (or parts of it) to the 'North' on a global scale. Everyone is obsessed with capital markets, but the regulation of international labour markets is a situation that one cannot run away from. Currently, everyone in the West is fascinated with India as a market, but there is more to the story than that.

What about the relative place of English and Indian languages as vehicles of different types of dicourse? After all, English as a language carries within it certain forms of thought. Can one be heard outside the English language in India?

I am certainly not comfortable with the hegemonic place that English has come to assume, over the nineteenth century to start with (under the aegis of the British empire), and especially in the last fifty years. In India, the reality is that it is more and more difficult to find 'social science discourse' in regional languages, even though they do survive in a humanistic vein, or as languages of literary expression. Actually, even where literature is concerned, it is obvious that many second-rate writers of fiction in English now receive more attention than the best writers in Indian languages. It is hard to imagine where we are heading with this, in the course of the next fifty years. If even French, which was once the great 'language of theory', is in the poor shape it is today, and given that German has receded enormously since 1945, what will happen to, say, Portuguese outside the song-text and the *telenovela* (or soap-opera)? The situation is grim for anyone who has an affective relationship with these languages. On the other hand the two languages that seem to hold their own on a world scale are Mandarin (Chinese) and Spanish. In fact, it would be quite different to do even this interview in English and in Portuguese. But I still do not think we have come to a point where the 'forms of thinking' that exist in other languages have been effaced by those in English. If you analyse my English or my Portuguese carefully, you will surely find traces of the deep structure of other languages there.

Fukuyama had spoken of the 'End of History' and now, after 9/11 has written of the 'Return of History'. Is this obsession with history a Western one? In India, is there the same type of historicism, or are there other dominant political and cultural trends?

Fukuyama and others are drawing both upon a hidden Christian millenarian vocabulary, and an explicitly Hegelian one. Neither of these has that much resonance in the intellectual world of modern-day Indians. Rather, I think the more worrying issue for me is the 'self-orientalizing' of Indian intellectuals in the context of post-colonial studies, where they insist that 'history' is a purely Western problem, and that they themselves should live outside history. This is the position of Ashis Nandy, Ranajit Guha, and others. I consider this both empirically fallacious—ignoring historical production in India before 1800—and tendentious in its view that some 'pure Indian self' exists and should be rescued in this way. It also shows to what extent dubious thinkers such as Mircea Eliade, with their glorification of a bogus version of the idea of 'myth', inform such thinking.

As regards the new 'Orientalism' in the West, particularly with regard to the Muslim world, what if any is its echo in India and its neighbourhood?

The problem here is that many right-wing political movements in India share the fear and hatred of Islam of a part of the Western media and establishment. This goes back to the Indian nationalist movement, and the two-nation theory, in which ideologues like V.D. Savarkar argued that Hindus and Muslims could never coexist within the same political space. In India this tendency, which finds plenty of support today in the middle class and elites, again came to the fore in the 1980s with the rise to power of the BJP, and the explicit political use of the idea that the Muslims had to pay the Hindus back for what had happened in the medieval period by way of sectarian violence. It still remains a potent force today. So, many on the right in India imagine that they are the natural allies of the West, with Islam as the common enemy. There are hundreds of blogs and sites on the internet devoted to diffusing this idea. In some sense, Samuel Huntington's conception is the template for this, with 'Western Civilization' and 'Hindu Civilization' allied againt 'Islamic Civilization'.

In the past centuries, many sorts of historical narratives played a crucial role in giving a sense of identity to particular groups, on the basis of their origins and so on. This in part was the subject of your book with Narayana Rao and David Shulman Textures of Time: Writing History in South India, 1600–1800. *Do you believe that the historian can still intervene in the formation of collective historical memory? Do you think the historian is socially useful?*

Obviously there is a vast distance that separates the world we looked at in *Textures of Time* from that today, most obviously because orality had a different place in that world, and also because of the multiplication of media that today have an interface with collective historical memory. And of course, as any number of observers have noted, we live in a world of excess and overflow. A work of history that was regarded as incredibly significant in 1985 may have thus been totally forgotten today. Some of these historical narratives that you refer to may have been seen as significant because they played a role in identity politics, in proving the grievances of one group with respect to another. Frankly, I am not interested in playing such a role today and I find the phenomenon of the historical *Black Book* (popular in some circles in Europe) rather disturbing as an instrumentalization of the historian. As for our 'social utility', are we really all that well placed to judge it? I am not even certain if I would know how to set up a thought experiment to judge the social utility of anything as large as the historian's role. But I do know that unlike what is claimed by so many post-colonial theorists, history is not just some evil, oppressive, and hegemonic device invented by the West.

What do you think are the advantages and disadvantages when one is an 'insider' while doing the history of a given country (or to use anthropological vocabulary, to be a participant-observer who controls the cultural codes), rather than an 'outsider'? How do you feel about the issue of 'closeness' and 'distance' in this respect?

It is not clear anyway who an 'insider' is in the context of the history of the sixteenth or seventeenth centuries. I do not usually do contemporary history, and most of the objects I study are separated from me by at least two centuries if not more. I don't have the sense of belonging any more to Calicut in 1498, than to Bahía in 1622. The problem however is twofold. First, much historiography is still organized in that way as I learnt to my cost when writing about Vasco da Gama. Some Portuguese historians, who had never worked on the subject, still thought it 'belonged' to them somehow and they interpreted the whole matter as a turf war, the outcome of which would decide who would get the plum positions in Portuguese expansion history in Europe and America. (This is quite funny in retrospect, given that I have nothing to do with those positions.) In a similar vein, Indian historians will sometimes—though less so now than fifty years ago—instinctively reject an English or American historian's views because of his nationality. At present, the worst of this in the USA is when historians of Indian origin (who grew up in the US) want to claim that they are somehow better placed to understand India by virtue of the 'fact' of their DNA. There is absolutely nothing to show that such persons control the cultural codes better than anyone else, nor is it the case that they can somehow automatically read or interpret a fifteenth-century text in Tamil or Telugu better than, say, a David Shulman. The second problem is that of dealing with the public at large. Here the matter is more complex, as people are often flattered by the fact that you will come and study 'their' history or enter 'their' archives. However, I want to stress that while a few things were easier (or obvious to me) when studying India, and no doubt it was correspondingly harder for me initially than for you or Jorge Flores to read and analyse documents in the Torre do Tombo, there is no clear or obviously sustained difference between 'insider' and 'outsider' here. In this sense, we are at quite a distance from the situation in anthropology.

Your relationship to Portugal is both intense and ambiguous. On the one hand, you have influenced a large number of historians, and your books can be found in any university library and are read and cited by both professors and students. You have thus shaped the discourse of the elites today to some extent. On the other hand, some of your readings of historical processes involving the Portuguese have been less than well received by the public at large. How do you see this paradox?

Actually, I do not believe that is entirely true, and the paradox is an illusion. First of all, at present I have three or four books translated into Portuguese. Two of these, one on the Bay of Bengal and one on the Portuguese empire, did not reach the general public for the most part. The problem arose with the third book, on Vasco da Gama. I have collected a large number of letters and responses I got to that book in Portugal. It is clear to me that the bulk of the hostility came from the university, and from precisely the elite circles you mention. What is obvious is that some of these were old-fashioned historians, who still defended the positions of the *Estado Novo* (or Salazarist state), and who hence found my view offensive. Some responses came from people who thought that I should stick to working on the Indian Ocean, and not meddle in Portuguese history. (Here we see a curious manifestation of the 'insider-outsider' issue.) But if you go back and read the newspapers and magazines of the time, you will see that the most violent and highly personal attacks actually came from certain tendencies in the so-called 'academic left', above all the school of Vitorino Magalhães Godinho. Part of this has to do with what I think of as a strand of European exceptionalism and (almost racist) arrogance that characterizes the positions of this school, which has never taken non-European historians (or materials in, say, Persian or Ottoman Turkish) seriously. Part of it has to do with the fact that some of them were fighting imaginary turf wars which I mentioned earlier. Of course, the fact that I had critiqued Godinho himself in a footnote, precisely for his Eurocentric arrogance, did not help. So far as the 'general public' was concerned, a few people (especially some claiming descent from Vasco da Gama himself) reacted angrily. But the truth is that I also got a number of very positive letters, and also letters asking for my help to track down details of this or that aspect of the history which someone was fascinated with. To the extent that the 'general public' was angry, I suspect it was because they were manipulated by motivated historians, this before the book had even been translated into Portuguese.

In your understanding, was there something specific about the Portuguese imperial experience? To what extent can we see an impact on this experience of the connections between South Asia, Africa, and South America?

This is a vast and fascinating subject. Yes, the Portuguese imperial experience is indeed specific, but it is also connected to others. To be sure, the specific and shifting links within the Portuguese empire are also of great interest, in particular the complex back-and-forth movement between the South Atlantic world and that of the Indian Ocean. Brazilian historians are now beginning to explore this with great profit. However, I also do not think we should exaggerate the uniqueness of the Portuguese empire, which was after all a large part of the mindset of the Estado Novo. There was a set of mutual influences with the Spanish empire that are worth exploring. Further, the British empire drew in some respects at least on the Portuguese example. I am thinking for example of the whole system of 'country trade', which obviously has more than a coincidental resemblance to the trade of the Portuguese *casado* traders in the Indian Ocean. At the same time, as Gervaise Clarence-Smith reminded us long ago, there was not one but several Portuguese empires, and the one that was reinvented in the nineteenth century itself bore traces of borrowings from other imperial experiences. It is not as if in Goa in the 1880s the dominant voice or vision was that of Afonso de Albuquerque or Dom João de Castro.

Looking at your academic career, one sees you have spent time in various centres of excellence in Europe and America, from the École des Hautes Études en Sciences Sociales, to the University of Oxford and now UCLA. How does one understand this? After all there are many Indian intellectuals in the great American universities, but many fewer in Europe.

My situation is indeed a bit peculiar, though it may seem a part of this movement of 'diaspora intellectuals' that Jackie Assayag and others have written about. Most of those you refer to left India at a much younger age than I did, often around

21 or 22, to do their doctoral research abroad. They were thus socialized into the British or American academic milieu, and have usually lived quite smoothly ever after in it. I stayed in India till my mid-30s, teaching at the Delhi School of Economics, when I moved for personal reasons to the EHESS, on the basis of my earlier links to Paris as a visitor. I had nearly a decade there, but eventually left for Oxford, partly because I was getting a bit dissatisfied with the French system—even though I do not regret a single moment I spent there. But the truth is that I had very few graduate students in Paris, because the subjects I studied were seen as marginal. When I and Serge Gruzinski proposed a change in the very structure of the EHESS, so that the 'area studies' were better integrated with history, we were rebuffed rudely by the administration and by many European historians. I think the historical part of the EHESS is now slowly beginning to pay a price for its provincialism, and its inability to keep up with the times. One cannot live forever on the glories of the past, or on a few 'stars' like Roger Chartier, Alain Boureau, Jean-Claude Schmitt, and Serge Gruzinski.

But I must admit I found things little better in Oxford, where once again the teaching of history was unbearably Eurocentric and conservative. For example, Indian history was only taught as a part of the history of the British empire. Though I had a Chair, I got the impression that my role there was meant to be decorative (and Sir John Elliott confirmed that he had sometimes felt this himself, as Regius Professor). This eventually prompted me to move to UCLA, though I had turned down offers earlier both from UCLA and other American universities such as Chicago. I had always been suspicious of the American academic system, based on my short visits there after 1987. And since indeed nothing in life is simple, I don't believe that my academic life here will be either. Here, I have more resources to be sure, better graduate students, and also see the potential for better integrating different parts of the world in a complex historical vision, without a blatant and anachronistic hierarchy between them. But it is still an uphill task. And I realize that the fact that I was never socialized into the Western academy at a young age will remain an obstacle, because I still find many of the conventions (that other intellectuals from India working in US universities accept easily) quite detestable, including the ghetto mentality of many of the Indian intellectuals themselves, and the obsession with the politics of ethnicity.

How do you see what some call the new 'hegemony' of the Indian intellectuals, especially where the Western academy is concerned?

I do not think there is any real intellectual hegemony, because in terms of deeper content, what is really so 'Indian' about it? These are authors who are essentially working within the same broad framework of references—Heidegger, Benjamin, Foucault, etc.—like so many others in the American academy. Their genealogy often takes them back, as many will now admit, to the Romantic critique of the Enlightenment, which also had nothing particularly Indian about it. I do agree that in the wake of Subaltern Studies, there has been a wave and a network effect, so that American universities have been vying for people to teach post-colonial theory and history in the 'subaltern' mode. And some have at times adopted terms like 'provincializing Europe' as slogans, without properly reading the book [by Dipesh Chakrabarty] to see what it argues. But I do not observe that any historian of Europe or the US has yet been shaken to the core by reading these works, perhaps because they are actually not that radical in relation to what they do already. Such work also does not basically challenge the established division of labour. That is also why so many pillars of the American historical establishment have accommodated it. We cannot treat all this as some sort of radical underground literature of *samizdat*. It is actually a particular, ethnically-tinted articulation of a more general phenomenon, which I think the American academy is perfectly comfortable with. Of course, this does not mean that there are not some very important individual works (whether books or essays), or very intelligent people at work here. However, if one thinks about it, the manner in which the larger movement occurred was probably as follows. There was in the 1960s and early 1970s, something called the 'Cambridge School' of Indian history. Those who belonged to it constantly denied it existed. But they still functioned as a collective, published together, acted as a network, a support group, so that the best of them like Chris Bayly or David Washbrook, carried the others along on this. Ranajit Guha and his disciples observed, followed, and greatly improved on this model. What they created is basically a lobby, a group for collective action and mutual support, which over the years gradually lost any real ideological (or even ideational) content. The received versions of this 'school' in, say, the Latin American or African historiography, are even more curious, because they are trying to infuse what is a shell of ethno-political action with deeper ideological content.

You left the Indian academic scene a good number of years ago, though you are still involved in various activities with colleagues, journals, and projects in the country. How do you see the transformations in the Indian academy in the past ten or fifteen years?

The situation in India is complicated, interesting for a few but depressing for many. Since the mid-1990s, Indian universities dealing with the humanities and social sciences have steadily been bled. Places like the Delhi School of Economics, where I taught, have lost a large proportion of their faculty to retirements, and they have not been replaced. Of course, the institutes of technology, management schools, law schools, and so on, are still doing well, because state funding has been replaced more and more by private and alumni support. But one cannot fund a history department in that way, at least not in India. At the same time, some independent research centres with few (at times, even no) teaching responsibilities are doing well, usually funded by private means, or the Ford and Rockefeller foundations. This may be one of the side effects of the retreat of the state from economic activity, because Indian universities were essentially state-funded. Still, some journals do work well. There are some places in which one can give an interesting talk before a lively audience. But these are less and less the university departments. I suspect this is a phase of transition, and that in another ten years' time the pendulum will swing the other way. But while it is going on we will have more and more elite, educated Indians, leaving to do their higher studies abroad, not at 21 or 22, but at 17 or 18. This is good for universities in the US or Australia, of course, and perhaps it is the thin edge of the wedge of labour movement I was mentioning (though I am in the final analysis sceptical about that).

21

History Speaks Many Languages

A Further Interview

This second interview with Sanjay Subrahmanyam was originally published in Paris on 27 January 2012 by the online journal *Books & Ideas*, English-language companion to *La Vie des Idées*. It was conducted by Anne-Julie Etter and Thomas Grillot.

What are you working on right now?

Right now I am working on a set of French materials from the seventeenth century—a very curious business. As you possibly know, I taught here at the École des hautes études en sciences sociales (EHESS) in Paris, from 1995 to 2002 or even 2004, as I spent the last two of those years between Oxford and Paris. At that time, I did work to some extent on French sources, at the Archives nationales and the Bibliothèque nationale. But it struck me at some point that, although I had already looked in some depth at other European sources, I had never gone beyond a very initial take on French materials. I was then in the committee of a student at UCLA, who was working on the embassy sent by the Safavid ruler of Iran to the court of Louis XIV in the early eighteenth century. I started reading these sources with her and realized that I understood these sources differently than she did because I had a quite different take on the Eurasian history of the period. As I was looking to take a year of sabbatical, I decided to write a project for a Guggenheim fellowship on French sources—which would also help me at a personal level because my wife, Caroline Ford, is an historian of France. This may sound like a very aleatory way of going about things. But behind it, there is a set of problems that have long interested me: how does one go back to write a history of Orientalism which is not the history of British colonial Orientalism, but something that existed before that?

When you do this kind of research, there are very obvious names you encounter, like that of François Bernier, who came from the Anjou region of France. Although there has been a certain amount of work done on Bernier, including a recent re-edition of some of his writings, there is a set of questions concerning him that nobody has really broached. And behind him there is a bunch of people that nobody has touched at all in three hundred years! The person I am focusing on right now is François le Gouz de la Boullaye, a gentleman who, like Bernier, was of Angevin extraction and who arrived in India in the 1640s, returned to France, and then went back and died in India in 1667 or so. What I want to do with these French sources is to cross them with the Dutch and English sources on the French, so as to give them more depth. Eventually, I am interested in looking at how the French looked at the Mughals and the Mughals looked at the French—there are very few direct sources, but implicitly one can understand a certain number of things.

Let me go back to François Bernier. He was a doctor trained at the famous Faculty of Medicine of Montpellier and was very close to Gassendi: he wrote an abrégé of Gassendi's philosophy and was there when he died. As such, he was read by Locke, and his influence can be felt from Montesquieu all the way through to Marx. Bernier was even a key thinker in the construction of the figure of the oriental despot and eventually of the Asiatic mode of production. Bernier went to

India and spent quite a long time there (between 1656 and 1668). Several of his writings were published not long after his return. But there are also very interesting materials that remained unpublished at the time. In one of these texts, he gives more or less confidential advice to Colbert, minister of finances to Louis XIV, on the functioning of the French East India Company. Peter Burke has written on Bernier and given what I think is a rather gilded view of who he is: the Bernier you see in the unpublished material is very different from the high and mighty philosopher of his *Letters*.* Bernier was actually very Machiavellian, even crudely political to an incredible extent.

I'll give you an example. There was a pirate called Hugo who showed up in the 1660s in the Indian Ocean and attacked ships carrying pilgrims to Mecca. This man was eventually captured in the Red Sea, his goods seized, and he was sent back to Europe. Colbert wanted to employ him. Bernier advises him there. It is very interesting how he approaches this. He does not discourage Colbert. He says: 'Wait a little bit of time until people have forgotten who this pirate is. Go on insisting that he is not French but Dutch. And when people have moved on, you'll be able to bring this character back into play.' And there is plenty of like advice in Bernier's lesser-known writings on India, including a strategy regarding misleading the Mughals on the extent and nature of French power in Europe. Overall, you see a very curious conception of politics that can nuance the view of how someone like Bernier functions—and he does so at two or three levels: ethnographic; as a student of comparative religion; as a distinctly Machiavellian actor.

---

*Peter Burke, 'The Philosopher as Traveller: Bernier's Orient', in Jaś Elsner and Joan-Pau Rubiés (eds), *Voyages and Visions: Towards a Cultural History of Travel* (London: Reaktion Books, 1999), pp. 124–37.

As an historian, you have often resorted to biographies and biographical vignettes . . .

Many historians have used individual trajectories, within very different contexts. My book on Vasco da Gama is not a biography in the normal sense of the term. There is a classical-type biography in French by Geneviève Bouchon, and French publishers, when approached for a translation of my own work, which had come out in English before hers, thought it would be redundant. But the two books are very different. Rather than only following the individual, I go back and forth between large contextual questions and Gama's individual trajectory, on which sources are silent. Gama does not write or talk much, so there is no way of entering his subjectivity, which is often the goal of the writer of biographies. It's simply impossible. And of course plenty of historians are confronted by these problems. Think of *The Cheese and the Worms* and microhistorians, or even people who do not think of themselves as microhistorians, like Linda Colley, who wrote a book specifically about a kidnapped woman in the eighteenth century (*The Ordeal of Elizabeth Marsh*, 2007), because of her interest in gender and the circulation of people in the modern world.

My own interest in large questions certainly comes from my background in the social sciences and my strong training in economics at the Delhi School of Economics. Social and cultural anthropology were huge there: M. N. Srinivas, André Béteille, and Veena Das were the major figures of that milieu at the time, in the 1970s. In a way, I didn't have to come to Paris: Paris and 'French theory' were already in Delhi. I have always tried to move between this level and a more individual-centred approach. At a basic level, it is the classic question of how deterministic you make your history, how much people are prisoners of context or active agents. What you need to do is constantly move between these levels of analysis. I did this from my very first book on. For instance, in *The Political Economy of Commerce: Southern India, 1500–1650*, which came out of my dissertation, I proposed the concept of portfolio capitalist. The only way that I was able to convince people that this concept was an interesting way to look at the development of a certain type of commercial capitalism was to track these capitalists, look at what resources they worked with and how they manipulated them. I wrote an entire chapter based on individual trajectories. Even at that time, in 1987–88, I was not into a very deterministic economic history. I really was never like some of my teachers who counted up ships and bills of lading, drew graphs and ran regressions—and also taught me how to do those things.

Why this difference from the start? One of my good friends, someone with whom I have had very interesting conversations over the years, Partha Chatterjee, was trained as a classic political scientist in Rochester, to work on game theory and the arms race. Now, one of the recent books that he wrote is entitled *A Princely Impostor?*, about the so-called Kumar of Bhawal case. It takes place in India in the early twentieth century: a prince dies of syphilis, but along comes this religious mendicant, a *sannyasi*, who claims he is the prince and is believed by the family. How does someone trained in political theory wind up studying this Martin Guerre story? Generally, I think that even Indian economists who stuck to economics have always had a more humanistic take on their discipline than many of their non-Indian colleagues. There is some kind of a cultural component there. I am thinking here of people like my friend and former teacher, Kaushik Basu. Perhaps Indian social scientists are also more prone than others to mix in their literary interests with their social scientific approach—now, of course, I am not saying here that in India there is no distinction between fiction and non-fiction.

Is this humanistic approach grounded in a different relationship with Indian readers?

Most historians in India, I think, do not write with a target audience in mind, much less so than in France for example, where a history book that does reasonably well can easily sell 5,000 copies. It's impossible in India—you write for ten people. I have never myself written with a large public or student audience in mind, except for *The Portuguese Empire in Asia*, which is somewhat close to a textbook. Even there, knowing that the book was never going to be used in India, I was addressing a much larger, worldwide audience. I think that for most of my colleagues in India, the larger audience just happens—or not. They don't write with it in mind.

It is also true that in India, authority counts for much more than, say, in the US. In America, seminar students are going to question you in a way that Indian students won't necessarily. But there is also a much greater tendency to conformity in the US, where you need to write like everybody writes. And there is a constant desire to classify you—and this is not just an intellectual thing, but clearly a marketing strategy, like you would put out any other product in a supermarket. In a refereed article, you are often invited to cite 'ten important books or articles' on the subject at the outset. But they are either often implicitly present in the argument, or irrelevant to it—so why cite them? It's just a matter of doffing your hat to those authors—three of whom are probably your referees anyway. If this sort of pressure—what I think of as academic food processing—did not exist, we might have a lot more creative work, and a greater desire to play with both form and content in history writing.

A considerable body of your work deals with connections between empires, spheres of trade, etc. You have also stressed that it implies redefining the objects of historical inquiry. What kind of historical objects emerge from paying attention to connections?

I belong to a generation which was not the generation of Indian Independence. This is the generation of Partha Chatterjee and Dipesh Chakrabarty. All of them were born more or less in 1947, the year of Indian Independence, or 1948. All are 'Midnight's Children'. Even my close collaborator Muzaffar Alam was born in 1947. They had already done a certain amount of the work of taking the inherited nationalist frame, which was the dominant frame of Indian history, and critiquing it. What is actually paradoxical is that, having critiqued it as a theoretical project, they still remained more or less prisoners of it, in terms of their own monographic production. None of them thought that it was interesting for instance to even write an article about some aspect of South East Asia or West Asia. They always write about India, or India in relation to the West. They are also completely dominated by the whole colonial encounter, which is understandable given their generation. This is for them a framing problem for all historical enquiries. Having the good fortune of coming a generation or half a generation after them, I could take some of this for granted. By the time I was doing my thesis, Partha Chatterjee's famous book (*Nationalist Thought and the Colonial World*, 1986) more or less existed; Benedict Anderson's *Imagined Communities* was out. For me it was pretty obvious that the nationalist frame was not the appropriate one.

But once you have done the theoretical critique of colonialism and of nationalist discourse, what are you going to construct as your objects? That is my real problem. When I seek connected histories, it is always in a particular context. If somebody is doing connected histories fifty years from now, it will be a very different context. It may be that by then the kinds of objects that we have established in my generation have become old and tired and are no longer interesting; people may want to make other connected histories. It is really a way of trying to constantly break the moulds of historical objects.

The difficulty is that if you go to an Indian history department, sixty-eight out of seventy people who are there may work
on India. There are usually two people who teach survey courses
on European history or maybe, in the older generation, on
Soviet history or Russian history because they had a link there of
some kind. Nobody in an Indian history department normally
does research on something else, even if they can teach by using
the usual textbooks. They will take Peter Burke's compendia on
new trends in European social history and teach European social
history out of that. But most of them would never dream of
going to an archive which is not an Indian or a British one.
Since I work on the pre-colonial period, it is even more obvious
to me that the relationship between Britain and India cannot be
my framing relationship for all questions or most questions I
ask. Take the example of Burmese history. In India practically
nobody ever thinks that it is worthwhile to do Burmese history.
Yet the history of northern Burma is very closely linked to the
history of parts of Eastern India, Bangladesh, and Northeastern
India. There is a whole sphere of circulation and state-formation. But with the exception of maybe two or three largely literary scholars in Bengal, it is not something that people would do.
And how many people in India work on South East Asia, which
is just down the road for us?

In India and I think here also in France, the national and the
nationalistic historiography is still the dominant historiography. There will always be a dominant historiography. It has
never been my concern to propose what is going to be the
dominant paradigm. I think of this much more as
Oppositionswissenschaft, a term that the early modern intellectual historian Peter Miller gave me. It is conceived to challenge
and go against the grain, not in a negative sense and not in a
mere sense of saying 'here are your theoretical errors', but to
propose other concrete projects, to implement them and tell
people, 'here is another project, tell me what is wrong with this

and why some other people cannot work in this style?' Of
course people will tell you that there are fifty thousand practical
reasons for which it cannot be done. It is very difficult to learn
languages, it is very difficult for people in India to go and access
these archives. When I was teaching in Portugal in the late
eighties, I used to tell students that, for some of the questions
concerning the Portuguese empire, one really has to go to
Dutch archives. They would say 'Dutch, what kind of a
language is that? Who in their senses can learn Dutch?'

The millenarian conjuncture of the sixteenth century was an
example I took of how one can look at connections and see a
hidden object emerge.* Unfortunately, in the debate that
followed, some people took it very literally and focused on the
example rather than the broader question. I chose that example
because I thought it was an unexpected one. If I had written
about silver circulation, people would have told me that Pierre
Vilar had done that kind of thing many years ago. Then it also
becomes a very material history, a history of prices and money.
I wanted to take something which was much more of a political
and cultural phenomenon, in order to show how you can actually play with it.

*Your research mainly deals with South India, the Mughal Empire,
and early modern Europe or, as you put it, 'early modern Eurasia'.
People in France are familiar with Serge Gruzinski's work on the
entangled worlds of the Catholic Monarchy. Can you tell us about
recent works of a similar vein that focus on other political and
cultural entities?*

It is true that I have worked on South India, the Mughal
Empire, and early modern Europe, but with Muzaffar Alam

* 'Sixteenth-Century Millenarianism from the Tagus to the Ganges',
From the Tagus to the Ganges: Explorations in Connected History (New Delhi:
Oxford University Press, 2004), chapter 5.

for instance, I have also worked on Central Asia, Iran, and South East Asia. I am also fairly well clued-up on Ottoman history, even though I do not actually work in the Ottoman archives. I teach Ottoman history and I use Ottoman history a lot, even in my examples, essentially with translated materials. Have a look at the examples of people circulating that are to be found in my most recent book, *Three Ways to Be Alien*: one of them is an Englishman who ends up in Spain, but spends a lot of his life in the East and the Mediterranean, the Ottoman Empire, and Iran. When I say Eurasia, I try to take it seriously within the limits of my competence in terms of archives. I sometimes get people to help me; I sometimes work closely with people.

Serge Gruzinski and I had a seminar together at the EHESS, which was called Amérique-Asie. Nathan Wachtel and others also took part in it, but Serge and I were the main motors behind it. In a way, he took it in a different direction from me, using more Iberian sources on Asia. That is what his last three books, including the one he has just finished, *The Eagle and the Dragon*, are trying to do. I have never got into the Latin American materials that much directly, though I have written a couple of articles that touch on this question. I have also recently done some work with Anthony Pagden on the relationship between the British Empire, the Spanish, and the Portuguese Empire.[*]

The difference between what I am doing and what Serge is doing may also lie in the fact that I am a bit more eclectic than he is, in my framework, and in the questions I choose. Serge has tended to take it more in a direction of thinking of this as a

---

[*] 'Roots and Branches: Ibero-British Threads across Overseas Empires', in Massimo Donattini, Giuseppe Marcocci and Stefania Pastore (eds), *L'Europa divisa e i Nuovi Mondi*, vol. 2, (Pisa: Edizioni della Normale, 2011), pp. 279–301.

problem of empire. He is interested in the circulation of texts and images within these empires and their peripheries. Empire is present in my work, but it is not always the dominant scheme within which I am working. I am also interested in histories which do not take place at the level of empire or are not articulated through it. A large part of South Indian history is not imperial at all. The Mughals, for example, were there for a relatively short time. *Symbols of Substance* (1992), which I wrote with David Shulman and Velcheru Narayana Rao, deals with very small states. Empire is not the question to which I am responding all the time. Neither am I trying to replace the nation with the empire as the paradigm within which one does history. I am much more interested in the intersection. This may also derive from the fact that I am coming out of the Indian Ocean world, whereas Gruzinski is coming out of the American world, where after 1500 you have these two massive facts of political life, first the Spanish Empire and then the British Empire. The Indian Ocean is a much messier place, even until the end of the eighteenth century. How much of the Indian Ocean does the British Empire really control even in 1800? We thus have different tastes, preferences, and objects, even though it all emerged from the same conversation.

What I would like people to do with it is to cross objects and archives, which one conventionally did not do. Some people have taken this on. A student of mine at UCLA, who has just started out on his thesis, wants to work on the zone between Gujarat and the Persian Gulf: that is Gujarat, and then you have the whole of the Gwadar, Makran, the Baluchistan area, and heading all the way through Oman, Masqat into the Persian Gulf. The historiography always keeps Gujarat separate as an object from the Persian Gulf. But we know that these are real spheres of circulation. And there is a whole set of questions which can be asked in relation to them: formation of small states, like the origins of the sultanate of Masqat and Oman in the seventeenth century; piracy and corsair activity in this area; religious circulation between these two sides and so on. That is a kind of connected history project which he is doing, but it is probably going to be a long haul for him, because he is trying to read materials in Persian and Arabic on the one hand and Dutch and French on the other, in order to see what he can do with all this for the late seventeenth and early eighteenth centuries.

One can also mention the 'entangled empires' type of projects, which I also find interesting. John Elliott wrote a book comparing the British and the Spanish Empires in the Atlantic (*Empires of the Atlantic World*, 2006). People like Eliga Gould have looked at South Carolina, Florida and the Caribbean in the late seventeenth and early eighteenth centuries, which is a world between the Spanish, the English colonists and the French. If you go to the historiography, what you will often get is either big macro-histories of the Atlantic, where people will list each empire and deal with it, or separate histories. You get the French in the Caribbean, the English in the Caribbean; there is a whole South Carolina historiography; for the late seventeenth to eighteenth centuries there is still a Spanish Caribbean or whatever historiography. But if you take these objects together, you see interactions of a type that you did not see before. Some people think it has something to do with the thing called 'connected histories', some do not. The name does not matter that much to me.

The examples you gave all point to the early modern era. Does that mean that a connected approach cannot be of help for later histori-cal periods?
It is true, studies which privilege these kinds of interaction deal mostly with the early modern period. It is for two reasons. One is probably that more early modern historians read Serge Gruzinski or me than late modern historians. Furthermore, the

hold of national history is much stronger when you cross 1800, which raises the issue of the constituted archives and habits. People will also tell you very frankly (and this is a chicken and egg problem) that there are no jobs which are defined like this for the nineteenth and twentieth centuries. In the earlier period, at least in the English-speaking world, many jobs are now defined in a way that would allow you to place yourself without people telling you 'Do you really do this or that?' Carlo Ginzburg was my colleague at UCLA. Upon his departure, some people tried to make an argument that since he had left, we needed an Italian historian. Is that really how you define Ginzburg? Is that what he has become, just an historian of Italy? That reflex is too often there.

But some people are starting to think differently with regard to the nineteenth and twentieth centuries. They are often historians of questions such as diasporas and mercantile networks, or sometimes people who are looking at certain kinds of intellectual history where you get the possibility of seeing things across normal boundaries. One can think of the conference on Italy and India which was organized recently in Paris: its project was to make a kind of a connected history of two nationalist movements, which are not often examined as connected.[*] Medievalists might eventually think that there is something to be done with it. But they have their own problems, which again deal with the nature of sources and the issue of the technical skills needed to read them.

Textures of Time (2001) is a book you co-authored with Velcheru Narayana Rao and David Shulman. It puts forward theses concerning genre and texture that enable you to identify diverse

---

[*] 'Italy and India: Intellectual Connections and the Circulation of Political Models in the 19th–20th Centuries', conference organized by Tiziana Leucci and Claude Markovits (Paris, EHESS, 2 December 2011).

historiographical traditions in pre-colonial South India, but are also meant to bear upon history-writing in general. This book has entailed a rich set of reactions in the field of Indian historiography. To what extent have its methodological proposals gone beyond the framework of Indian history?

The book has certainly had some reaction in Indian history. I believe someone is putting out a special number next year of the *Indian Economic and Social History Review* where people are trying to rethink Indo-Persian historiography in relation to our book. A forum was published in *History and Theory*. It was a debate where some differences were exposed. Still, it was dealing mainly with Indian materials. It was a bit disappointing that they did not also ask a non-Indianist to comment on it. When the book came out, South East Asianists were interested in it; even someone like François Hartog was quite interested in it and supported its translation into French at much the same time that he was working on 'regimes of historicity'. But the problem was that people who came from some historiographical traditions were comfortably sitting on a received wisdom, which said that there was no fundamental historiographical problem to be solved and that all the received categories were stable. For example, someone who writes on Arabic historiography has a whole tradition, which starts almost from the early centuries of Islam. There is a received wisdom on European historiography as well. Therefore a book which questions some of the categories and tries to offer new tools in order to redefine some of the boundaries is not something which immediately appeals to people who feel that this problem has been solved a long time ago.

If there is an interest outside India, I imagine it will come from regions where the issues are not so clear. It could be South East Asia or Africa, but also interestingly Persian historiography, which is not as secure in its self-perception as Arabic historiography. The issue of African historiography is a complicated one. The problem of Ethiopia or that of Mali is not the problem of Great Zimbabwe; there is also a line of influence there of Arabic-language historiography. A whole debate went on there, which began with Jan Vansina's writings on oral tradition. However, in spite of the obvious differences between the African and Indian experiences, a lot of it became about how history is this object which was imported from the West along with colonization. This is the cliché, which we have had for at least two hundred years. If people want to re-examine this question, I think that going to some of the ideas developed in *Textures of Time* could be useful to them. Unfortunately, this book has currently become too much mired in an Indian set of problems. We were expecting older-fashioned historians to react and say, 'This is not serious, this is not historiography, we know what historiography is, it is Gibbon and his Indian epigones, and so on.' But it was also depressing to see that many Indologists actually rejected it, given that they are invested in the idea that there is no *shastra* (theoretical texts, set of normative rules) of history. Moreover, they do not like to read Indian vernacular languages, in which languages most of our examples are. For them, anything worth saying in India must have been said in Sanskrit.

I am actually a bit disappointed with the reactions to both books I have written with Velcheru Narayana Rao and David Shulman. We took a lot of risks in *Symbols of Substance*. For the three of us—a literary scholar and folklorist, who has worked on oral literatures for a long part of his life, a classical Indologist specializing in religious studies, and an historian who comes out of economic history—to get together and write a book in the first place was taking a big risk. We wanted to work on South India, because all the historiography at the time was focused on North India. People sometimes put *Textures of Time* on reading lists now both in India and outside, but it has not made the impact we had hoped for it. Maybe we did not pose the problems in the right way, or clearly enough. As Americans would put it, perhaps our after-sales service was not good enough. If I had been a certain type of historian in an American university, I would have given ten talks about the book after it was published, showed up with piles of it, and sold it at a discount to people in the audience! But perhaps it is still too early to say what the real impact of these books will be. At any rate, we certainly enjoyed working on them and writing them—which is more than half the story.

Index